The Political Economy of Artificial Intelligence

NBER

NATIONAL BUREAU *of* ECONOMIC RESEARCH

National Bureau of Economic Research

Conference Report

NBER
NATIONAL BUREAU *of* ECONOMIC RESEARCH

The Political Economy of Artificial Intelligence

Edited by **Ajay Agrawal, Joshua Gans, Avi Goldfarb, and Catherine E. Tucker**

The University of Chicago Press

Chicago and London

The University of Chicago Press, Chicago 60637
The University of Chicago Press, Ltd., London

Published 2026
Printed in the United States of America

35 34 33 32 31 30 29 28 27 26 1 2 3 4 5

ISBN-13: 978-0-226-84704-7 (cloth)
ISBN-13: 978-0-226-84705-4 (ebook)
DOI: https://doi.org/10.7208/chicago/9780226847054.001.0001

Library of Congress Cataloging-in-Publication Data

Names: Agrawal, Ajay editor | Gans, Joshua, 1968– editor | Goldfarb, Avi editor | Tucker, Catherine (Catherine Elizabeth) editor
Title: The political economy of artificial intelligence / edited by Ajay Agrawal, Joshua Gans, Avi Goldfarb, and Catherine E. Tucker.
Other titles: National Bureau of Economic Research conference report
Description: Chicago ; London : The University of Chicago Press, 2026. | Series: National Bureau of Economic Research conference report | Papers from an NBER conference held in September 2024. | Includes bibliographical references and index.
Identifiers: LCCN 2025047294 | ISBN 9780226847047 cloth | ISBN 9780226847054 ebook
Subjects: LCSH: Artificial intelligence—Economic aspects—Congresses | Artificial intelligence—Political aspects—Congresses | Artificial intelligence—Military applications—Congresses | Artificial intelligence—Law and legislation—Congresses | BISAC: COMPUTERS / Artificial Intelligence / General | POLITICAL SCIENCE / Public Policy / Science & Technology Policy | LCGFT: Conference papers and proceedings | Conference papers and proceedings
Classification: LCC HC79.I55 P647 2026
LC record available at https://lccn.loc.gov/2025047294

♾ This paper meets the requirements of ANSI/NISO Z39.48-1992 (Permanence of Paper).

Authorized Representative for EU General Product Safety Regulation (GPSR) queries: **Easy Access System Europe**—Mustamäe tee 50, 10621 Tallinn, Estonia, gpsr.requests@easproject.com
Any other queries: https://press.uchicago.edu/press/contact.html

Relation of the Directors to the Work and Publications of the NBER

1. The object of the NBER is to ascertain and present to the economics profession, and to the public more generally, important economic facts and their interpretation in a scientific manner without policy recommendations. The Board of Directors is charged with the responsibility of ensuring that the work of the NBER is carried on in strict conformity with this object.

2. The President shall establish an internal review process to ensure that book manuscripts proposed for publication DO NOT contain policy recommendations. This shall apply both to the proceedings of conferences and to manuscripts by a single author or by one or more co-authors but shall not apply to authors of comments at NBER conferences who are not NBER affiliates.

3. No book manuscript reporting research shall be published by the NBER until the President has sent to each member of the Board a notice that a manuscript is recommended for publication and that in the President's opinion it is suitable for publication in accordance with the above principles of the NBER. Such notification will include a table of contents and an abstract or summary of the manuscript's content, a list of contributors if applicable, and a response form for use by Directors who desire a copy of the manuscript for review. Each manuscript shall contain a summary drawing attention to the nature and treatment of the problem studied and the main conclusions reached.

4. No volume shall be published until forty-five days have elapsed from the above notification of intention to publish it. During this period a copy shall be sent to any Director requesting it, and if any Director objects to publication on the grounds that the manuscript contains policy recommendations, the objection will be presented to the author(s) or editor(s). In case of dispute, all members of the Board shall be notified, and the President shall appoint an ad hoc committee of the Board to decide the matter; thirty days additional shall be granted for this purpose.

5. The President shall present annually to the Board a report describing the internal manuscript review process, any objections made by Directors before publication or by anyone after publication, any disputes about such matters, and how they were handled.

6. Publications of the NBER issued for informational purposes concerning the work of the Bureau, or issued to inform the public of the activities at the Bureau, including but not limited to the NBER Digest and Reporter, shall be consistent with the object stated in paragraph 1. They shall contain a specific disclaimer noting that they have not passed through the review procedures required in this resolution. The Executive Committee of the Board is charged with the review of all such publications from time to time.

7. NBER working papers and manuscripts distributed on the Bureau's web site are not deemed to be publications for the purpose of this resolution, but they shall be consistent with the object stated in paragraph 1. Working papers shall contain a specific disclaimer noting that they have not passed through the review procedures required in this resolution. The NBER's web site shall contain a similar disclaimer. The President shall establish an internal review process to ensure that the working papers and the web site do not contain policy recommendations, and shall report annually to the Board on this process and any concerns raised in connection with it.

8. Unless otherwise determined by the Board or exempted by the terms of paragraphs 6 and 7, a copy of this resolution shall be printed in each NBER publication as described in paragraph 2 above.

Contents

Acknowledgments

This volume was made possible by generous grants to the National Bureau of Economic Research (NBER) from the Alfred P. Sloan Foundation (grant #G-2023-19618) and Microsoft, with support from the TD Management and Data Analytics Lab and the Center for Innovation and Entrepreneurship at the Rotman School of Management at the University of Toronto. It is part of a multi-year research initiative at the NBER on digital economics and artificial intelligence. We are grateful to Daniel Goroff of the Sloan Foundation for his interest in and support for this project. We would also like to thank Helena Fitz-Patrick for outstanding assistance in the editorial process, Denis Healy and Abbie Murrell for expert grants management, and Brett Maranjian and Carol Deneka for outstanding support for the meeting at which the papers in this volume were presented.

Introduction

Ajay Agrawal, Joshua Gans, Avi Goldfarb, and Catherine E. Tucker

As the economic potential of artificial intelligence (AI) becomes clearer, a number of questions arise as to its impact on the political environment, including with respect to regulation, competition between nations, and political preferences. To provide some structure to future economics literature on these questions, we organized an NBER conference in September 2024 in Toronto with the aim, as set out in the invitation, "to set the research agenda for economics, emphasizing how AI might impact economic systems, their governance, and the relative power of individuals and nations." We brought together a mix of economists and political scientists to identify open questions and provide frameworks for research going forward.

This volume is the third edited collection to emerge from the NBER conference series on the economics of artificial intelligence. The first volume, *The Economics of Artificial Intelligence: An Agenda* (based on the first such

Ajay Agrawal is the Geoffrey Taber Chair in Entrepreneurship and Innovation and professor of strategic management at the University of Toronto's Rotman School of Management, and a research associate of the National Bureau of Economic Research.

Joshua Gans is a professor of strategic management and holder of the Jeffrey S. Skoll Chair of Technical Innovation and Entrepreneurship at the University of Toronto's Rotman School of Management, and a research associate of the National Bureau of Economic Research.

Avi Goldfarb is the Rotman Chair in Artificial Intelligence and Healthcare, and professor of marketing, at the University of Toronto's Rotman School of Management, and a research associate of the National Bureau of Economic Research.

Catherine E. Tucker is the Sloan Distinguished Professor of Management and a professor of marketing at MIT Sloan, and a research associate of the National Bureau of Economic Research.

For acknowledgments, sources of research support, and disclosure of the authors' material financial relationships, if any, please see https://www.nber.org/books-and-chapters/political-economy-artificial-intelligence/introduction-political-economy-artificial-intelligence.

conference in 2017), laid out a broad research agenda spanning AI's impacts on issues such as productivity, labor markets, scientific discovery, trade, and economic growth—several chapters have since become standard readings in many PhD curricula. The second volume, *The Economics of Artificial Intelligence: Health Care Challenges* (based on the 2022 conference), narrowed the focus to a single industry by examining economic issues associated with AI and health care. Building on these foundations, the present volume—born of the eighth NBER AI conference in September 2024—occupies a middle ground in scope, addressing the wide-ranging political economy of AI while remaining more focused than the inaugural collection and less narrowly sector bound than the health-care volume.

This volume contains a mix of invited articles and comments from that conference. It is organized into three key themes: the political economy of AI regulation, AI and military power, and AI and political identity. Consistent with NBER norms, our goal in putting this volume together was policy-relevant analysis without policy recommendations. We included papers with an eclectic mix of approaches—empirical studies, economic theory, thought pieces, and book summaries—to illuminate different facets of AI's political economy. Given the field's early stage and the limited availability of data on key dimensions of AI and political economy, this combination enables contributions that both identify what are likely to be the most important questions and begin to explore ways of answering them. While AI's impact is already being felt in areas such as content creation and health care, its implications for politics and nationhood remain comparatively underexplored.

I. The Political Economy of AI Regulation

Beraja and Yuchtman first discuss various ways that AI might be disruptive to existing economic structures, such as labor markets and the role of privacy in society. The chapter then points out a previously underappreciated aspect of AI's commercialization: that it will create new conflict over property rights for the inputs into AI applications. These include online content for generative AI, where current copyright policy does not provide clear guidance, and urban space for autonomous vehicles, including flying drones. The chapter, therefore, identifies important political forces that will shape the economic implications of AI, depending on how these property rights are ultimately allocated.

Farronato's chapter discusses one aspect of Beraja and Yuchtman's newly identified conflict over property rights: data. Building on the metaphor that Beraja and Yuchtman emphasized at the conference, that data is the new oil, Farronato notes that property rights over information are particularly complicated, as Arrow (1962) highlighted. Therefore, the underlying economic frameworks for developing property rights for information will need to be different from those developed for non-information goods such as oil.

In contrast to the chapters by Beraja, Yuchtman, and Farronato, which discuss the regulatory challenges in newly contested property rights, Callander's chapter examines how incentives affect relevant policy outcomes, particularly with respect to regulation. The chapter discusses the role of interest groups and asymmetric information between policymakers and innovative firms. Politics affects the path of technology, and through interest groups, the anticipated path of technology can affect politics.

The following two chapters turn to the regulation of algorithms. Like Callander, Gillis et al. emphasize asymmetric information between firms and regulators. They provide a detailed framework for assessing the relative benefits of different regulatory regimes. If the regulator emphasizes inputs into the algorithm, that can limit the upside potential of AI. If the regulator emphasizes the outputs, that can punish firms for bad luck. They point out that regulation can also occur *ex interim*, where the process can be scrutinized in ways that, under certain conditions, incentivize efficient deployment.

Gans's chapter also highlights trade-offs in regulating algorithms, noting that the economic approach to regulating through market design is generally more efficient than an approach that focuses on regulating the inputs to the algorithm or the algorithm itself.

Furman provides a broader discussion of the goals of AI regulation, emphasizing that there are meaningful differences between a "precautionary principle" approach and a cost-benefit approach. He identifies six principles to consider.

Together, these chapters suggest the contours of a research agenda for the political economy of AI regulation. How do alternative property-rights regimes for AI inputs—ranging from open-access licenses to exclusive copyrights—affect innovation incentives, market entry, and social welfare? Under what conditions do *ex interim* process-based regulation (e.g., model-audit requirements) outperform input- or output-based regimes in fostering both safety and dynamism? What are the equilibrium choices of interest groups and regulators when asymmetric information about AI capabilities is high, and how do these choices shape the pace and direction of technological diffusion? How can we quantify the welfare trade-offs between a precautionary-principle approach versus a cost-benefit analysis in AI oversight, particularly in high-stakes domains like finance or transportation? Finally, what empirical strategies can reveal the political feedback loops by which early regulatory decisions on data governance influence subsequent lobbying, public opinion, and legislative reform? These types of questions sketch an agenda for understanding the rich interplay between economic forces and the governance of AI.

II. AI and Military Power

Economic power and military power are interconnected. To emphasize this connection, we invited national security expert Paul Scharre to discuss his book *Four Battlegrounds*. His chapter serves as a transcript of his remarks at the conference. He examines each of the "battlegrounds" for AI dominance in military conflict: data, hardware, talent, and institutions. Gross's commentary on Scharre's chapter underscores that these four battlegrounds are primarily economic in nature, suggesting the issue could be framed as a "resource-based view of military performance." Consequently, the relative military power of nations relies heavily on a specific set of economic resources that countries apply to the military use of AI.

Another political scientist attending the conference, Jon Lindsay, argued that political science is probably the "more dismal science," partly because the consequences of military conflict are severe and partly because the implications of technological change on military power are difficult to ascertain. Thus, seemingly good news is often mixed with bad. Tying military outcomes to the role of judgment in decision-making (Agrawal, Gans, and Goldfarb 2018), Lindsay emphasizes that conflicts are often decided by willingness to pay costs as much as by military firepower. AI might not have much impact on national resolve, even if it changes the ability of nations to inflict harm on each other.

Together, these chapters point to a rich set of questions for the economics of AI and military power. How do marginal investments in the four battlegrounds—data acquisition, specialized hardware, human capital, and institutional frameworks—translate into shifts in national military effectiveness and bargaining power? What are the opportunity costs and spillovers when governments divert private-sector talent toward defense-oriented AI research, and how does that reshape civilian innovation ecosystems? Can we estimate models to quantify the trade-offs between stockpiling AI-optimized hardware versus investing in adaptive talent pipelines when facing uncertain future conflicts? How does asymmetric information about AI capabilities between rival states influence arms-race dynamics and the probability of preemptive strikes? What empirical strategies can uncover the causal impact of AI-driven military expenditures on both conflict escalation and deterrence? Questions such as these frame a research agenda for the economics of AI and military power.

III. AI and Political Identity

A third theme was the role of AI in shaping political identity. Fouka and Reich emphasize recent research on the role of education in shaping national identities. Nation building is a deliberate process, and it has long been recognized that education plays an important role in that process. Furthermore, there are reasons to expect that AI will lead to more effective and personalized education. Combining these ideas, they argue that AI could lead to more effective nation-building. They, therefore, connect disparate ideas on nation building, education, and AI to suggest a novel pathway through which AI might affect political identity.

Petrova et al. discuss a different way that AI can shape identity: through its impact on politicians and voters. They document that the automation of factories likely increased the activities of right-wing populist politicians in affected areas and, in related work, note that this in turn likely influenced election outcomes in the United States. Colantone offers some suggestions to enhance this research. Mansell et al. highlight that support for AI is not necessarily stronger on the left. Using data from Canada, they show that both the far left and the far right are more skeptical of AI, while traditional conservatives appear to be the most supportive.

Acemoglu et al. develop separate models of how AI's use in social media and targeted political advertising affect political preferences and political outcomes. For social media, curated news feeds lead to polarization. For advertising, two political parties aim to reach voters with digital ads, which can be crafted and targeted by AI. Naive voters may be convinced by incorrect information, and this increases the effectiveness of digital ads for political purposes. Thus, their models suggest that AI-powered media lead to polarization of voters, and that political parties respond to this by choosing polarizing policies. They note that competition between platforms will not solve these issues and instead explain how regulation of the algorithms (enforcing social media feed diversification or weaker ad targeting) could reduce polarization. In addition to touching on the theme of regulation, this concluding chapter provides specific mechanisms for an idea that is perhaps the central theme of this volume on AI and political economy, that politics affects technology and technology affects politics.

Political scientist Joshua Tucker commented on the presentation by Acemoglu et al. at the conference, which is related but distinct from the chapter those authors contributed to this volume. Tucker's comments highlight ideas similar to those of Beraja and Yuchtman, Farronato, and especially Callander, noting that regulation occurs in a contested environment. However, it remains unclear who would advocate for the policies in AI and online advertising that Acemoglu et al.'s research emphasizes.

These contributions invite a host of empirical and theoretical questions at the intersection of AI and political identity. How does personalized, AI-driven education alter measures of national cohesion and civic engagement, and what are the long-run welfare implications of such shifts? Can we estimate the causal effect of AI-mediated job displacement on the rise of populist identities, perhaps using regional variation in automation adoption as an instrument? What structural models can capture the feedback between AI-curated news feeds and the evolution of individual ideological sorting, and how might interventions—such as enforced content diversity—mitigate polarization without stifling user engagement? How do AI-powered targeted advertisements reshape voters' identity salience and turnout, and what are the comparative magnitudes of these effects across different electoral systems? Finally, what econometric strategies can uncover the role of social networks in amplifying AI-driven identity dynamics, and how might regulatory or platform-design changes alter these network effects? These types of questions set a research agenda for understanding how AI is reshaping the very fabric of political identity.

IV. Conclusion

This volume introduces an exciting new frontier at the intersection of artificial intelligence and political economy, laying out a research agenda for empirical and theoretical investigation. Two overarching challenges stand out.

First, bringing ideas from other disciplines into economics. AI's rapid and broad diffusion requires economists to engage with insights from military studies, political science, and data science—applying rigorous economic models to frameworks presented in nontraditional formats. For example, Scharre's resource-based view of AI in defense and Lindsay's political-science lens on conflict underscore the payoff from importing novel hypotheses into general equilibrium and game-theoretic settings. By recasting these narratives in the language of incentives, information asymmetries, and strategic complementarities, economists can both sharpen the underlying theory and generate testable empirical predictions.

Second, novel data generation and measurement. Understanding AI's political-economic impact hinges on new data such as lobbying expenditures, algorithmic audits, and platform governance. High-frequency measures of data sharing between firms and regulators, granular geo-coded records of automation adoption, and micro-level assessments of targeted political ads are examples of data that will be instrumental for identifying causal channels. These datasets will allow researchers to quantify welfare trade-offs—such as safety versus innovation—and to estimate structural parameters that govern interest-group dynamics, regulatory design, and the polarization of political identity.

Taken together, the contributions in this volume provide a conceptual scaffolding and methodological road map for researchers: from model construction and counterfactual simulation to field experiments and natural-experiment-based identification. We hope that this collection inspires the next generation of scholars to chart the dynamic interplay between AI, institutions, and social welfare to enhance our understanding of whether and how this rapidly advancing technology will impact the political economy.

I

The Political Economy of AI Regulation

1

Generalized Disruption
Society, Work, and Property Rights in the Age of AI

Martin Beraja and Noam Yuchtman

1.1 Introduction

Disruptive innovations are traditionally understood as those that threaten the rents—and even the existence—of incumbent firms (Aghion, Akcigit, and Howitt 2014; Christensen 2015). As a general-purpose technology, artificial intelligence (AI) will likely disrupt multiple industries, from digital services to health care, finance, and even manufacturing (Agrawal, Gans, and Goldfarb 2022). However, the broad applicability of AI means that disruption will not just stop at product markets. The technology has the potential for generalized disruption across multiple domains, much like electricity transformed many aspects of society in the 20th century (Gordon 2016).

In this chapter, we begin by discussing disruption in two domains that have already received attention: the sociopolitical sphere and labor markets. For example, facial recognition surveillance tools are already challenging civil rights (Beraja et al. 2023b), and large language models are likely to impact workers in many jobs (Eloundou et al. 2023). We then identify a new

Martin Beraja is an acting associate professor in the Economic Analysis & Policy Group at the Haas School of Business, UC Berkeley, and a faculty research fellow of the National Bureau of Economic Research.

Noam Yuchtman is the Drummond Professor of Political Economy in the Department of Economics at the University of Oxford and All Souls College.

We thank the participants at the NBER conference on AI and political economy, especially our discussant Chiara Farronato. Helpful and much-appreciated suggestions, critiques, and encouragement were provided by Avi Goldfarb, Shengwu Li, Sendhil Mullainathan, Steve Tadelis, Jean Tirole, and an anonymous referee. The authors have no conflict of interest, financial or otherwise, related to this study. For acknowledgments, sources of research support, and disclosure of the authors' material financial relationships, if any, please see https://www.nber.org/books-and-chapters/political-economy-artificial-intelligence/generalized-disruption-society-work-and-property-rights-age-ai.

domain that has heretofore been overlooked: the disruption of property rights over contestable inputs. That is, the resources that AI applications rely on—online content for generative AI, urban airspace for drones, genetic material for personalized medicine—are becoming valuable and contested inputs as rules and rights are often ill established.

The general-purpose nature of AI, therefore, means that the technology will not just be a driver of progress; it will be a generalized disruptive innovation that will demand new policies and regulations, especially as AI's influence extends into areas where laws are unclear or property rights are not well defined. In the sociopolitical sphere, concerns regarding citizen surveillance can lead to bans on AI technology in cities (Beraja, Yang, and Yuchtman 2023), and misinformation in the media can result in restrictions on algorithms and content moderation (Müller et al. 2023). In labor markets, worker displacement may provide a rationale for expanding social insurance or slowing down AI-based automation (Beraja and Zorzi 2024), and workplace monitoring may lead to calls for regulations to shield employees from excessive surveillance and a loss of autonomy. Last, as contestable resources like data or public space become valuable for AI applications, clearer property rights and usage frameworks will need to be established via litigation and regulation. These could include reforming intellectual property laws and definitions of fair use for online data, creating public repositories where individuals contribute genetic or biometric data subject to strong privacy protections, and designing zoning laws and auctions to allocate public space and electromagnetic spectrum for drones and other autonomous vehicles.

Importantly, the multiple ways that AI may disrupt economic, social, and political life may not act independently of one another. We close this chapter with a discussion of possible interactions among the various domains of disruption, a possibility with important policy implications, presenting both opportunities and challenges.

1.2 The Disruption of the Sociopolitical Sphere

In this section, we discuss how several AI-powered technologies might disrupt social interactions and political institutions. We consider, in turn, the development of technologies that will affect state capacity, the functioning of democratic institutions, social capital, and warfare.

1.2.1 State Capacity

Many dimensions of state capacity can be enhanced by AI technology, from bureaucratic decision-making to law enforcement, traffic regulation, and national defense (US Congress 2024). Governments have already installed "smart city" surveillance technologies and automated border control systems in airports, and are using algorithms to estimate tax liabilities.

An AI-supported state, however, may have ambiguous consequences for societal well-being.

1.2.1.1 Citizen Surveillance

Smart city technologies—which comprise surveillance cameras and associated algorithms that allocate public security, traffic, environmental, and public health resources—have been introduced by dozens of countries around the world. These technologies have the potential to inform and streamline a range of public services by collecting information and processing and responding to it intelligently in real time. For example, traffic regulation can improve with real-time monitoring, reducing commuting costs, lowering auto emissions, and allowing ambulances (and other public vehicles) to travel quickly.

While such surveillance capacity has the potential to improve state services and citizen well-being, it can also be used for purposes of political repression and social control—indeed, Beraja et al. (2023a) find that Chinese police procure surveillance AI technology and cameras following episodes of unrest and that such procurement makes unrest less likely to arise. Beraja et al. (2023b) find that weak democracies and autocracies import smart city AI technologies from China *precisely* in years when they experience domestic political unrest.

Concerns regarding government misuse of surveillance technology, as well as a more general citizen demand for privacy, have led to resistance to the introduction of facial recognition technology in parts of the US. Resistance to the use of AI-powered surveillance technology can be seen in San Francisco's ban on police use of facial recognition AI technology in 2019 (BBC News 2019a). As AI enhances the capacity of the state, its impact on welfare is likely to be heterogeneous and will depend fundamentally on the objectives of those who control the state.

1.2.1.2 Bureaucratic Bias

AI can also support bureaucratic decision-making, potentially reducing human error or bias. Such bias has been documented in, among other areas, lending (Atkins, Cook, and Seamans 2022), health care (Angerer, Waibel, and Stummer 2019), and judicial decision-making (Dobbie, Hull, and Arnold 2022).

Yet, it is not obvious that algorithms will succeed in undoing human biases—algorithms can improve on human performance, but whether they will do so depends on choices made by humans (e.g., the training data used), and algorithms can generate unintended harmful consequences without transparency (Christian 2021; Kleinberg et al. 2018). As with surveillance technology, the AI-empowered bureaucracy can enhance citizen well-being, but this is not guaranteed. Monitoring of AI technology's performance and efforts at AI transparency and accountability are now being pursued by civil society groups and legislators (Bains 2024).

1.2.2 Democracy and Media Consumption

Perhaps the most profound effect of AI on liberal democracies today is its impact on citizens' media consumption and thus their information sets and beliefs.[1] Social media is an increasingly important source of political news, and both news articles and political ads are algorithmically targeted toward viewers. This can create information bubbles and expose individuals to "fake news," for example, increasingly persuasive "deep fakes" in which AI produces realistic-looking and sounding—but fabricated—content. While evidence is ambiguous regarding the impact of social media exposure on political attitudes and voting behavior (Allcott and Gentzkow 2017; Allcott et al. 2024; Fujiwara, Müller, and Schwarz 2024), there exists evidence that users engage with "toxic" content (Beknazar-Yuzbashev et al. 2022) and that extreme content can generate extreme political views and even acts of hate in the real world (Müller and Schwarz 2021). Efforts to regulate speech are challenging in liberal democracies, but some suggestive evidence exists that social media content regulation may, in fact, moderate political discourse (Müller and Schwarz 2023).

1.2.3 Social Capital

AI has the potential to build social networks by improving matching across a range of platforms (from social media to dating to service provision). However, such matching might also produce polarization, or bubbles of like-minded individuals, and crowd out activity in the real world, where social interaction and the production of public goods remain paramount.

The use of AI algorithms in social media like Instagram has become so effective that scholars have begun to describe it as an "addiction" or as a "trap" (Allcott, Gentzkow, and Song 2022; Bursztyn et al. 2023). Evidence suggests that the development of online networks is characterized by homophily, which crowds out social interaction offline and erodes social cohesion (Enikolopov et al., 2024). Algorithms' success at capturing social media users' attention—while surely generating some consumer surplus—generates a range of negative externalities.

Concerns about self-control challenges, especially among children, as well as an understanding that reducing social media exposure may require *coordinated* behavior, have produced a range of public, civil society, and private sector responses. In the UK, the Online Safety Bill, passed in 2024, aims to regulate online content with the aim of protecting children from various forms of potentially harmful content (BBC News 2023). Civil society, in the

1. Concerns about the impact of AI on functioning of liberal democracy are discussed in Acemoglu (2021) and Tirole (2021).

form of parents' groups (e.g., Smartphone Free Childhood), has mobilized to coordinate commitment to delay smartphone access for children.[2] Finally, entrepreneurs, notably economist Leonardo Bursztyn, have developed coordinated commitment devices to reduce time spent online.[3]

1.2.4 Warfare

Potential military applications of AI include cyberwarfare as well as the use of AI in autonomous warfare, using drones. Concern about the potential dual use of frontier AI technology—both hardware and software—has led to restrictions on exports of the technology. The US currently restricts exports of AI technology and frontier microchips used to develop AI (e.g., to China) to preserve its lead in the AI arms race.[4] While this may have geopolitical benefits, it may also reduce the rate of technological progress in the field as international collaboration breaks down.

1.3 The Disruption of Labor Markets

In this section, we discuss how several AI-powered technologies will likely disrupt labor markets. We consider two technologies that will automate jobs and displace workers: autonomous vehicles and generative AI. We then analyze AI-based workplace monitoring technologies and their impact on worker well-being. Finally, and more speculatively, we describe how virtual worlds may lead to lower labor-force participation.

1.3.1 Autonomous Vehicles and Driver Displacement

Autonomous vehicles represent a transformative shift in transportation by using machine learning, advanced sensor technology, and vast data processing capabilities to operate without human intervention. Unlike traditional vehicles requiring drivers, autonomous systems rely on sophisticated algorithms, particularly in perception and decision-making, to navigate complex environments. Leading companies such as Tesla, Waymo, and Cruise are at the forefront, testing self-driving cars and trucks on public roads, with some already being used for limited commercial purposes.

Transportation and delivery services are a major sector of employment of middle- to low-income workers in the US. So far, these services require extensive human input for tasks like navigation, logistics management, and customer interactions. However, autonomous vehicles offer the potential

2. See Smartphone Free Childhood, https://smartphonefreechildhood.co.uk.

3. Bursztyn has developed the NOMOapp (*The Chicago Maroon 2024*).

4. Justifying this policy, Assistant Secretary of Commerce for Export Administration Thea D. Rozman Kendler, stated, "The PRC's [People's Republic of China's] Military-Civil Fusion strategy presents a significant risk that advanced node semiconductors will be used in military applications that threaten the security of the United States, as well as the security of our allies and partners." See US Department of Commerce (2024).

for continuous, round-the-clock operations, rendering certain roles less essential. As self-driving technology continues to advance, long-haul truck drivers, delivery drivers, and taxi operators face heightened vulnerability to job displacement, particularly those whose tasks are routine and repetitive.

Recent studies underscore the significant impact autonomous vehicles could have on employment in transportation and delivery services. A report by the US Department of Commerce estimates that about 15 million workers could be impacted to varying degrees (US Department of Commerce 2017). This represents about one in nine workers. Motor vehicle operators, in particular, are about one-third of these workers; they are predominantly male, older, less educated, and compensated less than the typical worker. A more conservative study finds that autonomous trucks could replace as many as 294,000 long-distance drivers (Viscelli 2018). Anecdotally, companies like Uber and Lyft are already experimenting with autonomous fleets for ride-sharing. For example, Uber has partnered with Waymo to offer self-driving cars in Austin and Atlanta (*The Wall Street Journal* 2024), and Lyft has announced partnerships with Mobileye and May Mobility to deploy autonomous vehicles on its platform (*The Verge 2024b*). In the logistics sector, Amazon's Prime Air program has received Federal Aviation Administration (FAA) approval to operate delivery drones beyond the visual line of sight (*The Verge 2024a*). Likewise, UPS has gained FAA clearance for its delivery drones to conduct longer-range flights (*The Verge* 2023).

The potential displacement of workers due to autonomous vehicles has sparked a debate about policy responses (Phillips 2023). Some policymakers propose implementing a "robot tax," drawing from economic rationales to slow down automation technologies more generally (Beraja and Zorzi 2024; Guerreiro, Rebelo, and Teles 2022). Indeed, the state of Nevada has already imposed an excise tax on the use of a dispatch center, software application, or other digital means by which an autonomous vehicle network company connects a passenger to a fully autonomous vehicle for transportation services (Nevada Revised Statutes § 372B.145—Excise Tax on Autonomous Vehicle Network Companies 2022). Others advocate for enhancing worker retraining and education initiatives to facilitate transitions into new roles. For example, the US Department of Transportation has emphasized the importance of workforce development programs to prepare employees for emerging opportunities in the evolving transportation sector (Groshen et al. 2018).

1.3.2 Generative AI and White-Collar Job Displacement

Generative AI refers to a category of artificial intelligence that creates new content by mimicking patterns from large datasets. Unlike traditional algorithms that simply process or classify data, generative AI models can produce original outputs, including text, images, code, and even complex simulations. These models are trained on massive datasets and leverage architectures like transformers to understand and generate human-like content. Firms such as OpenAI, Google DeepMind, and Anthropic have pioneered developments in generative AI, particularly through models like GPT-4, BERT, and other advanced language models.

The technology is increasingly seen as a disruptive force in the labor market, particularly for workers performing cognitive-intensive tasks. Traditionally, automation has affected manual labor, but generative AI's capabilities are more likely to impact white-collar jobs involving data analysis, writing, and creative design, such as those in marketing, journalism, legal research, and even software development. While these tools can augment human work by speeding up repetitive tasks and aiding creativity, they also pose a risk of job displacement. Employees performing repetitive cognitive tasks—such as copywriters, customer service agents, and junior analysts—are particularly vulnerable.

Recent work provides evidence of generative AI's disruptive impact on the labor market. For instance, a 2024 report by McKinsey estimated that up to 30 percent of hours currently worked across the US economy could be automated by 2030, a trend accelerated by generative AI (McKinsey 2024). In the media industry, platforms like Medium have experienced a surge in AI-generated content, leading to challenges in maintaining content quality and limiting opportunities for human writers (*Wired* 2024). Similarly, in customer service, companies are increasingly adopting AI-driven chatbots and virtual assistants, reducing the need for human agents and altering the employment landscape in this sector (*Time Magazine* 2024). Beyond these examples, the best systematic evidence to date comes from Eloundou et al. (2023), who found that large language models (LLMs) like ChatGPT could impact up to 80 percent of the US workforce, with 19 percent of workers potentially seeing over half of their tasks affected. This widespread influence spans all wage levels and sectors, positioning LLMs as a general-purpose technology that can automate jobs in cognitive-intensive occupations.

As is the case for autonomous vehicles, the rise of generative AI has resulted in calls for slowing down its adoption and offering worker retraining. For instance, the UK government has already introduced a national retraining scheme to support workers whose jobs may become obsolete due to AI, offering assistance in finding new careers or gaining additional skills (BBC News 2019b). Some, like pioneering AI developer Geoffrey Hinton, have gone as far as arguing for the need for a universal basic income to provide a stronger financial safety net for displaced workers (BBC News 2024).

That said, a key distinction between generative AI and autonomous vehicles—as well as with manufacturing automation from industrial robots in the past (Acemoglu and Restrepo 2022)—is the type of workers more likely to be displaced. Workers in high-paying, cognitive-intensive jobs in the case of generative AI and workers in middle- to low-income, routine-intensive jobs in the case of autonomous vehicles or industrial robots. This implies that economic rationales for policy intervention are weaker in the case of generative AI than they are for autonomous vehicles or they were for industrial robots (Beraja and Zorzi 2024). However, political pressure for policy interventions might be even greater in this case, given the higher levels of skill and greater de facto political power of highly paid workers.

1.3.3 Workplace Monitoring and Worker Well-Being

The application of AI as a monitoring technology in the workplace can transform employer-employee dynamics. AI-driven monitoring tools use algorithms to track employees' activities, assess performance metrics, and provide real-time feedback. For example, Amazon has deployed the Associate Development and Performance Tracker (ADAPT), an AI system that monitors worker productivity in its warehouses and can automatically fire them (Ye 2022). The use of AI for monitoring is not limited to manual labor, though; it extends to white-collar jobs, where it can, for instance, track online activity for hiring and performance evaluation (Dattner et al. 2019).

These systems are designed to optimize efficiency, but they also raise questions about the impact of monitoring on workers. Research has shown that constant surveillance can negatively impact workers' well-being and feelings of autonomy, linking it to increased stress and anxiety and also leading employees to feel distrusted (Ball et al. 2021). In particular, monitoring with technology has been found to be associated with negative mental health outcomes (American Psychological Association 2023). Moreover, concerns about data privacy and the potential for misuse add further complexity to the use of AI surveillance. That said, AI-powered monitoring could also lead to improvements in worker well-being by identifying factors causing dissatisfaction and providing targeted interventions to enhance job satisfaction and retention. For example, IBM's artificial intelligence has been shown to predict with 95 percent accuracy which employees are likely to quit (CNBC 2019).

Policymakers are advocating for stringent regulations to shield employees from excessive surveillance, proposing laws that restrict the methods and timing of workplace monitoring. For instance, New York City enacted a law in July 2023 requiring employers to conduct independent bias audits of their automated tools used in hiring and promotions (*The Week* 2023). Others emphasize the necessity for transparency, urging companies to inform employees about the extent and purpose of monitoring practices. In various regions, unions and advocacy groups have championed the "right to disconnect," aiming to protect workers from incessant monitoring and preserve work-life balance (UNI P&M 2020). These discussions highlight the importance of a balanced approach to AI-driven workplace monitoring, one that upholds employee well-being and privacy while allowing efficiency improvements.

1.3.4 Virtual Worlds and Labor Supply

Virtual worlds, immersive digital environments where users can interact and create experiences in real time, are becoming increasingly popular with advancements in AI-powered virtual reality technologies. Unlike traditional digital platforms, these worlds may in the future offer more engaging, highly interactive experiences that can simulate or even surpass real-world environments. Companies such as Meta, Epic Games, and Microsoft are investing heavily in these technologies, aiming to create virtual spaces where users can work, socialize, and entertain themselves, often referred to collectively as the "metaverse."

The rise of virtual worlds presents a unique impact on labor markets, as these immersive environments have the potential to draw users away from traditional work settings. Unlike autonomous vehicles or generative AI, which may directly displace jobs, virtual worlds influence labor participation indirectly by providing compelling alternatives to physical-world employment. Immersive virtual environments could lower real-world engagement and even reduce workforce participation by offering users a psychologically fulfilling escape from economic pressures and job responsibilities. Over time, the attraction of these digital spaces could lead to a gradual but notable decline in labor-force participation, especially among younger generations more open to digital and remote lifestyles. Early evidence hints at the social and economic allure of virtual worlds as an alternative to traditional labor market participation. Aguiar et al. (2021) have shown that immersive gaming, a precursor to the virtual world experience, is associated with a reduction in labor force participation among young adults. Furthermore, the economic opportunities within virtual worlds—such as virtual real estate, digital product sales, and paid interactions—allow users to earn income within these spaces, potentially decreasing the incentive to participate in traditional labor markets. For instance, platforms like Decentraland and Roblox enable users to monetize virtual assets, creating an economy within the virtual world itself.

While virtual worlds are still in their infancy, the potential shift away from traditional labor markets could prove as transformative as the shift from traditional retail to e-commerce. Just as e-commerce reshaped consumer behavior and the retail landscape, virtual worlds could similarly redefine workforce engagement, drawing individuals into immersive digital economies and reducing traditional labor market participation. Potential conflicts in regulatory and labor law are likely to arise, too, particularly regarding labor classification and taxation in digital economies. Policymakers may need to address whether economic activities in virtual worlds should be regulated as traditional employment, and how to protect workers' rights in a digital context, especially if these environments become primary sources of income for significant segments of the population.

1.4 The Disruption of Property Rights over Inputs

In this section, we discuss how novel AI applications will make previously overlooked resources valuable, leading to conflict and contestation regarding property rights over these inputs. We begin with conflicts over the use of online data in the case of generative AI and digital advertising, and then consider other forms of data, like genetic data for personalized medicine and biometrics for emotion recognition. We then describe how drones and other autonomous vehicles can lead to contestation over space and spectrum, inputs that can become congested. Last, and more speculatively, we discuss AI-powered technologies that might result in conflicts over biological or waste materials.

1.4.1 Online Data

1.4.1.1 Generative AI and Online Content

Generative AI companies identified online content (text and images) as a valuable input for training their models. The boundaries around online content ownership and its use had been only loosely defined before the advent of these tools. As such, generative AI has elevated text and image data to a fiercely contested input, sparking major legal disputes. For instance, OpenAI's ChatGPT was trained on vast amounts of text from books, websites, and other written sources, enabling it to produce responses to a variety of user prompts. *The New York Times* (NYT) has taken legal action against OpenAI, alleging unauthorized use of its articles in training ChatGPT. The core of the complaint is that OpenAI knowingly scraped NYT articles without obtaining a license, violating copyright law. The lawsuit claims that, when users prompt ChatGPT, the AI could generate outputs that closely mimic NYT articles—sometimes outright inventing them—or produce exact copies—what is known as "regurgitation"—thus misleading users and infringing on the newspaper's intellectual property rights. For example, the lawsuit states: "165. On information and belief, Defendants' infringing conduct alleged herein was and continues to be willful and carried out with full knowledge of The Times's rights in the copyrighted works. As a direct result of their conduct, Defendants have wrongfully profited from copyrighted works that they do not own" (The New York Times Co. v. OpenAI, Inc., et al., S.D.N.Y., 2023).

OpenAI argued that the NYT lawsuit lacks merit. For instance, OpenAI has asserted that its use of publicly available internet data, including from news sources, is protected by the fair use doctrine, which allows for limited use of copyrighted material for purposes like research and education. Moreover, they address concerns about regurgitation, explaining that such occurrences are unintentional and rare, and that efforts are made to minimize them.[5]

Similarly, Getty Images has filed a lawsuit against Stability AI, the company behind the tool Stable Diffusion. The tool is designed to generate high-quality images from user text prompts, making it a popular choice for AI-generated art. It was trained on a massive dataset of images and text descriptions, sourced from publicly available online platforms such as image-hosting websites, art communities, and social media. Getty alleges that Stability AI unlawfully scraped a vast number of its images, resulting in the unauthorized reproduction and potential modification of copyrighted material. The lawsuit also claims that Stability AI's actions were conducted with knowledge of the infringement. For example, the lawsuit states in *Getty Images Inc. v. Stability AI, Inc.* (D. Del. 2023): "58. Upon information and belief, Stability AI has knowingly removed Getty Images' watermarks from some images in the course of its copying as part of its infringing scheme. At the same time, however, as discussed above, the Stable Diffusion model frequently generates output bearing a modified version of the Getty Images watermark, even when that output is not bona fide Getty Images' content and is well below Getty Images' quality standards."

These cases illustrate generative AI's disruption of input markets where property rights related to their use were not clearly defined beforehand, leading to contestation. Arguably, the companies are banking on the expectation that courts and regulatory bodies would endorse their extensive data usage practices without explicit permissions. The evolution of the AI industry might change significantly if the legal framework were to enforce stringent protections for online content as intellectual property going forward.[6]

1.4.1.2 Digital Advertising and User Data

Digital advertising platforms have identified user data as an invaluable asset for AI-powered targeted advertising. Before the rise of these sophisticated platforms, the boundaries around user data ownership and its monetization were relatively undefined. As the platforms began harnessing data and AI algorithms to serve hypertargeted ads, they transformed personal data into a highly contested resource, raising profound privacy and ethical concerns.

5. See "OpenAI and Journalism," January 8, 2024, https://openai.com/index/openai-and-journalism/ for these and other counterarguments.

6. It is ironic that the *output* of large language models, like ChatGPT, has itself become a valuable, contestable input, functioning as training data used in "model distillation," in which a teacher model trains a student model. Such distillation may, in some cases, be unauthorized. This issue, which has recently come to prominence with the success of the AI firm DeepSeek, has placed incumbent firms, like OpenAI and Microsoft, in the position of trying to *prevent* an innovator from exploiting a novel input (see, e.g., *Forbes* 2025; Hulse et al. 2025).

For example, Google and Facebook collect vast amounts of user data, including browsing habits, location, and social connections, which are used to optimize advertising for individual users. Digital advertising is particularly valuable on these platforms precisely because of the data they can collect on their users, allowing companies to predict behavior and influence decisions. Zuboff (2023) describes it as a "surveillance capitalism" model, where user data is not only harvested but also transformed into a commodity to predict and manipulate consumer behavior.

Initial data collection practices by digital advertising companies often lacked transparent user consent (Esteve 2017). Users were largely unaware that their information was being monetized on such a large scale, and many continue to raise concerns about the extent of surveillance involved in these platforms' ad-targeting processes. The European Union's Digital Markets Act (DMA) and other regulatory efforts have recently sought to rein in the extensive data practices of digital platforms, mandating transparency and stricter data usage guidelines. Nonetheless, disputes persist. High-profile incidents, such as the Cambridge Analytica scandal, highlight the dangers of data leakages and unauthorized data sharing, demonstrating the societal risks and potential damages of AI-powered digital advertising.[7]

While companies like Google and Facebook assert that their data practices comply with legal standards, regulatory bodies continue to scrutinize their policies. The industry is currently at a crossroads, where clearer data property rights and privacy protections are increasingly being demanded. As regulatory frameworks evolve, the AI-powered digital advertising landscape may be forced to adapt, potentially limiting the unbounded data usage practices that have been foundational to its growth.

1.4.2 Other Forms of Data

1.4.2.1 Personalized Medicine and Genetic Data

With the advancement of AI in personalized medicine, genetic data may increasingly become a contested input for training models that predict health outcomes, tailor treatments, or identify disease risks. Companies like 23andMe have amassed extensive genetic databases from millions of customers, which are utilized to enhance personalized medicine and advance biomedical research. For instance, in 2018, 23andMe entered a collaboration with GlaxoSmithKline, granting the pharmaceutical company access to its genetic data to aid in drug discovery and development (Live Science 2018).

Ownership of genetic data is a pivotal issue in the debate surrounding AI-driven health care. Companies typically claim ownership over the aggregated

7. Cambridge Analytica used data harvested from millions of Facebook profiles to influence political campaigns, leading to widespread public outcry and scrutiny of Facebook's data protection policies (*The Guardian* 2018).

genetic data collected from their customers, often reserving the right to use or share this data with research partners or pharmaceutical firms. In many cases, companies assert control over the data under the terms of service agreements. This lack of transparent consent means that individuals may be unaware that their data is being shared or sold. The debate over ownership brings up complex questions: Should individuals have a proprietary claim over their genetic information, especially as it relates to their unique genetic makeup? Or does the aggregated and anonymized nature of the data shift the ownership to the collector?

In response to these challenges, regulation could treat genetic data as a public good. Public genetic data repositories—where individuals could contribute genetic data for research with stronger privacy protections—could emerge as an alternative to private databases. In the European Union, the General Data Protection Regulation is already impacting how companies collect, process, and share genetic data (PHG 2020), though specific provisions on genetic data ownership are still developing. As AI applications in health care expand, property rights over genetic data are likely to become even more contested, with potential implications for both individual privacy and the future landscape of health-care innovation.

1.4.2.2 Emotion Recognition AI and Biometrics

Emotion recognition AI can analyze how people react to content, advertisements, or instructions. As these systems become more sophisticated, companies could use gestures, facial expressions, and other biometric signals to tailor products, personalize marketing strategies, or even influence consumer decisions in real time. In turn, biometric data would become a highly valuable resource.

However, ownership over biometric data is ambiguous, especially in public or semiprivate spaces. For example, it is unclear who has the right to capture, analyze, or profit from someone's physical reactions at a live event, in a classroom, or even on public streets. This ambiguity could lead to legal conflicts between individuals, companies, and public entities over rights to access and analyze biometric signals, and it could drive regulators to step in and settle who "owns" the right to one's observable gestures and expressions.

1.4.2.3 Sports Performance Enhancement and Body Movements

AI applications in sports and physical performance optimization increasingly rely on analyzing athletes' body movements, often captured through motion sensors or video in training facilities, stadiums, and public spaces. These movement patterns are valuable for training AI models that can enhance athletic performance or prevent injuries. Yet, there is ambiguity in ownership rights over movement data in certain settings—particularly when movements are recorded during public events or in shared training spaces.

This ambiguity could lead to contestation, especially if organizations, athletes, or facility owners claim rights over motion data collected in these spaces. For instance, a sports venue might seek to monetize the body movement data of athletes or performers, whereas athletes themselves could argue that such data belongs to them. To address these issues, legal frameworks might need to define whether motion data captured in public or semipublic spaces is a collective or individual resource, and under what conditions it can be commercialized.

1.4.2.4 Sound Recognition and Natural Soundscapes

Beyond recent applications to voice recognition, AI-powered sound recognition applications could soon move to natural soundscapes like birdcalls, ocean waves, or ambient urban sounds. These soundscapes could thus become valuable resources for training and deploying AI in applications like wildlife conservation, urban planning, and smart city design. However, the rights to capture and analyze these sounds are often undefined, especially in public or communal environments.

For example, if an AI company uses urban noise data collected in a public park to train sound recognition algorithms for commercial applications, questions may arise around who controls access to the ambient soundscape. This could lead to debates over the ownership of public sound environments, with cities potentially asserting control over sound data generated within their limits, or communities demanding consent before companies can collect and commercialize soundscapes. Such regulations could treat ambient sounds as a shared resource, requiring companies to navigate new property rights considerations.

1.4.3 Congestible Space and Spectrum

1.4.3.1 Drones and Urban Airspace

As AI advances in areas like aerial surveillance and drone-based delivery, urban airspace will likely become a contested resource, particularly in densely populated cities. Unlike traditional airspace, which is regulated for commercial aviation, low-altitude urban airspace remains largely unregulated or limited to smaller drones with strict restrictions. However, AI's potential to manage fleets of delivery drones, inspection devices, and surveillance equipment has the potential to make this limited airspace highly valuable.

For example, companies like Alphabet's Wing and Amazon have begun testing drone delivery services, aiming to utilize urban airspace to expedite logistics for customers in metropolitan areas. Amazon, in particular, has lobbied the FAA to secure greater operational flexibility for its delivery drones, focusing on gaining access to airspace that allows for efficient delivery routes in urban settings (*Broadband Breakfast* 2023). Recently, the

FAA approved Wing drones to use an automatic dependent broadcast inside a major area of Dallas airspace where traditional aircraft are required to continually broadcast their position (*Robotics and Automation News* 2024).

The result could be conflicts between various industries (e.g., retail, logistics, security) vying for airspace usage rights. Cities may introduce "airspace zoning" laws or prioritize certain companies' or public services' access to air corridors based on public need, leading to increased regulation and potentially contested claims over airspace rights.

1.4.3.2 Delivery Robots and Sidewalk Space

Beyond airspace, ground-level public infrastructure such as roads and sidewalks could also become a contested resource as AI-driven delivery robots become popular. These autonomous systems require dedicated space to operate safely and efficiently, potentially competing with pedestrian traffic, traditional vehicles, and even other autonomous devices.

The competition for road and sidewalk space could lead to debates over prioritizing certain uses, especially in dense urban centers. Local governments may have to regulate these spaces more strictly, setting rules about which companies or types of autonomous devices can access which areas and at which times. Companies could lobby for priority access to reduce delivery times, while public advocates might push for pedestrian safety and access. The need for clear "public space rights" might spur a new layer of regulation, where companies lease specific areas for operation, similar to traditional utility easements.

1.4.3.3 Communication Networks and Electromagnetic Spectrum

With the growth of AI-driven devices and autonomous systems—drones, robots, Internet of Things devices, and more—the demand for wireless communication is expected to surge. Traditionally, governments have managed and auctioned off parts of the electromagnetic spectrum to telecom companies. But current allocation frameworks may not adequately address the requirements of these emerging technologies, leading to clashes over the allocation of spectrum resources.

For instance, AI-driven drone delivery systems depend on stable, high-bandwidth communication to operate safely and efficiently in dense urban environments. Companies like Amazon have already begun to lobby for dedicated spectrum allocations to ensure the reliability and safety of drone operations, particularly in areas with congested airspace (Altindex 2024). These efforts underscore the industry's recognition of the critical role that dedicated spectrum will play.

The regulatory landscape will have to evolve to address these challenges. Governments may have to balance spectrum availability between traditional telecom providers and emerging AI applications, perhaps creating new frameworks to designate "AI-exclusive" frequency bands. Otherwise, without clearer definitions and rights around spectrum usage, the deployment of next-generation AI technologies may face significant roadblocks.

1.4.4 Materials

1.4.4.1 Novel Drugs and Biological Materials

As AI accelerates the search for novel compounds in drug discovery, biological resources from remote ecosystems—like rainforests, coral reefs, and deep-sea environments—could become highly valuable. AI models can analyze genetic sequences from plants, fungi, and microorganisms to identify promising compounds for new drugs. However, the rights over these resources are often poorly defined, particularly in areas that aren't fully mapped, that are governed by local tribes, or that are in international waters.

For instance, if an AI model uses samples from organisms collected in an unclaimed deep-sea trench, questions may arise about whether these resources should belong to the global community, be protected as part of natural biodiversity, or be open to commercial exploitation. Similar disputes have already emerged in biotechnology, but AI's ability to exponentially scale these efforts could intensify the debate, with governments potentially intervening to set international standards that clarify access rights.

1.4.4.2 Recycling and Waste Materials

Traditionally seen as low-value byproducts, materials such as plastic, metals, and organic waste could in the future be repurposed by AI-enhanced recycling systems with unprecedented efficiency. Recycling companies using advanced AI sorting and processing technologies may begin to view waste as a valuable resource, sparking disputes over who holds the rights to these materials. Municipalities, private waste management firms, and recycling businesses could all claim ownership, especially as certain high-value waste streams like e-waste (discarded electronic devices and equipment) gain attention for their reusable components.

The courts may, in the future, need to clarify who owns valuable waste streams. Further, regulations might establish waste materials as shared resources, where municipalities, private firms, and recycling companies have structured access based on environmental and economic priorities. Moreover, as AI-enhanced recycling often involves processing hazardous materials, new environmental protections may become necessary to manage the risks associated with advanced sorting and repurposing technologies.

1.5 Conclusions

The general disruption induced by AI technologies has two features that we believe deserve particular attention from both academics and policymakers. First, AI's disruption in contestable input markets has the potential to generate enormous rents for innovators; to result in litigation among competing claimants; and, ultimately, to produce political conflicts to determine how property rights are established and rents are distributed. The political economy of groundbreaking innovation under contested property rights has not received significant attention from academic economists. But it is both of current policy interest (and of more general interest) to understand how innovation occurs when technologies use novel inputs and rules and rights are ill established beforehand.

Second, the generalized nature of AI disruption across multiple domains raises the possibility that disruptions will *interact*. For example, disruption in the labor market might typically produce a public policy response (e.g., implementation of redistribution or retraining programs). But AI's disruption of political institutions might shape the way public policy responds to the disruption of labor markets. A sanguine perspective is that AI may enhance state capacity to identify individuals with needs and to target retraining and redistribution: Disruption at one margin may be mitigated by disruption at another. A more pessimistic view is that the social costs of labor disruption will be compounded by AI's disruption of the functioning of democratic institutions; rather than strengthening the social safety net, labor market disruption may induce political extremism or attempts at political repression, enhanced by AI technology. Likewise, disruption in contestable input markets may prompt AI innovators—or competing stakeholders—to leverage AI's disruptive potential in the media to shape public opinion, influence litigation outcomes, and steer regulatory responses.

AI's disruptive capacity along novel, potentially interacting margins offers both opportunities and risks that policymakers and academics are now working to understand. By preparing for large-scale disruption, we can aim for policies that make such salutary spillovers more likely and that mitigate the pernicious consequences that we fear.

References

Acemoglu, Daron. 2021. "Harms of AI." Technical report. National Bureau of Economic Research.

Acemoglu, Daron, and Pascual Restrepo. 2022. "Tasks, Automation, and the Rise in US Wage Inequality." *Econometrica* 90 (5): 1973–2016.

Aghion, Philippe, Ufuk Akcigit, and Peter Howitt. 2014. "What Do We Learn from Schumpeterian Growth Theory?" In *Handbook of Economic Growth*, 2:515–63. Elsevier.

Agrawal, Ajay, Joshua Gans, and Avi Goldfarb. 2022. *Power and Prediction: The Disruptive Economics of Artificial Intelligence*. Harvard Business Press.

Aguiar, Mark, Mark Bils, Kerwin Kofi Charles, and Erik Hurst. 2021. "Leisure

Luxuries and the Labor Supply of Young Men." *Journal of Political Economy* 129 (2): 337–82.

Allcott, Hunt, and Matthew Gentzkow. 2017. "Social Media and Fake News in the 2016 Election." *Journal of Economic Perspectives* 31 (2): 211–36.

Allcott, Hunt, Matthew Gentzkow, Winter Mason, Arjun Wilkins, Pablo Barberá, Taylor Brown, Juan Carlos Cisneros, Adriana Crespo-Tenorio, Drew Dimmery, Deen Freelon, et al. 2024. "The Effects of Facebook and Instagram on the 2020 Election: A Deactivation Experiment." *Proceedings of the National Academy of Sciences* 121 (21): e2321584121.

Allcott, Hunt, Matthew Gentzkow, and Lena Song. 2022. "Digital Addiction." *American Economic Review* 112 (7): 2424–63.

Altindex. 2024. "Amazon's Lobbying Push in Q3: Technology, Copyright, and Strategic Influence." https://altindex.com/news/amazon-lobbying-focus.

American Psychological Association. 2023. "Work in America Survey." https://www.apa.org/pubs/reports/work-in-america/2023-work-america-ai-monitoring.

Angerer, Silvia, Christian Waibel, and Harald Stummer. 2019. "Discrimination in Health Care: A Field Experiment on the Impact of Patients' Socioeconomic Status on Access to Care." *American Journal of Health Economics* 5 (4): 407–27.

Atkins, Rachel, Lisa Cook, and Robert Seamans. 2022. "Discrimination in Lending? Evidence from the Paycheck Protection Program." *Small Business Economics*: 1–23.

Bains, Chiraag. 2024. "The Legal Doctrine That Will Be Key to Preventing AI Discrimination." Brookings Institution, September 13. https://www.brookings.edu/articles/the-legal-doctrine-that-will-be-key-to-preventing-ai-discrimination/.

Ball, Kirstie, et al. 2021. *Electronic Monitoring and Surveillance in the Workplace*. European Commission Joint Research Centre.

BBC News. 2019a. "San Francisco Is First US City to Ban Facial Recognition." May 19. https://www.bbc.co.uk/news/technology-48276660.

BBC News. 2019b. "UK Workers Who Lose Jobs to AI Will Be Retrained." July 17. https://www.bbc.com/news/business-49019390.

BBC News. 2023. "Online Safety Bill: Divisive Internet Rules Become Law." October 26. https://www.bbc.co.uk/news/technology-67221691.

BBC News. 2024. "We'll Need Universal Basic Income—AI 'Godfather.'" May 18. https://www.bbc.com/news/articles/cnd607ekl99o.

Beknazar-Yuzbashev, George, Rafael Jiménez Durán, Jesse McCrosky, and Mateusz Stalinski. 2022. "Toxic Content and User Engagement on Social Media: Evidence from a Field Experiment." https://papers.ssrn.com/sol3/papers.cfm?abstract_id=4307346.

Beraja, Martin, Andrew Kao, David Y. Yang, and Noam Yuchtman. 2023a. "AI-tocracy." *Quarterly Journal of Economics* 138 (3): 1349–1402.

Beraja, Martin, Andrew Kao, David Y. Yang, and Noam Yuchtman. 2023b. "Exporting the Surveillance State via Trade in AI." Working Paper No. 31676. National Bureau of Economic Research. https://www.nber.org/papers/w31676.

Beraja, Martin, David Y. Yang, and Noam Yuchtman. 2023. "Data-Intensive Innovation and the State: Evidence from AI Firms in China." *Review of Economic Studies* 90 (4): 1701–23. https://doi.org/10.1093/restud/rdac056.

Beraja, Martin, and Nathan Zorzi. 2024. "Inefficient Automation." *Review of Economic Studies* 92 (1): 69–96.

Broadband Breakfast. 2022. "Amazon Asks FCC to Allow Drones in 60–64 GHz Band in Preparation for New Delivery Service." November 23. https://broadbandbreakfast.com/amazon-asks-fcc-to-allow-drones-in-60-64-ghz-band-in-preparation-for-new-delivery-service/

Bursztyn, Leonardo, Benjamin R Handel, Rafael Jimenez, and Christopher Roth.

2023. "When Product Markets Become Collective Traps: The Case of Social Media." Technical report. National Bureau of Economic Research.
The Chicago Maroon. 2024. "30-Foot Inflatable Dog Promotes NOMO App's Anti-Social Media Challenge." October 24. https://chicagomaroon.com/44360/news/30-foot-inflatable-dog-promotes-nomo-apps-anti-social-media-challenge/.
Christensen, Clayton M. 2015. *The Innovator's Dilemma: When New Technologies Cause Great Firms to Fail*. Harvard Business Review Press.
Christian, Brian. 2021. *The Alignment Problem: How Can Machines Learn Human Values?* Atlantic Books.
CNBC. 2019. "IBM Artificial Intelligence Can Predict with 95% Accuracy Which Workers Are About to Quit Their Jobs." *CNBC Work*, April 3. https://www.cnbc.com/2019/04/03/ibm-ai-can-predict-with-95-percent-accuracy-which-employees-will-quit.html.
Dattner, Ben, Tomas Chamorro-Premuzic, Richard Buchband, and Lucinda Schettler. 2019. "The Legal and Ethical Implications of Using AI in Hiring." *Harvard Business Review* 25: 1–7.
Dobbie, Will, Peter Hull, and David Arnold. 2022. "Measuring Racial Discrimination in Bail Decisions." *American Economic Review* 112 (9): 2992–3038.
Eloundou, Tyna, Sam Manning, Pamela Mishkin, and Daniel Rock. 2023. "GPTs Are GPTs: An Early Look at the Labor Market Impact Potential of Large Language Models." Technical report. arXiv.org.
Enikolopov, Ruben, Maria Petrova, Gianluca Russo, and David Yanagizawa-Drott. 2024. "Socializing Alone: How Online Homophily Has Undermined Social Cohesion in the US." https://papers.ssrn.com/sol3/papers.cfm?abstract_id=4738801.
Esteve, Asunción. 2017. "The Business of Personal Data: Google, Facebook, and Privacy Issues in the EU and the USA." *International Data Privacy Law* 7 (1): 36–47.
Forbes. 2025. "OpenAI Believes DeepSeek 'Distilled' Its Data for Training—Here's What to Know About the Technique." January 29. https://www.forbes.com/sites/siladityaray/2025/01/29/openai-believes-deepseek-distilled-its-data-for-training-heres-what-to-know-about-the-technique/.
Fujiwara, Thomas, Karsten Müller, and Carlo Schwarz. 2024. "The Effect of Social Media on Elections: Evidence from the United States." *Journal of the European Economic Association* 22 (3): 1495–1539.
Gordon, Robert J. 2016. *The Rise and Fall of American Growth: The US Standard of Living Since the Civil War*. Princeton University Press.
Groshen, Erica L., Susan Helper, John Paul MacDuffie, and Charles Carson. 2018. "Preparing US Workers and Employers for an Autonomous Vehicle Future." Technical report. US Department of Transportation, June. https://avworkforce.secureenergy.org/wp-content/uploads/2018/06/Groshen-et-al-Report-June-201811.pdf.
The Guardian. 2018. "Revealed: 50 Million Facebook Profiles Harvested for Cambridge Analytica in Major Data Breach." March 17. https://www.theguardian.com/news/2018/mar/17/cambridge-analytica-facebook-influence-us-election.
Guerreiro, João, Sergio Rebelo, and Pedro Teles. 2022. "Should Robots Be Taxed?" *Review of Economic Studies* 89 (1): 279–311.
Hulse, Robert, Tyler G. Newby, Stuart P. Meyer, and Fredrick Tsang. 2025. "DeepSeek, Model Distillation, and the Future of AI IP Protection." Fenwick, February 3. https://www.fenwick.com/insights/publications/deepseek-model-distillation-and-the-future-of-ai-ip-protection
Kleinberg, Jon, Himabindu Lakkaraju, Jure Leskovec, Jens Ludwig, and Sendhil Mullainathan. 2018. "Human Decisions and Machine Predictions." *Quarterly Journal of Economics* 133 (1): 237–93.
Live Science. 2018. "23andMe Is Sharing Its 5 Million Clients' Genetic Data with

Drug Giant GlaxoSmithKline." *Live Science*, July 26. https://www.livescience.com/63173-23andme-partnership-glaxosmithkline.html.

McKinsey. 2024. "Generative AI and the Future of Work in America." Research paper, July 26. https://www.mckinsey.com/mgi/our-research/generative-ai-and-the-future-of-work-in-america.

Müller, Karsten, and Carlo Schwarz. 2021. "Fanning the Flames of Hate: Social Media and Hate Crime." *Journal of the European Economic Association* 19 (4): 2131–67.

Müller, Karsten, and Carlo Schwarz. 2023. "The Effects of Online Content Moderation: Evidence from President Trump's Account Deletion." https://papers.ssrn.com/sol3/papers.cfm?abstract_id=4296306.

Nevada Revised Statutes § 372B.145—Excise Tax on Autonomous Vehicle Network Companies. 2022. https://law.justia.com/codes/nevada/2022/chapter-372b/statute-372b-145/.

PHG. 2020. "The GDPR and Genomic Data." PHG Foundation Report.

Phillips, Fisher. 2023. "How Will Employment Policymakers Respond to Autonomous Vehicles?" Insights 8.21.18. https://www.fisherphillips.com/en/news-insights/autonomous-vehicles-blog-driving-the-future/how-will-employment-policymakers-respond-to-autonomous-vehicles.html.

Robotics and Automation News. 2024. "Google-Owned Wing Wins FAA Authorization for Drone Deliveries." *Robotics and Automation News*, January 16. https://roboticsandautomationnews.com/2024/01/16/wing-wins-faa-authorization-for-drone-deliveries/76638/.

Time Magazine. 2024. "As Employers Embrace AI, Workers Fret—and Seek Input." June 21. https://time.com/6990637/ai-employers-workers.

Tirole, Jean. 2021. "Digital Dystopia." *American Economic Review* 111 (6): 2007–48.

UNI P&M. 2020. "Legislating a Right to Disconnect." UNI Guide. https://uniglobalunion.org/wp-content/uploads/uni_pm_right_to_disconnect_en.pdf.

US Congress. 2024. "Bipartisan House Task Force Report on Artificial Intelligence." Technical report, December. https://www.speaker.gov/wp-content/uploads/2024/12/AI-Task-Force-Report-FINAL.pdf.

US Department of Commerce. 2017. "The Employment Impact of Autonomous Vehicles." Technical report, August 11. https://www.commerce.gov/data-and-reports/reports/2017/08/employment-impact-autonomous-vehicles.

US Department of Commerce. 2024. "Commerce Strengthens Export Controls to Restrict China's Capability to Produce Advanced Semiconductors for Military Applications." Technical report. Bureau of Industry and Security, December 2. https://www.bis.gov/press-release/commerce-strengthens-export-controls-restrict-chinas-capability-produce-advanced-semiconductors-military.

The Verge. 2023. "FAA Clears UPS for Long-Range Delivery Drones." September 6. https://www.theverge.com/2023/9/6/23861764/faa-ups-delivery-drones-amazon-prime-air.

The Verge. 2024a. "Amazon's Prime Air Delivery Drones Can Fly Even Farther After FAA Approval." May 30. https://www.theverge.com/2024/5/30/24167776/amazon-prime-air-delivery-drones-faa-bvlos-approval.

The Verge. 2024b. "Lyft Is Also Partnering with Robotaxi Companies." November 6. https://www.theverge.com/2024/11/6/24289475/lyft-may-mobility-mobileye-nexar-autonomous-robotaxi.

Viscelli, Steve. 2018. "Driverless? Autonomous Trucks and the Future of the American Trucker." UC Berkeley Center for Labor Research and Education.

The Wall Street Journal. 2024. "Waymo to Offer Self-Driving Cars on Uber in Austin and Atlanta." September 13. https://www.wsj.com/tech/waymo-to-offer-self

-driving-cars-on-uber-in-austin-and-atlanta-ac651aa3?utm_source=chatgpt.com.

The Week. 2023. "The (Ongoing) Fight Against Workplace AI Surveillance." January 15. https://theweek.com/tech/workplace-ai-surveillance.

Wired. 2024. "AI Slop Is Flooding Medium." October 28. https://www.wired.com/story/ai-generated-medium-posts-content-moderation.

Ye, Alice. 2022. "Amazon's ADAPT and Its Harm on Workers." *Behind the Data: Humans and Values* (UC Berkeley Data Science blog), March 2. https://blogs.ischool.berkeley.edu/w231/2022/03/02/amazons-adapt-and-its-harm-on-workers/.

Zuboff, Shoshana. 2023. "The Age of Surveillance Capitalism." In *Social Theory Re-Wired*, 203–13. Routledge.

2

Data as the New Oil
Parallels, Challenges, and Regulatory Implications

Chiara Farronato

The impact of technological innovation often relies on harnessing previously overlooked or underutilized resources, as illustrated by the historical progression of oil and the contemporary role of data. Just as the development of drilling and refining technologies revolutionized the utility of oil in the second half of the 19th century, a series of technological developments over the past few decades, most recently exemplified by the advent of generative artificial intelligence (GenAI), is unlocking the new potential of data. This series of innovations turned raw inputs—crude oil and raw data—into valuable outputs, fundamentally reshaping industries. However, the emergence of such technologies also raises critical questions about property rights and other forms of regulation. The metaphor "data is the new oil" often arises in discussions, both within academic circles—such as at the NBER conference for this handbook—and beyond. In this short article, I delve into this analogy, exploring the similarities and differences between oil and data as transformative resources.

The association between data and oil is widely attributed to Clive Humby, a British mathematician and data scientist.[1] In 2006, Humby emphasized that data, like crude oil, is valuable only in combination with technologies

Chiara Farronato is the Glenn and Mary Jane Creamer Associate Professor of Business Administration at Harvard Business School, a research associate of the Centre for Economic Policy Research, and a faculty research fellow of the National Bureau of Economic Research.

For acknowledgments, sources of research support, and disclosure of the author's material financial relationships, if any, please see https://www.nber.org/books-and-chapters/political-economy-artificial-intelligence/data-new-oil-parallels-challenges-and-regulatory-implications.

1. Nisha Talagala, "Data as the New Oil Is Not Enough: Four Principles for Avoiding Data Fires," *Forbes*, March 2, 2022, https://www.forbes.com/sites/nishatalagala/2022/03/02/data-as-the-new-oil-is-not-enough-four-principles-for-avoiding-data-fires/.

that refine it into useful outputs, be it consumer insights for product improvements or response suggestions to customer service inquiries. This metaphor highlights the shared trajectory of oil and data: Both have become transformative resources only through significant technological advancements that unlocked their potential. However, this parallel also highlights an important challenge. Just as oil's extraction and use brought about complex regulatory and societal issues, the emergence of data as a valuable resource introduces equally difficult questions about regulatory and societal implications.

The fact that innovation brings about regulatory uncertainty is not a new phenomenon. In fact, new businesses often exploit legal gray areas to drive innovation. There are many such examples in the most recent digital age. Electronic commerce enjoyed a tax advantage in the early days because a 1992 Supreme Court ruling required businesses to have a physical presence in a state for the sales taxes to be applicable.[2] Companies like Amazon and eBay (Einav, Knoepfle, et al. 2014) could thus charge lower prices compared to brick-and-mortar retailers, contributing to the growth of e-commerce. Eventually, in 2018, the Supreme Court overturned its initial ruling,[3] thus allowing states to collect sales taxes from online retailers. More recently, ride-sharing and short-term rental platforms also entered markets while avoiding the regulations that govern incumbents. At least initially, Uber and Lyft avoided requirements such as taxi medallions and commercial licensing and insurance. Similarly, Airbnb avoided lodging taxes and was exempt from complying with zoning laws. Eventually, regulators caught up with the new service platforms by applying the existing regulations to the new providers, creating new regulations, or banning the new providers altogether.

These examples have in common the fact that the innovators' approach relied on exploiting gaps and ambiguity in several existing laws (Einav, Farronato, and Levin 2016), of which Beraja and Yuchtman (2025) in this handbook emphasize property rights. In these contexts, it is often impossible to clarify the applicable regulation ex ante. First, the parties with whom the innovator would have to contract are many and fragmented: states in the case of sales taxes and local jurisdictions in the case of lodging taxes and taxi medallions. Second, regulators can often be influenced by incumbents (Callander and Li 2024), who have more lobbying resources and a strong interest in not being disrupted. Finally, regulation can take a long time, increasing investment costs and the risks of innovation obsolescence. As an example, news aggregators such as Google News, which will be discussed later, emerged in the early 2000s, whereas regulation over the aggregators' use of snippets and hyperlinks from original publishers was not approved until at least 2019 in the European Union and even later in other countries.

2. Quill Corp. v. North Dakota, 504 U.S. 298 (1992), https://supreme.justia.com/cases/federal/us/504/298/.

3. South Dakota v. Wayfair, Inc., 585 U.S. ___ (2018), https://www.supremecourt.gov/opinions/17pdf/17-494_j4el.pdf.

Oil and data are alike in that radical innovations have leveraged these inputs. However, it is worth highlighting that it was not a single technological innovation that unleashed their potential. For oil, the drilling of oil wells was not enough. In fact, shortly after 1859, when Edwin Drake drilled his first well in Titusville, Pennsylvania, the well was shut down because it was not profitable. The price of crude oil, which was mostly usable only in its raw form as lamp fuel, was too low to justify the project.[4] The oil well was followed by a long series of technological advancements over the following several decades—from distillation to cracking to more complex refining processes—which allowed for oil to be transformed into usable (and very valuable) products, such as gasoline or plastics (Yergin 2011).

In this respect, the "data as oil" metaphor is fitting. Humby's 2006 quote, over a decade before the current GenAI revolution, was likely motivated by the early applications of data science and machine learning to electronic commerce. Google's PageRank algorithm was one of the earliest applications of using information about web pages to rank them in search results (Page et al. 1999). Amazon pioneered collaborative filtering to suggest products on the basis of customers' own behavior and the behavior of similar users (Linden, Smith, and York 2003). Like oil, the data refining supply chain is a complex set of processes (Iansiti and Lakhani 2020) that, over the past decades, has been experiencing a long sequence of technological innovations. Most recently, that is exemplified by the introduction of generative adversarial networks (Goodfellow et al. 2020) and transformers (Vaswani et al. 2017) in combination with computing technology—such as graphics processing units (GPUs)—that allows for parallelization and scaling up of massive models. Such evolution has led to data generating more and more insights across an increasing number of applications. There is no reason to think today is the end of the journey.

That is where the similarities between oil and data stop. The two differ in several important dimensions that will affect how property rights and other forms of regulation will be defined in the age of artificial intelligence (AI). When it comes to data, the task of regulating property rights is made more challenging than with oil by the fundamental difficulty of pricing information, also known as Arrow's information paradox (Arrow 1962). Data generates information whose value can be assessed only after knowing what kind of information is generated. Ex ante, it is very hard to know whether an AI model would provide information that is actually valuable. For example, even now that large language models have been available for some time, hallucinations (instances when the models produce incorrect or nonsensical output that appears plausible) are a critical area of investigation (Huang et al. 2023).

4. "When First Oil Flowed," *New York Times*, July 22, 1934, https://timesmachine.nytimes.com/timesmachine/1934/07/22/110042820.html?pageNumber=133.

Further, data comes in at least two forms: data that tends to be static or slowly changing, like a person's date of birth or address, and data that frequently and dynamically changes, like a person's recent online searches or purchases. The first type is more similar to oil than the second type. Static data maintains its relevance to generate insights over time, making its value (and thus its transaction price) easier to determine. Dynamic or behavioral data, though, can be quite difficult to value because its relevance is often tied to specific contexts or periods, and it quickly loses significance as behaviors or circumstances change. This distinction highlights a core challenge in defining property rights for data: static data, being more enduring, aligns slightly better with traditional notions of ownership and transferability, similar to tangible assets like oil. Behavioral or dynamic data, however, is ephemeral, context dependent, and often co-created by multiple entities, such as platforms and users, in interconnected ways.

The recombinant nature of AI models, especially those based on GenAI, further complicates the issue by making it difficult to assess the contribution of individual data sources. GenAI learns simultaneously from multiple fragmented inputs, which are often small and diverse, leading to challenges in determining the value of each independent source. This difficulty is exacerbated by the uncertain substitutabilities and complementarities between these sources, as their combined effects may differ significantly from their individual impacts.

Despite their intrinsic differences, both static and dynamic data defy traditional notions of ownership and transferability because they are inherently nonrivalrous and can be replicated, shared, and reused without diminishing their original value. This makes it difficult to assign exclusive ownership rights in the same way that we do for physical assets. In the recent context of GenAI, the most relevant form of property right is copyright, which protects creative works such as newspaper articles, images, and music. Judging from the large number of lawsuits against GenAI companies,[5] it is clear that current copyright owners like *The New York Times* and Getty Images consider the use of their works to train GenAI models to fall outside of the fair use doctrine.[6] (The fact that incumbents will fight to maintain the status quo is very eloquently described in Callander and Li 2024.)

Although an evaluation of whether fair use applies in the context of

5. DAIL is the Database of AI Litigation, https://blogs.gwu.edu/law-eti/ai-litigation-database/.

6. The fair use doctrine in copyright law allows for use of copyrighted material without the permission of the copyright owner under a limited set of circumstances. Fair use is established by four factors: the purpose and character of the use (e.g., transformative or educational), the nature of the copyrighted work (e.g., fictional or non-fictional), the amount of original work used, and the effect on the market for the original work. Common examples of fair use include criticism, commentary, research and teaching, and news reporting. See Copyright Law of the United States, chap. 1 "Subject Matter and Scope of Copyright," para. 107, https://www.copyright.gov/title17/92chap1.html#107.

GenAI is beyond the scope of this commentary, it is important to emphasize the economic effects that such innovations can have on the market for creative works (Waldfogel 2012). On the one hand, it may reduce the returns to creative works because some demand will substitute for the output from GenAI models. As an example, some people may rely on ChatGPT instead of *The New York Times* to find information about past events. On the other hand, it may also reduce the costs of producing and distributing creative works in the first place (Kretschmer and Peukert 2020). Indeed, writers at *The New York Times* may be able to write an article about current events faster with the help of ChatGPT. Or somebody searching for past events may be directed to *New York Times* articles via ChatGPT. Together, the two forces have opposite effects on the incentives to produce creative works given the current stringency of copyrights, making it uncertain whether copyrights should be strengthened or weakened to maintain the current level of creative works (assuming such a level is even optimal).[7]

As previously mentioned, news aggregators were the subject of similar speculations a few years ago. Copyright issues with news aggregators like Google News arose from their use of headlines, snippets, and links to display news content without compensating publishers. Publishers argued that these practices infringed on copyright and reduced traffic to their websites, thus undermining their ad revenue and subscriptions. Aggregators claimed fair use, asserting that snippets were factual and their services increased traffic to original sources, especially small publishers (Athey, Mobius, and Pal 2021). Eventually, legislation caught up with the business model of news aggregators. Among the new regulations, the European Union's 2019 copyright directive allowed for unlicensed hyperlinks and short snippets, whereas Australia in 2021 and Canada in 2023 opted for the compensation of publishers by news aggregators through "link taxes."[8]

The fact that data is endogenously produced (unlike oil, whose quantity is fixed) creates an additional challenge. Although the first iteration of an AI model often uses "naturally occurring" data, like text from classic books or paintings from the Renaissance, that is unlikely to be the case in the future. If AI models are used to generate new creative works, a circularity of input-output relationships emerges between the data used for training AI models and the use of those models to generate even more data. Subsequent rounds of model deployments mean that previous versions of AI models are influencing (and changing) the data-generating process of data that is the input to future model iterations. This feedback loop raises critical questions (Sühr, Samadi, and Farronato 2024) about the quality and diversity of data used in

7. This is a delicate balance that affects virtually all intellectual property rights, including copyrights (Waldfogel 2012) and patents (Romer 1990; Scotchmer 2004), and that sometimes is resolved with public investment in innovation (Greenstein 2015).

8. Nana Ama Sarfo, "What's Going on with Digital Link Taxes?" *Forbes*, October 2, 2023, https://www.forbes.com/sites/taxnotes/2023/10/02/whats-going-on-with-digital-link-taxes/.

training subsequent iterations of AI models, as well as additional property rights questions over who owns that data.

There is one final commonality between data and oil worth highlighting, which involves externalities. For oil, it is pollution; for the use of data, it is the risk of erosion of privacy and potential misuse, as in the case of deep fakes. Just as the widespread use of oil has led to environmental degradation and climate change, the extensive collection and use of data may generate significant societal costs. These include the risk of surveillance, data breaches, and the perpetuation of biases through algorithmic decision-making. In both cases, these externalities are often borne by individuals and communities that are distinct from the entities that profit from the resource, creating an imbalance that likely needs to be addressed by regulatory intervention or other innovative solutions.

While the analogy between oil and data provides useful insights into their transformative potential, it is essential to recognize their fundamental differences. Unlike oil, which is finite and primarily tied to physical extraction, data is an endogenously generated and nonrivalrous resource. Its value is heavily contingent on the technologies and contexts in which it is applied. In addition, oil's externalities are predominantly environmental, whereas data's societal risks involve privacy, fake news, surveillance, and algorithmic biases. These distinctions highlight that the challenges and solutions for regulating data and assigning property rights are likely to diverge significantly from those applied to oil.

In reflecting on the rhetoric surrounding data and AI, it is important to question other popular claims that often circulate in industry and policy conversations, such as "AI will democratize access to knowledge" and "AI scales effortlessly." These statements may sound compelling, but they risk ignoring the complexities of how data is collected, governed, and used effectively. Taking a more realistic view that acknowledges both the potential and limitations of data-driven technologies is essential for developing meaningful approaches to regulation, ownership, and societal impact.

References

Arrow, Kenneth. 1962. "Economic Welfare and the Allocation of Resources for Invention." In *The Rate and Direction of Inventive Activity: Economic and Social Factors*, Universities-National Bureau Committee for Economic Research, and Committee on Economic Growth of the Social Science Research Council, 609–26. Princeton University Press.

Athey, Susan, Markus Mobius, and Jeno Pal. 2021. "The Impact of Aggregators on Internet News Consumption." NBER Working Paper No. 28746. National Bureau of Economic Research.

Beraja, Martin, and Noam Yuchtman. 2025. "Generalized Disruption: Society,

Work, and Property Rights in the Age of AI." In *The Political Economy of Artificial Intelligence*, edited by Ajay Agrawal, Joshua Gans, Avi Goldfarb, and Catherine E. Tucker. University of Chicago Press.
Callander, Steven, and Hongyi Li. 2024. "Regulating an Innovative Industry." Paper presented at Economics of Artificial Intelligence conference, September 19–20, 2024, Toronto.
Einav, Liran, Chiara Farronato, and Jonathan Levin. 2016. "Peer-to-Peer Markets." *Annual Review of Economics* 8 (1): 615–35.
Einav, Liran, Dan Knoepfle, et al. 2014. "Sales Taxes and Internet Commerce." *American Economic Review* 104 (1): 1–26.
Goodfellow, Ian, et al. 2020. "Generative Adversarial Networks." *Communications of the ACM* 63 (11): 139–44.
Greenstein, Shane. 2015. *How the Internet Became Commercial: Innovation, Privatization, and the Birth of a New Network*. Princeton University Press.
Huang, Lei, et al. 2023. "A Survey on Hallucination in Large Language Models: Principles, Taxonomy, Challenges, and Open Questions." *ACM Transactions on Information Systems* 43 (2): 1–55.
Iansiti, Marco, and Karim R. Lakhani. 2020. *Competing in the Age of AI: Strategy and Leadership When Algorithms and Networks Run the World*. Harvard Business Press.
Kretschmer, Tobias, and Christian Peukert. 2020. "Video Killed the Radio Star? Online Music Videos and Recorded Music Sales." *Information Systems Research* 31 (3): 776–800.
Linden, Greg, Brent Smith, and Jeremy York. 2003. "Amazon.com Recommendations: Item-to-Item Collaborative Filtering." *IEEE Internet Computing* 7 (1): 76–80.
Page, Lawrence, et al. 1999. "The PageRank Citation Ranking: Bringing Order to the Web." In *The Web Conference*. Technical report. Stanford InfoLab. http://ilpubs.stanford.edu:8090/422/.
Romer, Paul M. 1990. "Endogenous Technological Change." *Journal of Political Economy* 98 (5): pt. 2, S71–S102.
Scotchmer, Suzanne. 2004. *Innovation and Incentives*. MIT Press.
Sühr, Tom, Samira Samadi, and Chiara Farronato. 2024. "A Dynamic Model of Performative Human-ML Collaboration: Theory and Empirical Evidence." arXiv preprint 2405.13753.
Vaswani, Ashish, et al. 2017. "Attention Is All You Need." In *Advances in Neural Information Processing Systems*.
Waldfogel, Joel. 2012. "Copyright Research in the Digital Age: Moving from Piracy to the Supply of New Products." *American Economic Review* 102 (3): 337–42.
Yergin, Daniel. 2011. *The Prize: The Epic Quest for Oil, Money & Power*. Simon and Schuster.

3

Regulating AI
The Race Between Policymakers and the Rise of a New Interest Group

Steven Callander

3.1 Introduction

It is not unusual for the textbook version of an institution to differ from how that institution works in practice. This gap is nowhere greater than with politics. In the textbook version, policymaking reflects a careful balancing of benefits and harms in the public interest. In practice, politics is a brutal battle between interest groups in which fairness and the public interest play at best an incidental role.

The emergence of new technologies—and their possible regulation—brings this distinction to a sharp point. As a technology emerges, firms enter the market, and an industry develops around it. As the industry grows in the market, it also grows in stature in politics. The industry becomes an *interest group*. In the idealized version of politics, the industry would inject its expertise into policy deliberations and improve social welfare. In practice, the industry uses its political power to shape regulations in a way that is favorable to the industry itself.

For an established and stable technology, the textbook recommendation for economic efficiency is to impose socially optimal regulation before the industry grows and obtains political strength. For new technologies like AI, the problem is that we don't yet know what those regulations should be. The policymaker can wait to learn, but by the time she identifies the optimal

Steven Callander is the Herbert Hoover Professor of Public and Private Management and Professor of Political Economy at Stanford Graduate School of Business.

I thank the audience and organizers of the NBER Economics of AI conference for stimulating discussion and an anonymous referee for helpful comments. For acknowledgments, sources of research support, and disclosure of the author's material financial relationships, if any, please see https://www.nber.org/books-and-chapters/political-economy-artificial-intelligence/regulating-ai-race-between-policymakers-and-rise-new-interest-group.

regulation, the AI industry may have grown so strong politically, and it will be too late to stop it.

Regulating a new industry is a race—a race between policymakers and the rise of a new interest group. Policymakers race to learn about the technology and how to regulate it before the industry is able to build political power and wield it to shape regulation in its favor. In this chapter, we describe the nature of this race and speculate on how it will develop. How can a socially minded policymaker structure and compete in this race such that the winner is society? This is a hard problem, to be sure, although not an intractable one. This article sketches several paths toward a solution.

3.2 Disruptive Technologies: Learning About Benefits and Harms

The impact of a new technology can often be learned only by doing. Only by developing and applying a technology does its power reveal itself and the harm it causes become evident. A challenge for policymakers is to learn about harms before they occur. If learning can occur in a lab, independent of industry growth, then a precautionary principle applies, and regulators can wait to learn about harms before allowing the industry to flourish (Acemoglu and Lensman 2024). In practice, lab learning is limited, and most learning, particularly the impact a technology has on society, can be learned only by applying the technology in practice. Gans (2024) characterizes when it is optimal to let the industry grow despite the risks and, indeed, when it is optimal to speed up industry development to bring forward learning. Callander and Li (2024) introduce the possibility that the firms developing AI hold superior information about potential harms. They show that it is difficult for the policymaker to extract this information, given the firms' hope to profit from AI, and that this difficulty increases the more competition there is in the market.

The problem we address in this chapter is related yet different. In the papers cited here, the question is whether the policymaker can learn about harms before they occur. If she can, she can update regulations and avert the harms. The question of this chapter is whether the policymaker will still hold enough political power to update regulations by the time she learns whether harm will occur.[1] We follow Gans (2024) in supposing that learning is by doing and that the rate of learning depends on industry growth. To this, we add the observation that industry growth also translates into growth in political power, and the industry can use that political power to stop the policymaker from intervening in its use of AI.[2]

1. Gans (2024) studies two cases: when AI adoption is and is not reversible. In this chapter, the policymaker's ability to reverse AI adoption is endogenous, declining in time as the industry grows.

2. The crypto industry provides an example. The crypto industry leveraged the enormous market valuations of its largest firms to become the largest political contributor in the 2024 electoral cycle in the US.

3.3 Political Outcomes Result from Interest Group Competition

An axiom of politics is that elected officials care about votes. Even public-minded policymakers must get reelected, and not all policymakers are that. The desire for votes need not create bad incentives. After all, satisfying citizens and winning their vote is the intent of representative democracy. The problem is that votes are not represented equally. If a voter is unaware of an issue, or if the issue will not swing her vote and she won't otherwise get involved, policymakers are free to ignore the voter's preferences. Rather, it is those who care enough about an issue for their vote to hinge on how the policymaker acts who receive representation. In fact, it is not even necessary to be a voter to be represented. If an individual or group can deliver votes in some other way—via campaign donations, a positive message, or organization—then policymakers will represent their preferences. These are the *interest groups*. Olson (1971) taught us that the political process should be understood through the lens of interest groups. To predict a political outcome, Olson argued, we shouldn't look too much at polls of public opinion; instead, we should look at the weight of the interest groups on either side of the issue.

The political power of an interest group depends on several characteristics. Importantly, these characteristics are correlated with but not in direct proportion to a group's market or social power. To be powerful, an interest group must be organized. It must be able to act on its preferences and deliver votes to a policymaker. The number of votes that can be delivered, whether directly or indirectly, depends on (1) numbers, or how many votes lie within the firm or industry and in its value chain; (2) message, or how sympathetic the public is to the interest group; (3) money; and (4) coverage, or where the votes are located, given the electoral rule in place.

As the AI industry grows, it will acquire political power to the extent that its market power translates into these characteristics. As it does so, a socially minded policymaker's ability to control policy will endogenously erode.

3.4 Politics Combined with Market Competition Generates Path Dependence in Technology

Politics not only creates a contest between policymakers and the AI industry; it creates competitive pressures within the industry. The combination of the two forces can generate a path dependence in the technology itself. This path dependence can lock in the technological approach adopted by early entrants, cutting off experimentation and innovation prematurely.

Path dependence emerges because first movers in the market are also first movers in politics. Later entrants must play catch-up in the market as well as in politics. The need to catch up in politics can shape their market strategy and, indeed, their approach to the technology.

To see why, observe that the first movers use the political power they acquire to not only keep a policymaker off their back but also keep at bay the threat of market competitors. If later entrants are poised to overtake them with new technological approaches, first movers can stop them by lobbying for standards that favor their own technological approach. This may not be good for AI broadly, but it is good for the first movers.

The strategic pressure on later entrants, therefore, is to hew closely to the technological and market approach of the early entrants, to beat them on their own terms in the market so that political power cannot be turned against them. This pressure to conform leads to a technological path dependence that locks in whatever approach happened to be tried first, leaving other approaches unexplored.

Politics provides a novel source of technological lock-in. It complements existing explanations of path dependence and technological lock-in, such as learning by doing and the idiosyncrasy of early decisions (Bryan 2017). Unlike lock-in from learning by doing, there are no redeeming features of lock-in from politics. When driven by politics, technological lock-in represents a pure inefficiency due to rent seeking that distorts and restrains the innovation process.

3.5 What Can Be Done?

The problem addressed here is not easy. In the face of extreme uncertainty, nonspecialist policymakers must navigate a fine line between fostering innovation and not losing their authority over it. Here I sketch out two possible paths to solving the problem. Both paths derive from the problem itself.

The first possible path is to drive a firmer wedge between markets and politics. If the industry cannot translate its market power into political power, then it can be allowed to flourish without fear that it will overwhelm the political process. There are several ways that the political process can be shielded from market power. One is to delegate AI regulation to an independent government agency. Although the bureaucracy always sits under legislative oversight, an agency is protected from political pressure by supermajority provisions in the legislature (e.g., the filibuster in the US Senate) or other statutory requirements. This approach raises the possibility of capture of the regulator by the industry, so it is important which agency is granted authority and the nature of that authority.

One way to reduce the probability of regulatory capture is for the legislature to create a new agency dedicated to the regulation of AI. Imagine how the finance industry would look different today if the Consumer Finance Protection Bureau (CFPB) had been created before rather than after the industry practices that contributed to the global financial crisis. Another, more minimalist, approach is to preemptively assign authority over AI to an existing agency. The overlapping jurisdiction of the multitude of government agencies, particularly at the federal level in the US, allows firms as well as activist groups to "venue shop" for a favorable agency. The legislature can retain control by clearly and preemptively delegating authority over AI. Do policymakers prefer that the agency in control of AI regulation be staffed by lawyers or economists or even social theorists? Or should those with technical training in the technology itself control the regulation of the technology? This choice matters, and it is one policymakers in the legislature have ex ante control over.

A second path to solving the problem is to target market power before it can be translated into political power. A blanket approach to limiting market power would be destructive to AI innovation. Fortunately, that is not necessary to solve the problem. It is sufficient to limit only the structure of market power so that the translation into political power is muted. As detailed above, the mapping from market to political power is not one to one. The AI industry can be allowed to flourish, with some firms even allowed to obtain substantial market power, so long as the form of that market power does not hold the elements of substantial political power. Regulating with this connection in mind means that regulation can be minimal and focused on shaping industry growth rather than limiting it.

This approach may involve regulation that separates the various functions of the industry into different firms so that the ingredients for political power don't accumulate. For example, the parts of the industry with the most money and resources could be separated from the parts of the industry with many jobs and a message that resonates with the public. This should be a consideration in the decision of where to apply AI regulation—at the large language model level or the app level—as it will shape how divisions within the industry develop.

In the best case, these interventions will shape the industry so that vibrant competition emerges within the AI industry and translates into competition in the political domain as well. If the industry can be fractured politically, policymakers may obtain the best of both worlds: an industry without the unified strength to overwhelm the political system and incentives that induce AI firms to reveal their private information about the technology through lobbying that will lead to more effective policymaking.

Whether policymakers can pull this off and solve their problem remains to be seen and depends on whether they can allow the industry to develop and flourish while mitigating the political threat. The longer policymakers delay, the stronger the AI industry becomes, and the harder the problem becomes. The clock is ticking.

References

Acemoglu, D., and T. Lensman. 2024. "Regulating Transformative Technologies." *American Economic Review: Insights* 6 (3): 359–76.

Bryan, K. A. 2017. "The Perils of Path Dependence." In *Survive and Thrive: Win-*

ning Against Strategic Threats to Your Business, edited by J. Gans and S. Kaplan. Dog Ear Publishing.

Callander, S., and H. Li. 2024. "Regulating an Innovative Industry." Working paper.

Gans, J. S. 2024. "How Learning About Harms Impacts the Optimal Rate of Artificial Intelligence Adoption." *Economic Policy*: 3–21.

Olson, M. 1971. *The Logic of Collective Action: Public Goods and the Theory of Groups*. Harvard University Press.

4 Regulating Algorithms
What and When

Talia Gillis, Scott Nelson, and Jann Spiess

4.1 Introduction

In many high-stakes domains of algorithmic decision-making, those who develop and deploy complex AI systems may have different objectives from the regulators overseeing them. Firms deploying algorithmic systems may prioritize profitability or other private benefits, while regulators may have additional or differing concerns, such as the distributional effects of algorithmic decisions and their impact on safety and market stability. These differences in preferences, compounded by information and technological asymmetries and the costs of regulation, present a fundamental challenge—how should algorithmic decisions be regulated?

This chapter examines regulatory approaches available for overseeing algorithmic decision-making, with a particular focus on the temporal design of rules and their evaluation. Our goal is to illuminate the trade-offs between different approaches and highlight the unique opportunities afforded by algorithmic settings compared to more traditional decision-making contexts.

In our framework, a firm develops and deploys a policy for automated

Talia Gillis is a professor of law at Columbia Law School.

Scott Nelson is an assistant professor of finance and Cohen and Keenoy Faculty Scholar at the University of Chicago Booth School of Business.

Jann Spiess is an associate professor of operations, information, and technology at Stanford Graduate School of Business.

Authors are listed in alphabetical order. We thank Laura Blattner for earlier input and discussions, Avi Goldfarb, Haggai Porat, and an anonymous reviewer for insightful comments, and Ritha Sarf for excellent research assistance. For acknowledgments, sources of research support, and disclosure of the authors' material financial relationships, if any, please see https://www.nber.org/books-and-chapters/political-economy-artificial-intelligence/regulating-algorithms-what-and-when.

decision-making—such as a lender creating a loan-underwriting model to maximize profits—while a regulator considers additional societal objectives like fairness, safety, and systemic risk. The regulator aims to design a regulatory regime that addresses the misalignment of preferences while accounting for information and cost constraints. The interaction between regulator and lender plays out around two key phases of algorithmic development and deployment. In the training phase, some initial data become available, and the firm uses these data to implement its algorithm. Next, in the deployment phase, the resulting algorithmic policy is applied for decision-making on new data—such as real-time loan applications—the particulars of which might not have been fully knowable during training.

We argue that in algorithmic settings, there is a distinctive opportunity to design regulation around these two phases of model training and deployment. We highlight two temporal dimensions of regulation. The first dimension concerns the stage of the algorithmic pipeline targeted by a legal rule: *ex ante* (before the training phase), *ex interim* (after training but before deployment), or *ex post* (after deployment). *Ex ante* rules put coarse constraints on the models that can be trained, even before the data become available. For instance, such rules might limit the permissible inputs (e.g., prohibiting the use of protected-class variables) or restrict the models to certain types, such as simple or self-interpretable models. These restrictions can shape the model design space before any training data are observed. *Ex interim* rules apply after the model has been trained but before deployment, and constrain the models adopted by the firm. For example, one way these rules can operate is by allowing regulators to inspect and test models before the models' deployment. Finally, *ex post* rules target the deployment stage, where regulators evaluate the outcomes produced by the deployed model. These outcomes reflect not only the algorithmic policy but also the particulars of the real-world environment—deployment state—that are only knowable at this stage. For example, regulators may investigate disparities in realized lending decisions, which arise from the interaction between the deployed algorithmic policy and the actual distribution of applicants.

The second temporal dimension concerns the timing of evaluating compliance with a rule. A legal rule can be scrutinized at a stage later than the one it targets. For example, an *ex ante* rule might be scrutinized not only during the *ex ante* stage but also at the *ex interim* or *ex post* stages following model development and/or deployment. Similarly, *ex interim* rules may be scrutinized either during the *ex interim* stage or later at the *ex post* stage. By explicitly considering these two temporal dimensions—the timing of rules and the timing of scrutiny—this chapter maps the space of possible regulatory regimes and explores the trade-offs associated with different approaches.

We leverage this framework to classify emerging approaches in AI regulation. Specifically, we develop a temporal taxonomy that maps regulatory approaches according to both the stage of the algorithmic decision-making pipeline targeted by the rule and the timing at which compliance with the rule is assessed. This taxonomy allows us to systematically examine how current regulations, proposed frameworks, and policy discussions address the full range of regulatory options.

Our main insight is that *ex interim* rules represent a potentially powerful tool for regulating algorithmic policies. Unlike *ex ante* interventions, *ex interim* rules are less rigid because they account for the specific models developed based on the training data. Compared to *ex post* interventions, *ex interim* rules are less blunt since they more directly target the *conduct* of the firm, as they do not depend on the (potentially random) realization of outcomes that the firm has no direct control over. Crucially, *ex interim* rules, particularly when scrutinized before deployment, can help prevent the materialization of harmful outcomes. This offers an important opportunity in algorithmic settings compared to more traditional decision-making contexts. For example, in decision-making based on human discretion, there is often no *ex interim* stage where a policy is fully described or describable prior to deployment, leaving only rigid *ex ante* or blunt *ex post* regulation as feasible options. When decisions are taken by algorithms, on the other hand, they are mathematical objects that can be described, tested, and evaluated under controlled conditions even before they are applied.

To illustrate the potential value of *ex interim* rules, consider a financial regulator overseeing algorithmic credit decisions by a lender. The regulator may, for example, aim to ensure that not too many loans are extended to risky borrowers. However, the number of risky loans issued and the number of actual defaults depend not only on the lender's algorithmic policy but also on factors beyond the lender's control, such as which borrowers apply and how economic conditions affect repayment behavior. While the algorithm is under the lender's control, some of these external factors are not. When regulation is designed to target conduct rather than outcomes alone, targeting the lender only on the basis of realized outcomes may be inefficient, as it risks penalizing the lender for bad luck rather than for unreasonable decisions. Evaluating whether the algorithmic policy itself was reasonable based on information available at the time of development may lead to a more targeted and effective regulatory policy. Furthermore, such scrutiny is possible even before the lending rule is deployed, allowing regulators to intervene before harm is done.

The desirability of *ex interim* rules, however, depends crucially on the cost of scrutinizing compliance by the firm at each stage. If scrutiny of compliance with *ex interim* rules is more resource-intensive than scrutinizing *ex post* rules—for instance, because *ex post* rules leverage easily measurable outcomes, while scrutinizing *ex interim* rules may require accessing the training data and evaluating a highly complex algorithmic process—then regulation based on *ex interim* rules may be less attractive for a resource-constrained regulator. Despite these caveats, we illustrate in a stylized example that *ex interim* scrutiny can have value even in cases when it has a higher cost, since targeting the firm's conduct directly allows the regulator to align preferences in a more precise way than overly static or overly noisy *ex ante* and *ex post* rules can. The effectiveness of *ex interim* rules also depends on factors such as the relationship between information available during training and the deployment state. For example, if the training data used by a lender closely resembles the real-world distribution of borrowers, the outcomes of the deployment stage are more likely to reflect the decisions made during the training phase. In such cases, *ex post* rules are less likely to target noise or unexpected factors unknown to the developer at the training stage.

Our chapter contributes to the interdisciplinary literature on regulatory design as it relates to AI, spanning economics, law, political science, computer science, and data science more broadly. Recent work examines the design of regulations for algorithmic decision-making and the trade-offs faced by regulators when aligning firm incentives with broader societal objectives (Cowgill and Tucker 2020; Guerreiro, Rebelo, and Teles 2023; Rambachan et al. 2020). The work in Kleinberg et al. (2018) and Kleinberg et al. (2020) emphasizes the opportunities for *ex interim* legal rules in algorithmic settings, where algorithmic policies are specified before deployment. Our work extends these insights by emphasizing additional temporal dimensions in the regulatory pipeline. Specifically, we study the trade-offs between regulating algorithms before and after deployment, building on our previous work introducing the concept of algorithmic explainers (Blattner, Nelson, and Spiess 2024) and stress testing (Gillis and Spiess 2019) at the *ex interim* stage.[1]

Other related work examines current and emerging AI regulatory frameworks across countries (Comunale and Manera 2024) and specific regulatory tools, such as licensing and auditing (Anderljung et al. 2023; Guha et al. 2023; Hadfield and Clark 2023), which we consider within our temporal framework. Our work also builds on literature documenting and considering the various AI risks, such as existential risks (Acemoglu 2023; Jones 2024), privacy (e.g., Acquisti, Taylor, and Wagman 2016; Goldfarb and Tucker 2012), and fairness (e.g., Hardt, Price, and Srebro 2016), and the tensions between innovation and addressing potential risks (Agrawal, Gans, and Goldfarb 2023; Callander and Li 2024). By relating these different policy considerations to the regulatory timing in algorithmic pipelines, we demonstrate the trade-offs associated with legal rule timing and compliance evalua-

1. Another related literature has studied the welfare implications of personalized pricing when firms use "big data" to price discriminate (Bergemann, Brooks, and Morris 2015; Porat 2022; Dubé and Misra 2023; Ali, Lewis, and Vasserman, 2023; Bar-Gill, Sunstein, and Talgam-Cohen 2023; Rhodes and Zhou 2024). While this literature has largely focused on the policy question of how and whether to restrict what data firms can use, we show that there are additional regulatory possibilities that, while allowing broad access to rich consumer data, regulate the pricing models that use these data.

tion timing. While we highlight some representative examples here, this list is not exhaustive, as the literature on AI regulation continues to grow rapidly.

Our analysis also relates to the classic law and economics literature on optimal regulatory design, which discusses the choice of regulatory restriction types (Kaplow 2013; Shavell 2018), the design of legal enforcement mechanisms (Shavell 1984), and the impact of enforcement costs on optimal legal rules (Kaplow and Shavell 1994; Shavell 1993).

The remainder of this chapter proceeds as follows. Section 4.2 provides a high-level temporal framework of algorithmic decision-making and regulation. Section 4.3 presents our taxonomy of regulatory approaches within that framework, distinguishing between when rules apply in the algorithmic pipeline and when compliance with those rules is assessed. Section 4.4 builds on this taxonomy by formally modeling regulation as a game between a firm deploying an algorithm and a regulator overseeing its use, and illustrates key considerations through a simple, stylized example. Section 4.5 highlights the model's key insights and situates them within related work, emphasizing the unique opportunity that algorithmic regulation provides to scrutinize decisions before deployment and the materialization of harm. This section also discusses some important limitations of our framework. Finally, Section 4.6 proposes some directions for future research.

4.2 A Temporal Framework for the Regulation of Algorithms

We consider a high-level framework of algorithmic deployment and its regulation. This multistage framework covers the interaction between a firm deploying an algorithm and a regulator overseeing its use. The firm chooses an algorithmic policy. For example, the firm could be a lender that designs an algorithm to make credit-application-approval decisions. The regulator puts constraints or imposes penalties on the algorithm and its implications. For example, a financial regulator may restrict the variables that are permissible for use in credit decisions or penalize a lender for unfair lending practices. This interaction between the two can be seen as a principal–agent game where the regulator plays the role of the principal and the firm represents the agent, which we formalize in Section 4.4.

In our framework, there is a *training phase* in which the firm selects the algorithmic policy on the basis of some initial data and a subsequent *deployment phase* in which it is implemented. For example, a lender uses historical repayment data to train a model in the training phase, and then leverages this model to decide whom to approve for a loan in the deployment phase. This perspective on the genesis of algorithmic decisions suggests three targets for regulatory intervention (fig. 4.1): First, regulatory interventions could impose *ex ante* restrictions that target the training phase and its inputs, such as which training data the firm is allowed to use, how it can be processed, and the types of models that can be trained on it. Second, the regulator

ex ante → training phase *ex interim* → deployment phase *ex post* →

Fig. 4.1 Stylized temporal structure of the algorithm pipeline and its regulation

could formulate an *ex interim* regulation that concerns the actual algorithmic policy after it is computed, but before it is deployed. Finally, *ex post* regulation could target the actual decisions and outcomes that follow the implementation of the algorithmic policy.

To understand the full range of legal strategies available for regulating algorithmic systems, we distinguish between two dimensions of regulation along the temporal axis: *rule timing* and *scrutiny timing*. Rule timing refers to the stage in the algorithmic life cycle that a legal rule is designed to govern. For example, rule timing distinguishes between restrictions to the inputs that can be used for training (an *ex ante* rule) and requirements for a model to undergo stress testing before deployment (an *ex interim* rule). Scrutiny timing, by contrast, refers to when compliance with the rule is actually assessed. These two dimensions are conceptually distinct: an *ex ante* rule, such as an input restriction, could be scrutinized at different points—before training (*ex ante* scrutiny, e.g., during licensing), later during model development (*ex interim* scrutiny, e.g., through submitted documentation), or even after deployment (*ex post* scrutiny, e.g., through post hoc audits). Similarly, an *ex interim* rule (e.g., a stress-testing requirement for the chosen model) may be scrutinized *ex interim* (before deployment) or *ex post* (only after deployment).

Critically, the separation between rule timing and scrutiny timing allows for the design of combined regimes or conditional scrutiny: a regulator may decide to evaluate compliance with an *ex ante* or *ex interim* rule only if an issue at deployment arises (e.g., post hoc audits of allowed inputs in response to realized harm). Such distinctions frame the legal strategies we explore in greater detail in the taxonomy in Section 4.3.

4.3 A Taxonomy of Emerging Regulatory Approaches

This section introduces a temporal taxonomy of regulatory approaches. Building on our framework from Section 4.2, we categorize regulatory approaches by the stage of the algorithmic pipeline they target and the timing at which compliance is assessed. By making this structure explicit, we clarify how emerging regulatory proposals, as well as long-standing doctrines such as disparate impact liability, fit into this framework, and how regulators may choose between upstream prevention and downstream enforcement. As we show, algorithmic systems create opportunities for *ex interim* regulation, which is limited in traditional human decision-making contexts. Moreover, scrutiny timing offers additional flexibility: Even when

Table 4.1. **Temporal taxonomy of regulatory options**

Scrutiny timing →	*Ex ante* (before training)	*Ex interim* (during development)	*Ex post* (after deployment)
Rule timing ↓			
Ex ante (before training)	Rule targets *ex ante* stage and is scrutinized *ex ante*. Example: input restrictions checked for licensing.	Rule targets predevelopment stage but is scrutinized only at development stage. Example: verifying compliance with input restriction through a conformity assessment before model deployment.	Rule targets predevelopment stage but is only scrutinized *ex post*. Example: verifying compliance with an input restriction through *post hoc* analysis after deployment harm has materialized.
Ex interim (during development)	N/A	Rule targets development stage and is scrutinized pre-deployment. Example: an explainer of model weights documented and reported pre-deployment.	Rule targets development stage but is only scrutinized at deployment. Example: evaluation of whether inappropriately trained model parameters caused disparities at deployment.
Ex post (after deployment)	N/A	N/A	Rule targets outcomes and is scrutinized at deployment. Example: deployment impact analysis showing true impact of model on different groups.

interim scrutiny is costly or infeasible, regulators can use *ex post* scrutiny of *ex interim* rules, using realized outcomes to trigger more targeted assessments of whether earlier constraints were met.

The taxonomy here outlines the temporal options and illustrates how different regulatory instruments, ranging from mandates to evaluation obligations, populate this design space. While *ex ante* rules can theoretically be scrutinized at any stage, practical constraints limit when other rules can be meaningfully assessed. For instance, rules governing deployment outcomes can be evaluated only after deployment has occurred. These temporal constraints create the pattern of available regulatory options shown in table 4.1, where certain combinations are marked as "N/A" because they are temporally impossible.

While the choice of *what* and *when* to regulate—*ex ante*, *ex interim*, or *ex post*—determines the timing of intervention or scrutiny, it does not dictate the *type* of regulatory tool used. Regulatory-tool type, though not the focus of our chapter, presents another important consideration for regulatory design: Across all points in the rule or scrutiny timeline, regulators can employ either mandates or evaluation obligations. *Mandates* are rules that prescribe specific conduct. These may take the form of clearly defined requirements, such as prohibitions on using certain inputs, or more flexible standards that still require compliance with a concrete obligation, like ensuring dataset representativeness. *Evaluation obligations*, by contrast, do not typically dictate particular actions. Instead, they require firms to engage in processes such as identifying risks, documenting model development, or demonstrating that certain factors were considered in decision-making (Engler 2023; Kaminski 2023).[2] The remainder of this section examines how these rules can be deployed at different stages of algorithmic development and decision-making.[3]

4.3.1 *Ex Ante* Rules

Ex ante rules, applied prior to the development of an algorithm, cover a range of regulatory tools, including restrictions or requirements regarding future functions the firm may develop. One common type of *ex ante* rule limits the inputs a firm can use when developing or training a model. For example, the prohibition on AI systems from using personal characteristics, such as social behavior or personality traits, when those characteristics were not collected for the intended use, or the prohibition on the use of emotion recognition in workplaces or educational institutions (except for medical and safety reasons) can be found in Article 5(1) of the EU AI Act (European Union 2023). Regulation could also prohibit the development of certain models altogether, such as the EU AI Act's prohibition on social scoring, which is considered an "unacceptable risk." These restrictions all target the *ex ante* stage. Below we consider how *ex ante* rules can be scrutinized at any point in the pipeline.

***Ex ante* scrutiny**. There are several reasons a regulatory regime might

2. Some legal requirements may blur the line between the categories of mandates and evaluation obligations. For example, a law might require a firm to establish a risk management system. If the law prescribes exactly how the system should be structured and what documentation must be maintained, it functions as a mandate. If it simply requires that the firm engage in risk identification and mitigation without prescribing the details, it operates more like an evaluation obligation. Article 9 of the EU AI Act (European Union 2023), which requires a risk management system to consider foreseeable risks to "health, safety or fundamental rights," is an example of an evaluation obligation. Although the requirement applies at the *ex interim* stage, it emphasizes process-oriented compliance rather than prescribing a specific outcome. Both categories of legal rules—mandates and evaluation obligations—can, in principle, correspond to any combination of rule timing and scrutiny timing represented in table 4.1.

3. Our focus here is primarily on public regulatory scrutiny, although private enforcement, such as private litigation, can also play a role in ensuring compliance. In many cases private enforcement, such as tort litigation, statutory claims or other civil recourse, operates *ex post* and is often triggered by the materialization of harm. See, e.g., Sharkey (2024).

choose to scrutinize *ex ante* rules already during the pre-development stage. If the mere collection and storage of data introduce significant risks—such as when dealing with highly sensitive information like biometric data or if there is a concern about models leaking or being stolen—it may be preferable to ensure compliance before development begins rather than defer scrutiny to a later stage. Additionally, in high-risk domains that pose substantial safety concerns, regulators may seek to limit which entities are permitted to develop AI for certain purposes, requiring these entities to demonstrate that they have sufficient safeguards in place. Anderljung et al. (2023), for example, propose requiring a governmental license for developing AI models in certain safety-critical and high-risk industries such as air travel, power generation, and manufacturing.

Ex ante scrutiny often takes the form of a licensing regime, where a firm is permitted to proceed to the development stage only after meeting specific conditions. These conditions might include demonstrating compliance with input restrictions or adequately addressing potential risks through documented risk assessments.

***Ex interim* scrutiny.** Rather than scrutinizing an *ex ante* rule during the pre-development stage, a regulator might opt to scrutinize compliance during the *ex interim* development stage. For example, the EU AI Act requires deployers of high-risk AI systems to produce a report demonstrating that their systems comply with the act's requirements (see Annex VII of European Union 2023). In some cases, a "notified body"—a designated third party—is tasked with certifying these conformity assessments. These assessments often include *ex ante* restrictions, such as prohibitions on the use of certain sensitive personal data or requirements to identify and mitigate risks at the pre-development stage. In certain circumstances, a notified body's refusal to certify the assessment may halt further development, effectively making the third-party approval an *ex interim* scrutiny of certain *ex ante* requirements. Similarly, Anderljung et al. (2023) suggest that certain AI models should require a government license pre-deployment, depending on the developer's ability to demonstrate compliance with certain safety standards, which could include *ex ante* restrictions or requirements.

***Ex post* scrutiny.** *Ex post* scrutiny refers to evaluating compliance with legal rules after an AI system has been deployed. Scrutinizing an *ex ante* rule at this later stage may be particularly desirable when the cost of auditing and assessing compliance is high, in which case the regulator might selectively scrutinize the *ex ante* rule when observing a particular outcome at deployment. For instance, a regulator might choose to consider whether a firm has complied with input restrictions on using protected characteristics only if the deployed model results in significant racial disparities. In line with this approach, Article 79 of the EU AI Act (European Union 2023) allows for market surveillance authorities to evaluate an already deployed AI system with respect to its compliance with the act's obligations, covering rules that target any stage of the algorithmic life cycle, including rules that relate to pre-development. Similarly, self-assessments required for *ex ante* licensing may only be scrutinized *ex post*, potentially resulting in license revocation. While this approach allows regulators to focus costly enforcement efforts, it also raises challenges in cases where immediate intervention is needed to prevent ongoing or widespread harm.

4.3.2 Rules for Consistency

Ex interim rules apply to the model development stage, after training data are available but before deployment, and therefore relate to rules that restrict or constrain the algorithmic function once it is being trained. At this point, the regulator can impose rules that relate to the training data and the concrete function trained on that data. *Ex interim* rules can be restrictions on the function that may depend on the training data itself. For instance, a regulator might assess whether the selected algorithmic rule is appropriate or whether a more desirable algorithmic rule could be implemented based on the information available during training, using tools such as explainers or stress-testing frameworks.[4] For example, Article 9 of the EU AI Act requires a risk management system that considers the foreseeable risks to "health, safety or fundamental rights" at deployment. Similarly, the proposed Canadian Artificial Intelligence and Data Act (AIDA) (Canada 2024) requires that firms developing high-impact AI systems establish measures to "identify, assess, and mitigate risks of harm or biased output" before the system is deployed. The Algorithmic Accountability Act, proposed in 2023 (US Senate 2023), similarly requires concrete impact assessments before deployment (Kaminski 2023).

A type of requirement that could be interpreted as *ex ante* or *ex interim* puts restrictions on the training dataset—which can be understood as targeting how the data itself is processed—serves as an example of *ex interim* rules. For instance, Article 10 of the EU AI Act mandates that AI systems use training, validation, and testing datasets that satisfy quality standards, such as relevance, representativeness, and absence of prohibited biases.

In practice, precisely defining the boundaries of the *ex interim* and *ex post* stage can be challenging, particularly when developers engage in iterative testing or smaller-scale internal evaluations that blur the line between development and deployment. This ambiguity complicates the enforcement of *ex interim* rules, especially when scrutiny is intended to take place before individuals are impacted by an AI system.

4. In our framework, we jointly consider obligations for both developers of AI systems and those who deploy them. However, in practice, the deployer of an AI system may not be the same as the developer. For instance, a lender (user) might use a credit scoring model created by a third party (developer). Legal frameworks such as the EU AI Act recognize this distinction and impose separate obligations on developers and deployers. For tractability, we consider these obligations jointly.

As noted earlier, *ex interim* rules cannot be scrutinized at the *ex ante* stage because compliance with a future requirement cannot be assessed before the relevant activities have taken place. Therefore, scrutiny of *ex interim* rules occurs during the *ex interim* or *ex post* stages.

***Ex interim* scrutiny.** *Ex interim* scrutiny implies the evaluation of compliance with *ex interim* rules during the model development stage, prior to deployment. This type of scrutiny ensures that developers adhere to requirements in real-time as the system is being developed rather than after deployment. Under the EU AI Act, providers of high-risk AI systems are required to maintain detailed documentation of their development processes, including demonstrating how training data meets specified standards. Regulators or third-party entities, such as notified bodies, may review this documentation during the development phase to verify compliance, so that these *ex interim* evaluation obligations are scrutinized before deployment (*ex interim* scrutiny of an *ex interim* rule). Several scholars have suggested that firms should be required to demonstrate that their models are fair and non-discriminatory to receive permission to deploy the models, similar to Food and Drug Administration approval (Malgieri and Pasquale 2022; Tutt 2017).

Ex interim scrutiny is particularly valuable for addressing risks that may be difficult or costly to mitigate after deployment. However, this approach often requires significant regulatory resources and access to the development process, which can be burdensome. As a result, regulators may prefer to allocate enforcement resources to *ex post* scrutiny, where compliance is prioritized based on realized outcomes.

***Ex post* scrutiny.** *Ex post* scrutiny refers to the evaluation of compliance with an *ex interim* rule after the deployment of the AI system. This approach may be especially practical when assessing compliance with an *ex interim* rule is costly or resource-intensive. In such cases, a regulator might choose to assess compliance only if harm materializes at the *ex post* stage—thereby using realized harms as a trigger for selective, targeted scrutiny of *ex interim* constraints.

Discrimination law often functions as an *ex post* scrutiny of *ex interim* decision-making. For example, while review under the disparate impact doctrine is triggered by *ex post* disparities,[5] the primary consideration of whether an entity engaged in prohibited disparate impact, for example, an employer who uses a screening tool that selects men at a higher rate than women, is whether there is a "business justification" for the policy that led to the disparity. Because this justification relates to whether the AI system was meant to predict job performance, for example, this would be scrutiniz-

5. See, for example, EEOC v. Greyhound as an example of a singular focus on *ex post* outcomes. The court stated that "[t]his conclusion should be as obvious as it is tautological: there can be no disparate impact unless there is a disparate impact." 635 F.2d at 191–92.

ing the model development stage. Similarly, the Community Reinvestment Act triggers scrutiny of banking lending policies when financial institutions fail to adequately provide loans to low- and moderate-income areas they serve. In this vein, Kleinberg et al. (2018) argue that algorithms provide an important opportunity for transparency by enabling the inspection of the training model—which they refer to as the "screener" algorithm—once decision disparities are detected, to enforce discrimination laws.

4.3.3 *Ex post* Rules

Ex post rules are designed to address materialized harm rather than anticipated risks. Unlike *ex ante* or *ex interim* rules, which focus on preventing potential issues before deployment, *ex post* rules are reactive: They assess harm that has, at least in part, already occurred. This materialized harm reflects not only the firm's algorithmic policy but also factors that are only knowable at the time of deployment and may lie beyond the firm's control. For example, a lending policy that results in a high rate of loan defaults may stem from both the lender's application policy and external factors—such as the characteristics of borrowers who apply or how economic conditions affect repayment behavior.

Rules that hold developers or deployers accountable when a deployed AI system causes physical harm or other damage—such as tort liability for autonomous vehicle accidents—are examples of *ex post* rules. Particularly in strict liability regimes, where a deployer's reasonable risk-mitigation efforts do not absolve liability, the firm effectively becomes a de facto insurer against harm.

Similarly, obligations to engage in ongoing monitoring, measure outcomes, and report harms often target the *ex post* stage. For example, Article 79 of the EU AI Act requires post-market monitoring in light of real-world outcomes, creating an *assessment obligation* at the *ex post* stage. The proposed Canadian Artificial Intelligence and Data Act (Canada 2024) includes provisions for monitoring and reporting incidents of harm or biased outputs from high-impact AI systems. The NIST AI Risk Management Framework (NIST 2023), a nonbinding framework in the US, calls for comparing system performance at deployment to the assessments made pre-deployment, reinforcing the importance of *ex post* scrutiny.

Some rules combine *ex post* and *ex interim* elements. *Ex post* rules enable regulators to focus enforcement efforts on actual harms rather than theoretical risks that may never materialize. However, liability that extends beyond the monitoring and reporting requirements—such as a determination of illegal disparate impact—may also require scrutiny of an *ex interim* rule. In such cases, the ultimate finding of liability often hinges on whether the deployer or developer complied with *ex interim* rules, such as demonstrating that the model's design and data usage were justified and aligned with legitimate business purposes.

Ex post rules are less desirable in high-risk domains where regulators may prioritize preventing harm before it materializes. The trade-offs involved in harm regulation, including negligence-based and strict liability approaches, have been extensively examined in the law and economics literature (e.g., Polinsky and Shavell 2000).

4.4 A Stylized Model of Algorithm Deployment and Regulation

In this section, we formally model the regulation of algorithms within the framework of Section 4.2 as a game between the firm that deploys an algorithm and the regulator that oversees its use. The regulator can impose rules that constrain the algorithmic policies selected by the firm, with the type of restriction depending on the stage in the decision-making pipeline. Rules that target the *ex ante* stage are limited to simple restrictions that do not directly rely on training data, such as restrictions on inputs or the types of models that can be trained. Rules that target the *ex interim* stage focus on restricting aspects of algorithmic policies that emerge after the firm accesses the training data. Finally, rules targeting the *ex post* stage impose restrictions based on the observed impact of the algorithmic policies after deployment. Additionally, the regulator must decide when to scrutinize compliance with a rule, which can also impact the cost of regulatory oversight.

Following the classification in Section 4.2, within our model, we consider regulatory regimes that vary in their rule and scrutiny timing. We argue that the regulator's choice of the timing of the rule and its scrutiny generally depends on the relative costs of each approach, and whether the approach can sufficiently address the regulator's objectives. As an illustration, we provide a simple example to demonstrate the trade-offs between different regulatory options, highlighting the opportunity for regulation to target algorithmic decisions even before they have been deployed and possibly scrutinize compliance before harm can materialize at deployment.

4.4.1 Setup

We formally model the setting from Section 4.2 as a stylized game between a firm (agent) deploying an algorithm and a regulator (principal) overseeing its use. The firm chooses an algorithmic policy f from some set $\mathcal{F}$. We think of this algorithmic policy as a mapping $f : X \rightarrow \mathcal{A}$ from features $x \in X$ to a decision $f(x) \in \mathcal{A}$. For example, the firm could be a lender who decides whether to give credit ($a \in$ {extend credit, deny credit} $= \mathcal{A}$) to a borrower with financial history x. The regulator puts constraints or imposes penalties on the algorithmic decisions f. For example, a financial regulator may restrict the variables that are permissible for use in credit decisions or penalize a lender for unfair lending practices.

We assume that the firm and the regulator may have different preferences over algorithmic decisions. The firm wants to maximize profit $\Pi_\theta(f)$, such as the net return to lending. The regulator aims to maximize utility $U_\theta(f)$, which may differ from the firm's goal, such as by additional fairness or risk considerations. Both objectives could depend on the state of the world $\theta \in \Theta$ when the algorithmic policy f is deployed. For example, this state of the world may determine the joint distribution of some outcome of interest y (such as repayment) and the covariates x (such as the financial histories of actual loan applicants).

We assume that there is a training phase in which the algorithmic policy is chosen and a deployment phase in which it is applied. In the *training phase*, the firm chooses an algorithmic policy $\hat{f}_\tau \in \mathcal{F}$ based on a training signal $\tau \in T$. This signal represents the training data that is used by the firm when deciding between functions $f \in \mathcal{F}$. In the *deployment phase*, the state of the world $\theta \in \Theta$ is realized, leading to lender profit $\Pi_\theta(\hat{f}_\tau)$ and regulator utility $U_\theta(\hat{f}_\tau)$. We model the idea that this training signal is informative about the deployment state by assuming that $(\tau,\theta) \in T \times \Theta$ comes from a joint distribution P. For example, the training data may be a sample from the same distribution as the deployment. We assume that both the regulator and the firm begin the game knowing the joint distribution P, and later learn τ.

Without any regulation, a firm that maximizes expected profit would choose an algorithmic policy $\hat{f}_\tau$ during the training phase that maximizes $E[\Pi_\theta(f)|\tau]$ over all available policies $f \in \mathcal{F}$, leading to realized profit $\Pi_\theta(\hat{f}_\tau)$ to the firm and utility $U_\theta(\hat{f}_\tau)$ to the regulator. However, the firm's first-best choice may have undesirable properties from the regulator's perspective, such as when a lender's credit-scoring policy excludes part of the target population or leads to excess systemic risk. The regulator, therefore, may want to restrict the firm's choice of algorithmic policy.

4.4.2 Target and Timing of Regulation

Following the setting in Section 4.2, regulatory interventions in our game can target and happen at three points in time: before the training phase (*ex ante*), between the training and deployment phases (*ex interim*), and after deployment (*ex post*). *Ex ante*, the regulator can decide on general restrictions on how the firm is allowed to process training data that do not depend on the particular training data that is later realized. For example, the regulator may generally rule out that policies use some prohibited features. Alternatively, a rule targeting the *ex interim* stage, after the training sample τ is available and the firm chooses its algorithmic policy, can determine whether a particular algorithmic rule $\hat{f}_\tau$ is permissible for use in the specific context. For example, a regulator concerned with financial stability may, based on the results of a stress test of a lending rule and its performance in an adverse scenario even before it is deployed, determine whether the use of a lending rule is permissible. Finally, *ex post* rules relate to the stage at which the deployment state θ is realized and the algorithmic rule is deployed. At this stage, the regulator can observe outcomes and sanction the firm based

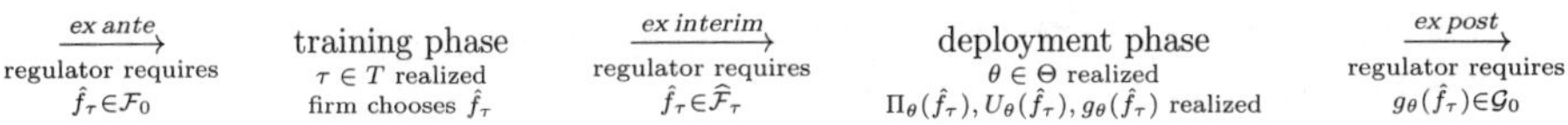

Fig. 4.2 Rule timing of regulatory interventions

on them. For example, a banking regulator concerned with fairness may check for disparities in realized lending decisions and decide, on the basis of those disparities, whether to penalize the lender.

In all three cases, we assume that regulatory rules define a set of permissible algorithmic policies $\hat{f}_\tau$ that the lender can choose without facing sanctions. However, the nature of these restrictions differs across different types of regulation (fig. 4.2).

Ex ante rules make simple general restrictions about the way that algorithmic rules can be chosen in the first place, such as restrictions on how training data is allowed to be used or which algorithmic rules can be searched over in the first place. For simplicity, we focus on one specific way of capturing such restrictions: we assume that *ex ante* rules simply limit the permissible algorithmic policies to some fixed set. That is, these rules take the form $\hat{f}_\tau \in \mathcal{F}_0$ for some *ex ante* chosen $\mathcal{F}_0 \subseteq \mathcal{F}$. This captures, for example, that specific characteristics cannot be used by the final policy, like an input restriction, or that some model classes are not allowed to be considered.[6]

For *ex interim* rules, restrictions are directly on the function $\hat{f}_\tau$ and may depend on the training data itself. That is, these rules take the form $\hat{f}_\tau \in \hat{\mathcal{F}}_\tau \subseteq \mathcal{F}$. In this case, the regulator checks whether the selected algorithmic rule is appropriate, potentially using the training data to make this determination. For example, a regulator may check whether a better algorithmic rule is available (when scrutinized *ex interim*) or would have been available (when scrutinized *ex post*) based on the information available during training.

For *ex post* rules, tests take the form whether $g_\theta(\hat{f}_\tau) \in \mathcal{G}_0$, where $g_0(f)$ are some realized outcomes of deploying a function $f \in \mathcal{F}$ in state θ. That is, *ex post* rules only depend on the implications of the algorithmic rule in the realized state θ. Here, the function $g_\theta(\cdot)$ is fixed and predefined and expresses the outcomes that *ex post* regulation can be based on, while the choice of the set $\mathcal{G}_0$ represents the regulator's restriction.[7] When there are disparity concerns, then $g_\theta(f)$ may capture the realized differences in lending rates

6. There are alternative options for capturing the idea of rigid *ex ante* rules from our taxonomy in Section 4.3. For example, we could restrict the way that training data is allowed to be processed and limit the firm to only use some coarser information CleanedData(τ), where the regulator chooses the mapping CleanedData. Or we could think more generally of putting some coarse, easy-to-implement restrictions on the mapping $\tau \mapsto \hat{f}_\tau$.

7. This formulation allows for cases where the regulator can set *ex post* rules that depend on the exact deployment state θ, which we can express by setting $g_\theta(f) = (\theta, \tilde{g}_\theta(f))$. Similary, our model allows for cases where the function f is fully observed *ex post*, which we can express by $g_\theta(f) = (f, \tilde{g}_\theta(f))$, But the model also allows for cases where the regulator only observes

across protected groups, and $\mathcal{G}_0$ the range of differences the regulator is willing to accept.

We assume that determining the legal rule and compliance with it can be costly to the regulator, and that ensuring $\hat{f}_\tau \in \mathcal{F}_0$ costs $c_{ex\ ante}$, that testing $\hat{f}_\tau \in \hat{\mathcal{F}}_\tau$ comes at a cost $c_{ex\ interim}$, and that checking $g_\theta(\hat{f}_\tau) \in \mathcal{G}_0$ comes at a cost $c_{ex\ post}$.[8]

Following our general framework, we distinguish between the rule timing, that is, which information the specific rule is based on, and the scrutiny timing, that is, when compliance with the rule is assessed. We assume here that the cost of testing some rule only depends explicitly on the timing of the rule, not on the timing of the scrutiny. That is, whether an *ex interim* rule is scrutinized *ex interim* or *ex post* comes at the same cost. However, *ex post* scrutiny of an *ex interim* rule may still be cheaper if it is performed only when bad outcomes materialize, thus reducing the expected cost.

We assume that *ex interim* scrutiny implies that the regulator forces the firm to choose a permissible function $\hat{f}_\tau$ that complies with *ex ante* and *ex interim* rules, whereas for *ex post* scrutiny the regulator decides whether to allow the firm to collect profits $\Pi_\theta(\hat{f}_\tau)$ or to punish the firm by reducing profits to $\underline{\Pi}$. The timing of the scrutiny, therefore, matters for the overall cost to the regulator. *Ex post* scrutiny of *ex interim* rules—such as when a regulator uses materialized harm for targeting auditing efforts of *ex interim* compliance—may involve the cost $c_{ex\ post}$ of testing *ex post* as well as the cost $c_{ex\ interim}$ of *ex interim* testing, for firms that are selected for auditing. Throughout, we consider the case where the regulator commits to a deterministic regulatory policy (in the form of *ex ante* rules $\mathcal{F}_0$, *ex interim* rules $\tau \mapsto \hat{\mathcal{F}}_\tau$, *ex post* rules $\mathcal{G}_0$, and the decision when to scrutinize each rule).[9]

4.4.3 Regulatory Regimes

We now make different regulatory options concrete by listing five specific regulatory regimes that mirror our taxonomy in Section 4.3. In the example here, we consider the case where *ex ante* rules can be scrutinized for free, $c_{ex\ ante} = 0$, which expresses the idea that simple restrictions on inputs or functional form may be easy to verify. Typically, we would assume that *ex post* rules are cheap to enforce while checking *ex interim* rules may be more costly ($c_{ex\ interim} > c_{ex\ post} \geq 0 = c_{ex\ ante}$) since they require inspecting the com-

some coarse summary information about the consequences of the deployed policy in the realized state.

8. A more general formulation would make the costs depend on the specific restrictions; for example, $c_{ex\ ante}$ may depend on the specific restriction $\mathcal{F}_0$, as some restrictions may be cheaper to verify than others.

9. Natural extensions include cases where the regulator imposes a fine in the *ex post* and possibly also in the *ex interim* stage, cases with audits that only happen with a given probability, cases with limited commitment, and repeated interactions where an infraction in a first interaction leads to additional regulatory obligations in the next.

plex algorithm (and possibly the training data) beyond the realized consequences of algorithm deployment. The five regulatory regimes we consider are the following:

1. *No regulatory constraints*: In the laissez-faire regime, there are no regulatory constraints, and the firm is free to choose any $\hat{f}_\tau \in \mathcal{F}$ after observing the training signal τ.
2. *Ex ante restriction*: If the regulator imposes *ex ante* rules $\mathcal{F}_0$, the firm is forced to choose $\hat{f}_\tau \in \mathcal{F}_0$ but otherwise is unrestricted. (Here, since we assume that *ex ante* rules can be checked without cost to the regulator, we assume that they can also be perfectly enforced; in particular, we do not consider different scrutiny timing options.)
3. *Ex post rule*: If the regulator imposes *ex post* rules, then the regulator does not put any *ex ante* or *ex interim* restrictions. Instead, the regulator can pay $c_{ex\ post}$ to choose $\mathcal{G}_0$. In this case, the firm obtains profit $\Pi_\theta(\hat{f}_\tau)$ if $g_\theta(\hat{f}_\tau) \in \mathcal{G}_0$ and $\underline{\Pi}$ otherwise. The regulator obtains utility $U_\theta(\hat{f}_\tau) - c_{ex\ post}$ since the algorithmic policy is already deployed.
4. *Ex interim audit*: If the regulator performs an *ex interim* audit, the regulator pays $c_{ex\ interim}$ and chooses $\hat{\mathcal{F}}_\tau$, and the firm chooses $\hat{f}_\tau \in \hat{\mathcal{F}}_\tau$. This case corresponds to *ex interim* scrutiny of an *ex interim* rule.
5. *Ex interim rule scrutinized by ex post audit*: If the regulator imposes *ex interim* rules based on an *ex post* audit, the regulator first tests based on an *ex post* rule $g_\theta(\hat{f}_\tau) \in \mathcal{G}_0$, at cost $c_{ex\ post}$, whether to perform an in-depth audit. If the rule is violated, the regulator pays an additional $c_{ex\ interim}$ to assess whether $\hat{f}_\tau \in \hat{\mathcal{F}}_\tau$. In this case, the firm obtains profit $\Pi_\theta(\hat{f}_\tau)$ if $\hat{f}_\tau \in \hat{\mathcal{F}}_\tau$ and $\underline{\Pi}$ otherwise. The regulator obtains utility $U_\theta(\hat{f}_\tau)$ net of the costs of the audits. Writing δ for the probability that the *ex post* rule is violated ($g_\theta(\hat{f}_\tau) \notin \mathcal{G}_0$), this means that the expected cost of the regulator is $c_{ex\ post} + \delta c_{ex\ interim}$. This option corresponds to *ex post* scrutiny based on *ex interim* and *ex post* rules in the parlance of Section 4.2.

While these regulatory options could be combined in principle, we consider them separately to simplify our analysis. Throughout, we assume that the regulator and the firm maximize expected utility and profit, respectively.

4.4.4 Regulation in an Illustrative Example

To illustrate insights from our general model, we now provide a simple instance. Specifically, we consider a lender who selects between three decision rules for allocating credit, namely a risky rule that expands credit to many borrowers, a conservative rule that provides credit only to very safe borrowers, and an imprecise rule that adds unnecessary noise, $f \in \mathcal{F} =$ {risky, conservative, imprecise}. We assume that the deployment state can either be high or low, $\theta \in$ {high, low}, which could represent, for example, a period of financial stability (high) or instability (low). The immediately observed outcome can be one of $g_\theta(f) \in$ {great, good, bad}.

Table 4.2. Lender and regulator payoffs in the example

	Lender Profit $\Pi_\theta(f)$		Regulator Utility $U_\theta(f)$		Realized Outcome $g_\theta(f)$	
	θ = high	θ = low	θ = high	θ = low	θ = high	θ = low
f = risky	6	2	5	−1	Great	Bad
f = conservative	4	1	2	2	Good	Good
f = imprecise	2	0	1	0	Bad	Bad

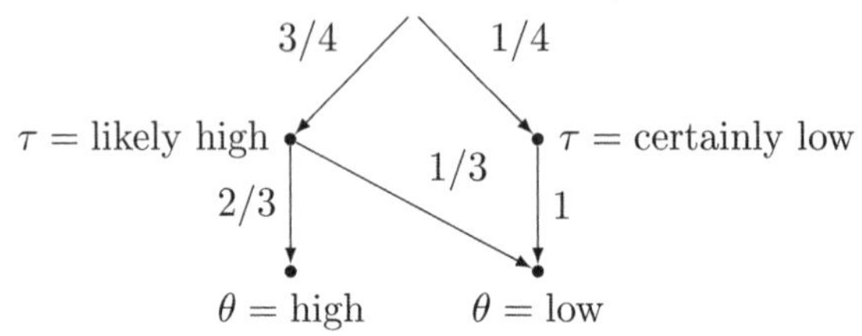

Fig. 4.3 Joint distribution of training and deployment signals in the example

The lender generally prefers the risky to the conservative policy. The financial regulator prefers expanding credit access in the high state, but is concerned about harm to marginal borrowers who cannot repay their loans in the low state. So the regulator prefers the risky rule to be used in the high state and the conservative rule in the low state. Neither the regulator nor the lender prefers the imprecise rule. Concrete profits and regulator utility that represent these rank orderings are provided in table 4.2.

In the training phase, we assume that the lender receives a noisy signal $\tau \in T$ = {likely high, certainly low} about the future deployment state, with $P(\tau$ = certainly low) = 1/4. (These signals represent training data that are indicative of the repayment probabilities of borrowers in the deployment phase.) If the training signal is τ = certainly low, then the deployment state will be low, $P(\theta$ = low | τ = certainly low) = 100%. If it is τ = high low, then there is a 2/3 chance of the high state occuring, so $P(\theta$ = high | τ = likely high) = 2/3. This distribution is also represented in figure 4.3.

The lender observes the training signal τ and chooses an algorithmic policy $\hat{f}_\tau$ to maximize expected profit, subject to potential regulatory constraints. If the training signal is τ = likely high, then regulator and lender agree that the risky algorithmic policy is optimal. But if τ = certainly low, then the regulator prefers the conservative policy, while the lender still prefers the risky policy.

We now consider the different regulatory regimes from Section 4.3 in this example. Throughout, we assume that the regulator aims to maximize expected utility, that the regulator can punish the lender by setting profit to $\underline{\Pi} = -6$ (e.g. by excluding it from making profits in the future), that the cost for *ex interim* tests is $c_{ex\ interim} = c$ with $0 < c < 3$, and that *ex ante* and *ex post* tests are not costly ($c_{ex\ ante} = 0 = c_{ex\ post}$). The different regulatory regimes then play out as follows:

1. *No regulatory constraints*: In the laissez-faire regime without regulatory constraints, the lender always chooses the risky algorithm, leading to expected lender profit of 4 and regulator utility of 2.

2. *Ex ante restriction*: If the regulator can only impose *ex ante* rules of the form $\hat{f}_\tau \in \mathcal{F}_0$, then the regulator could force the lender to avoid the risky rule (and pick the safe rule instead), $\mathcal{F}_0 = \{\text{conservative}\}$. With our parameters, this would still lead to safe regulator utility of 2 (but reduce expected lender profit to 2.5).

3. *Ex post rule*: If the regulator imposes an *ex post* rule, they can punish the lender as a function of the outcome in the deployment state. In the example, a plausible option would be to require outcomes $g_\theta(\hat{f}_\tau) \in \mathcal{G}_0 = \{\text{good, great}\}$ and punish the lender (by imposing profit $\underline{\Pi} = -6$) whenever the bad outcome materializes ($g_\theta(\hat{f}_\tau) = \text{bad}$). In this case, the lender would not choose the risky option in either the high or the low training state, since even in the high training state the expected profit (net of regulatory sanctions) from deploying the risky algorithmic rule is now 2, relative to an expected profit of 3 for deploying the conservative policy. Hence, regulator profit would still be 2, but lender profit would be reduced to 2.5.

Of course, the effectiveness of these *ex post* audits depends on the severity of punishment. If, for example, the regulator could impose a lighter punishment of, say $\underline{\Pi} = 0$, then this policy could effectively rule out the choice of the risky algorithmic option in the low training state only. However, such a policy would still be limited in a different instance of our model: if there is a possibility of the high state occurring even after a low training state, then limited liability (in the sense of $\underline{\Pi} = 0$) for the lender may make *ex post* sanctions ineffective since they may not be enough to force the choice of the conservative algorithmic policy even in the low training state.

4. *Ex interim audit*: If the regulator intervenes at the interim stage, they can pay a fee of c to impose restrictions on the choice of the lender based on the training signal. Here, this would imply a restriction to the regulator's preferred choice,

$$\hat{f}_\tau \in \hat{\mathcal{F}}_\tau = \begin{cases} \{\text{risky}\}, & \tau = \text{likely high}, \\ \{\text{conservative}\}, & \tau = \text{certainly low}. \end{cases}$$

In this case, the overall expected regulator utility, net of cost, is $2.75 - c$, which is an improvement over the other options as long as the cost is small enough ($c < .75$). The expected lender profit in this case is 3.75.

5. *Ex interim rule scrutinized by ex post audit*: The regulator could also intervene in the *ex post* stage, but still use *ex interim* information. In this case, a natural policy would be to only scrutinize the training phase if the risky

algorithmic policy was deployed in the low state. In this case, if the regulator threatens to pay a cost c to check whether the lender chose $\hat{f}_\tau$ = risky for τ = certainly low, but only in the case that θ = low and $g_\theta(\hat{f}_\tau)$ = bad are realized, then it would push the lender to implement the preferred choice

$$\hat{f}_\tau = \begin{cases} \text{risky}, & \tau = \text{likely high}, \\ \text{conservative}, & \tau = \text{certainly low}. \end{cases}$$

However, the expected cost is now lowered to $c/4$, since the *ex interim* scrutiny only happens in the case of a low deployment state following the optimistic training signal, for an expected regulator utility (net of cost) of 2.75 – $c/4$. Expected lender profit is unchanged at 3.75.

This specific example highlights the potential of targeted *ex interim* rules for algorithmic regulation, even in cases where they are more costly to enforce than *ex ante* and *ex post* rules. In addition, disentangling rule and scrutiny timing can yield regulatory solutions with lower cost.

4.4.5 Frictions from Algorithmic Complexity

Our approach to *ex interim* regulation of algorithms is built around tests of the form $\hat{f}_\tau \in \hat{\mathcal{F}}_\tau$ that check whether the algorithmic decision function belongs to some permissible set. In practice, the algorithmic policies chosen by the firm may be very complex. For example, a lender may utilize deep neural networks or other machine learning methods to determine who should receive credit. In such cases, the regulator may not be able to parse all the nuances of the firm's choice $\hat{f}_\tau$, or the firm may be limited in its ability to share all the algorithm's details for privacy or intellectual property reasons. Instead, the regulator may have to rely on simplified (typically low-dimensional) descriptions of algorithmic decisions. In practice, these could take the form of variable-importance measures, simpler proxy models, or evaluations at a limited number of data points. In our model, we can capture the restriction that the regulator may not be able to fully capture complex AI algorithms by restrictions on *SimpleDescription* ($\hat{f}_\theta$) rather than on $\hat{f}_\theta$. Concrete examples from our previous work include audits based on simple explainers (Blattner, Nelson, and Spiess 2024) and "discrimination stress testing" based on assessing an algorithmic policy by evaluating it at specific test points (Gillis and Spiess 2019).

In the stylized example from Section 4.4.4 above, such frictions could imply that the regulator cannot distinguish between all algorithmic policies in $\mathcal{F}$, and instead only observes whether a given choice falls within a coarse partition. *Which* functions the regulator can distinguish between then depends on the technology used to explain or describe the algorithm and its output (Blattner, Nelson, and Spiess 2024). For example, we could consider different coarse ways of describing algorithms, each of which partitions the space $\mathcal{F}$ = {risky, conservative, imprecise} into two non-trivial parts.

A first way focuses on the overall behavior of the algorithmic policy. If the risky and conservative options are overall more similar to each other than to the imprecise policy, then such a coarsening may only make it possible to distinguish the imprecise policy from the others, leaving it impossible for the regulator to distinguish between $f \in$ {risky, conservative} and rendering effective regulation infeasible. Instead, an effective way of summarizing complex functions has to be mindful of the source of preference misalignment. Here, this would mean that a coarsening into, say, {risky} and {conservative, imprecise} would be more effective, since it preserves all the information relevant to the misalignment between lender and regulator.

4.5. General Implications for Regulating Algorithms

The prior sections introduced a framework of a regulator leveraging *ex ante*, *ex interim*, and *ex post* tools to regulate a firm that deploys an algorithmic policy. In this section, we highlight three key implications within the context of the formal model in Section 4.4, and discuss them in connection with other related work.

4.5.1 The Value of *Ex interim* Regulation

First, we observe that the *ex interim* stage—something we argue is unique to the algorithmic context—has value from a regulatory perspective. To see this, contrast the option of *ex interim* intervention with several possible *ex post* regulatory regimes. One such *ex post* regime is to penalize the firm for undesirable outcomes. While this helps align preferences, it risks penalizing the firm for deployment-state realizations beyond its control, such as external market conditions. This undermines the primary goal of many legal rules, which is to target specific unwanted conduct rather than impose strict liability for all adverse outcomes. The regulator then faces a trade-off, as in a classic delegation problem, between a penalty being either so mild that it leads to excessive realizations of bad outcomes from the regulator's perspective or so strict that it leads to overly conservative behavior by a risk-averse firm. *Ex interim* regulation, in contrast, allows the regulator, in principle, to target precisely the aspects of the firm's conduct that are under the firm's control

In our framework, *ex interim* rules can even lead to first-best outcomes for the regulator. As an extreme case, if there is no cost to *ex interim* tests ($c_{ex\ interim} = 0$ in the model from Section 4.4), then *ex interim* audits generally dominate *ex ante* and *ex post* rules. First, *ex interim* tests of the form $\hat{f}_\tau \in \hat{\mathcal{F}}_\tau$ are strict generalizations of *ex ante* tests of the form $\hat{f}_\tau \in \mathcal{F}_0$. Second, relative to *ex post* tests, *ex interim* rules are more precise because they directly scrutinize the use of training data, rather than relying on the (possibly noisy) realization of the deployment state over which the firm has no control. Third, *ex interim* rules can be applied before deployment, which avoids bad outcomes before they can happen. In the extreme case when there are also no frictions in imposing restrictions on algorithmic policies, the regulator can ensure that their first-best choice is deployed by performing an *ex interim* audit with $\hat{\mathcal{F}}_\tau = \{\hat{f}_\tau^*\}$ with $\hat{f}_\tau^* \in \arg\max_{f \in \mathcal{F}} E[U_\theta(f)|\tau]$. In this world, the regulator effectively chooses the algorithmic policy.

The opportunity of the *ex interim* stage for regulation is also pointed out by Kleinberg et al. (2018), which argues that *ex interim* rules in algorithmic settings offer a distinctive advantage by leveraging the transparency and specificity of algorithmic processes, enabling clear attribution of disparities to particular modeling choices. When the regulator either cannot observe the training state or cannot fully understand the algorithm, optimal regulation is more subtle. Blattner, Nelson, and Spiess (2024) analyze a setting similar to that in Section 4.4 and characterize when it is optimal for a regulator to use *ex interim* regulation in the form of an *explainer* that, by projecting the firm's algorithmic policy into a lower-dimensional representation that shows how it behaves in a few (carefully chosen) dimensions, can constrain the firm's behavior in ways targeted at the principal–agent preference misalignment; in general, this leads to second-best outcomes unless misalignment is very severe and high-dimensional. Gillis and Spiess (2019) develop a related *ex interim* regulatory approach that involves deploying the algorithmic policy on test data—an approach they refer to as "stress testing" an algorithm. Inspired by bank stress testing, under this approach, a model is tested under a hypothetical materialization of the deployment state θ that is unknown to the developer during model training. In contrast with Blattner, Nelson, and Spiess (2024), whose explainer tool can be thought of as examining *ex interim* how an algorithmic policy behaves on several columns (variables) of data, the Gillis and Spiess (2019) approach can be thought of as examining algorithm behavior on several rows (individual observations) of data. Each approach may be preferable in different circumstances, depending on whether misalignment is best summarized through a few (high-dimensional) examples or through a few data features.

Another consideration is that the form of optimal regulation depends on the relationship between the training and deployment state, as well as the effectiveness of *ex post* punishments. In settings where training and deployment data are very similar, scrutiny based on *ex interim* rules may be unnecessary and scrutiny based on *ex post* outcomes may be sufficient, provided that effective *ex post* punishment leads to high compliance with the *ex post* rule. On the other hand, if there is substantive additional uncertainty about the deployment state, then optimal regulation is likely to include *ex interim* rules. When there is limited room for *ex post* punishment, there is a stronger case for enforcing such rules at the interim stage.

More broadly, the distinction between *ex interim* and *ex post* regulation parallels the distinction between certification regimes and enforcement regimes. Consider how the US regulates car safety, which at a high level can be viewed as a combination of (1) supervising car manufacturers' car development process and certifying a car model as meeting safety standards at the preproduction stage and (2) periodically investigating cars' safety performance in the "deployment" state of being driven, either through annual safety inspections (as mandated in some US states) or through National Highway Traffic Safety Administration–ordered recalls (at the federal level). (*Ex ante* regulation of cars, meanwhile, might take the form of restrictions on which types of cars can even be designed, for example, maximum allowable axle length.) Algorithmic decision-making enables such *ex interim* regulation to be used for a broader set of economic activity.

4.5.2 The Optimal Form of *Ex post* Scrutiny

A second implication of our framework is that, even if regulation is more feasible or cost-effective to apply *ex post*—for example, because of the cost $c_{ex\ interim}$ of formulating rules that involve the training data in the formalization of Section 4.4—*ex post* regulatory tools should often also include *ex interim* information, provided that *ex interim* scrutiny is not too expensive. This follows from a logic similar to that in the preceding subsection: effective regulation should optimally target the actual conduct, rather than only possibly noisy consequences.

There are cases where *ex post* scrutiny based on *ex post* rules alone can be effective or desirable. For example, if the regulator in an extension of our model would be able to impose arbitrary penalties, then they could align preferences based on realized outcomes alone (e.g., by imposing a penalty $\Pi_\theta(\hat{f}_\tau) - U_\theta(\hat{f}_\tau)$). However, if the firm has limited liability, transfers are limited otherwise, or it is infeasible to observe or estimate the necessary utility differences even *ex post*, then regulation without *ex interim* scrutiny may become inefficient.

4.5.3 Cases for *Ex ante* Regulation

A third important takeaway from our framework is an understanding of cases in which *ex ante* regulation may be valuable. To recap, in our framework, *ex ante* restrictions refer to limitations on algorithms that do not rely on any training or deployment data. This *ex ante* regulation can take several forms. In our model, they capture the *ex ante* exclusion of specific inputs and models before training starts. In a broader sense, we could think of simple *ex ante* restrictions as easily enforceable high-level restrictions to the data-processing and training process.

The two leading cases in which *ex ante* regulation makes sense within our framework are when the cost of implementing *ex post* and especially *ex interim* rules is very high (e.g., when accessing training and deployment data is complicated), and when misalignment can be easily captured by preferences over which inputs to use (e.g., when the regulator wants to enforce that only certain variables are used for pricing by a firm). But when *ex interim* and *ex post* rules are easily enforced, then they subsume any *ex ante* rules. However, the trade-offs between *ex ante* and downstream rules can become more complex when additional frictions are involved.

In a related model that introduces frictions through algorithm complexity, Blattner, Nelson, and Spiess (2024) considers when it might be optimal to *ex ante* restrict an algorithmic agent to use only simple models. Their analysis points to several such conditions. First, if the loss from restricting to simple models is small, or if misalignment between regulator and lender is particularly severe (in a sense that Blattner, Nelson, and Spiess [2024] formalize), then *ex ante* restrictions to simple models can be beneficial. Second, if the regulator cannot observe the training state and if their regulator's prior is relatively uninformative about the training state, *ex interim* tools may have less use. Concerns about artificial intelligence presenting an existential risk for society (e.g., Jones 2024) often reflect some combination of these conditions: an uninformative prior about the training of AI tools, or a perception of severe misalignment, or a belief in the loss from using simple models being modest.

A specific case of *ex ante* regulation involves restricting which inputs an algorithm can access. Typically, such input restrictions are considered in the context of antidiscrimination regulation for protected characteristics, such as race or gender. While input-based regulation is often considered fraught in the era of "big data" (Kleinberg et al. 2018; Gillis 2021), given how high-dimensional combinations of permitted inputs can be used to proxy for a forbidden input (Mullainathan and Spiess 2017), Liang et al. (2021) makes the case for input-based restrictions to achieve certain fairness goals. Relative to Blattner, Nelson, and Spiess (2024), the setup in Liang et al. (2021) highlights several conditions that contribute to *ex ante* restrictions being valuable: The principal has limited uncertainty about the training or deployment state, so that the form of optimal regulation is relatively knowable from the *ex ante* perspective; and the principal and agent have particularly strong misalignment (in the form of strong fairness preferences of the regulator).[10]

4.5.4 Other Considerations

Our framework necessarily excludes some features that may also be relevant for the context-specific regulation of algorithms. One crucial consideration not included here is the demand for privacy and other normative considerations in algorithmic regulation. *Ex ante* restrictions on specific

10. An interesting intermediate case is whether input restrictions can productively be combined with the Blattner, Nelson, and Spiess (2024) explainer tool. For example, if the explainer that a regulator has access to is too low-dimensional to sufficiently capture the misalignment with the firm, but the regulator additionally has access to *ex ante* restrictions on model inputs, then combining an *ex interim* explainer that targets some model features with an *ex ante* restriction on using other model features may be optimal.

model inputs, for example, may be justified either by privacy concerns or by concerns about whether including these features per se in a model would be ethically undesirable (e.g., Acquisti, Taylor, and Wagman 2016; Goldfarb and Tucker 2012, 2024; Kiviat 2019).

In addition, our model focuses on the regulator scrutinizing the algorithmic policy actually chosen by the firm. Some regulatory approaches focus instead on the *procedure* that generated these algorithmic decisions from training data, beyond pre-processing of the data. This procedure—that is, the actual algorithm—is represented in our model as the mapping from training data to algorithmic policy, $\tau \mapsto \hat{f}_\tau$. The regulator in our model scrutinizes the algorithm's output $\hat{f}_\tau$ for the *realized* training data τ, rather than the full mapping from *any* training data τ to the algorithmic policy $\hat{f}_\tau$. In our model, we focus on the chosen policy since only this realization ultimately gets deployed and enters the regulator's utility. In addition, in practice, training algorithms may involve manual steps that are hard to capture fully. Nevertheless, there could be cases where scrutiny already happens *before* training data is available or in which communicating the training data may be infeasible. In those cases, scrutinizing how training data is generally processed—that is, analyzing the full mapping $\tau \mapsto \hat{f}_\tau$—may be part of effective regulation as a variant of our *ex interim* approach.

Another relevant question we have not addressed is how the regulator learns about the markets they are regulating, which may be particularly relevant in some emerging algorithmic settings where regulatory precedent is scant. The regulator's data collection may also interact with competing firms' incentives to differentially disclose data to the regulator.[11] We also do not consider the question of how frequently to audit a firm, or how to target these audits (e.g., the resource-constrained regulator's problem of whether to audit a small firm with probable rule violations, or a larger firm with less likely, but potentially more widespread, rule violations).

Finally, we only consider the decision of the firm on how to turn training data into algorithmic policies, but not their decision on which training data to acquire in the first place. Questions of fairness can be decided as much by which data is used as by how an algorithm is trained (Blattner and Nelson 2024; Caro, Gillis, and Nelson 2025), and obtaining high-quality data that represent the deployment distribution well may be a costly investment that firm and regulator have different preferences over.

4.6 An Agenda on Building Tools for AI Regulation

The unique opportunity for novel approaches to regulation in algorithmic settings also suggests a broad agenda for future research. We close with a few highlights from what we see as a wide-open area.

11. For an interesting, related analysis, see work in Callander and Li (2024).

On the one hand, this chapter argues that there are already clear opportunities for the effective regulation of algorithms. Among those is that regulation in an algorithmic setting can intervene at an *ex interim* stage where a firm has designed an algorithmic policy but has not yet deployed it. The framework developed here, building on some of our other work (e.g., Blattner, Nelson, and Spiess 2024; Gillis and Spiess 2019), helps articulate why this *ex interim* stage has value. Our framework also shows the broad—but not universal—conditions under which a regulator would prefer *ex interim* regulation over more traditional *ex ante* or *ex post* interventions. Drawing on insights from the landscape of emerging AI regulation in practice, we also show how the option to delay the scrutiny of these *ex interim* processes until a later *ex post* stage can have added benefit beyond an *ex interim* approach alone.

On the other hand, we see a long list of unanswered questions, including some related to how our conclusions above extend (or do not) to settings with other characteristics than those considered here. Among other open issues discussed in Section 4.5, we see it as particularly exciting to understand how the demand for privacy or other ethical considerations interact with algorithmic regulation, how the algorithmic development process itself might be regulated distinctly from the trained algorithmic policy, and how competitive forces and dynamic incentives among firms might shape the information available to regulators at the *ex ante* stage when deciding their approach to regulation, and to firms at the training stage when they form algorithmic policies.

Taking a step back from the economics of regulation, we also see it as important to ask what market solutions might address the regulatory challenges studied here. For example, could a market emerge for *ex interim* certification, and under what conditions? What might be the advantages and risks of relying on private firms to provide such certification services in lieu of a regulator? And—*quis custodiet ipsos custodes*—might that certification market itself benefit from regulation?

References

Acemoglu, Daron. 2023. "Harms of AI." In *The Oxford Handbook of AI Governance*, edited by Justin B. Bullock, Yu-Che Chen, Johannes Himmelreich, Valerie M. Hudson, Anton Korinek, Matthew M. Young, and Baobao Zhang, 660–706. Oxford Handbooks (2024), https://doi.org/10.1093/oxfordhb/9780197579329.001.0001.

Acquisti, Alessandro, Curtis Taylor, and Liad Wagman. 2016. "The Economics of Privacy." *Journal of Economic Literature* 54 (2): 442–92.

Agrawal, Ajay, Joshua S. Gans, and Avi Goldfarb. 2023. "Do We Want Less Automation?" *Science* 381 (6654): 155–58.

Ali, S. Nageeb, Greg Lewis, and Shoshana Vasserman. 2023. "Voluntary Disclosure and Personalized Pricing." *Review of Economic Studies* 90 (2): 538–71.

Anderljung, Markus, Joslyn Barnhart, Anton Korinek, Jade Leung, Cullen O'Keefe,

Jess Whittlestone, Shahar Avin, Miles Brundage, Justin Bullock, Duncan Cass-Beggs, et al. 2023. "Frontier AI Regulation: Managing Emerging Risks to Public Safety." arXiv preprint arXiv:2307.03718.

Bar-Gill, Oren, Cass R. Sunstein, and Inbal Talgam-Cohen. 2023. "Algorithmic Harm in Consumer Markets." *Journal of Legal Analysis* 15 (1): 1–47.

Bergemann, Dirk, Benjamin Brooks, and Stephen Morris. 2015. "The Limits of Price Discrimination." *American Economic Review* 105 (3): 921–57.

Blattner, Laura, Scott Nelson, and Jann Spiess. 2024. "Unpacking the Black Box: Regulating Algorithmic Decisions." arXiv preprint arXiv:2110.03443.

Blattner, Laura, and Scott Nelson. 2024. "How Costly Is Noise? Data and Disparities in Consumer Credit." https://doi.org/10.48550/arXiv.2105.07554.

Callander, Steven, and Hongyi Li. 2024. "Regulating an Innovative Industry." Technical report, National Bureau of Economic Research. Presented at NBER Conference on Economics of Artificial Intelligence, September 19–20, 2024, Toronto.

Canada. 2024. Artificial Intelligence and Data Act (AIDA). Proposed Legislation.

Caro, Spencer, Talia Gillis, and Scott Nelson. 2025. "Modernizing Fair Lending." Forthcoming in the *Journal of Legal Analysis*.

Comunale, Mariarosaria, and Andrea Manera. 2024. "The Economic Impacts and the Regulation of AI: A Review of the Academic Literature and Policy Actions." Working paper. International Monetary Fund.

Cowgill, Bo, and Catherine E. Tucker. 2020. "Algorithmic Fairness and Economics." *Research paper.* Columbia Business School.

Dubé, Jean-Pierre, and Sanjog Misra. 2023. "Personalized Pricing and Consumer Welfare." *Journal of Political Economy* 131 (1): 131–89.

Engler, Alex. 2023. "The AI Regulatory Toolbox: How Governments Can Discover Algorithmic Harms." *Brookings Institution*, October.

European Union. 2023. Regulation of the European Parliament and of the Council Laying Down Harmonized Rules on Artificial Intelligence (Artificial Intelligence Act) and Amending Certain Union Legislative Acts. Proposal for a Regulation.

Gillis, Talia B., and Jann L. Spiess. 2019. "Big Data and Discrimination." *The University of Chicago Law Review* 86 (2): 459–88.

Gillis, Talia B. 2021. "The Input Fallacy." *Minnesota Law Review* 106: 1175.

Goldfarb, Avi, and Catherine E. Tucker, eds. 2024. *The Economics of Privacy*. University of Chicago Press.

Goldfarb, Avi, and Catherine Tucker. 2012a. "Privacy and Innovation." *Innovation Policy and the Economy* 12 (1): 65–90.

Goldfarb, Avi, and Catherine Tucker. 2012b. "Shifts in Privacy Concerns." *American Economic Review* 102 (3): 349–53.

Guerreiro, Joao, Sergio Rebelo, and Pedro Teles. 2023. "Regulating Artificial Intelligence." Working Paper 31921. National Bureau of Economic Research.

Guha, Neel, Christie Lawrence, Lindsey A. Gailmard, Kit Rodolfa, Faiz Surani, Rishi Bommasani, Inioluwa Raji, Mariano-Florentino Cuéllar, Colleen Honigsberg, Percy Liang, et al. 2023. "AI Regulation Has Its Own Alignment Problem: The Technical and Institutional Feasibility of Disclosure, Registration, Licensing, and Auditing." Forthcoming in the *George Washington Law Review*.

Hadfield, Gillian K., and Jack Clark. 2023. "Regulatory Markets: The Future of AI Governance." arXiv preprint arXiv:2304.04914.

Hardt, Moritz, Eric Price, and Nati Srebro. 2016. "Equality of Opportunity in Supervised Learning." *Advances in Neural Information Processing Systems* 29.

Jones, Charles I. 2024. "The AI Dilemma: Growth Versus Existential Risk." *American Economic Review: Insights* 6 (4): 575–90.

Kaminski, Margot E. 2023. "Regulating the Risks of AI." *Boston University Law Review* 103: 1347.

Kaplow, Louis, and Steven Shavell. 1994. "Accuracy in the Determination of Liability." *Journal of Law and Economics* 37 (1): 1–15.

Kaplow, Louis. 2013. "Rules Versus Standards: An Economic Analysis." In *Scientific Models of Legal Reasoning*, 11–84. Routledge.

Kiviat, Barbara. 2019. "The Moral Limits of Predictive Practices: The Case of Credit-Based Insurance Scores." *American Sociological Review* 84 (6): 1134–58.

Kleinberg, Jon, Jens Ludwig, Sendhil Mullainathan, and Ashesh Rambachan. 2018. "Algorithmic Fairness." *AEA Papers and Proceedings* 108: 22–27.

Kleinberg, Jon, Jens Ludwig, Sendhil Mullainathan, and Cass R. Sunstein. 2018. "Discrimination in the Age of Algorithms." *Journal of Legal Analysis* 10: 113–74.

Kleinberg, Jon, Jens Ludwig, Sendhil Mullainathan, and Cass R. Sunstein. 2020. "Algorithms as Discrimination Detectors." *Proceedings of the National Academy of Sciences* 117 (48): 30096–30100.

Liang, Annie, Jay Lu, Xiaosheng Mu, and Kyohei Okumura. 2021. "Algorithm Design: A Fairness-Accuracy Frontier." arXiv preprint arXiv:2112.09975.

Malgieri, Gianclaudio, and Frank Pasquale. 2022. "From Transparency to Justification: Toward Ex Ante Accountability for AI." *Brooklyn Law School, Legal Studies Paper* (712).

Mullainathan, Sendhil, and Jann Spiess. 2017. "Machine Learning: An Applied Econometric Approach." *Journal of Economic Perspectives* 31 (2): 87–106.

NIST. 2023. Artificial Intelligence Risk Management Framework (AI RMF) 1.0. January.

Polinsky, A. Mitchell, and Steven Shavell. 2000. "The Economic Theory of Public Enforcement of Law." *Journal of Economic Literature* 38 (1): 45–76.

Porat, Haggai. 2022. "Behavior-Based Price Discrimination and Data Protection in the Age of Algorithms." https://papers.ssrn.com/sol3/papers.cfm?abstract_id=4254326.

Rambachan, Ashesh, Jon Kleinberg, Sendhil Mullainathan, and Jens Ludwig. 2020. "An Economic Approach to Regulating Algorithms." Working Paper No. 27111. National Bureau of Economic Research.

Rhodes, Andrew, and Jidong Zhou. 2024. "Personalized Pricing and Competition." *American Economic Review* 114 (7): 2141–70.

Sharkey, Catherine M. 2024. "A Products Liability Framework for AI." *Columbia Science and Technology Law Review* 25 (2).

Shavell, Steven. 1984. "Liability for Harm Versus Regulation of Safety." *The Journal of Legal Studies* 13 (2): 357–74.

Shavell, Steven. 1993. The Optimal Structure of Law Enforcement." *The Journal of Law and Economics* 36 (1, pt. 2): 255–87.

Shavell, Steven. 2018. "A Model of the Optimal Use of Liability and Safety Regulation." In *Economics and Liability for Environmental Problems*, 77–86. Routledge.

Tutt, Andrew. 2017. "An FDA for Algorithms." *Administrative Law Review* 69: 83.

US Senate. 2023. Algorithmic Accountability Act of 2023. S. 2892, 118th Congress. https://www.congress.gov/bill/118th-congress/senate-bill/2892.

5

Algorithmic Fairness
A Tale of Two Approaches

Joshua Gans

5.1 Introduction

As algorithms based on artificial intelligence proliferate, an important regulatory challenge is whether and how to regulate their use to meet various goals associated with achieving fairness and/or preventing discrimination. To date, policymakers have focused on computer science-led approaches to these issues. However, an emerging body of literature from economists challenges this approach to regulation.

The computer science approach, as outlined by Barocas et al. (2023), focuses on imposing fairness constraints directly on algorithmic systems. This typically involves mathematical definitions of fairness—such as demographic parity, equal opportunity, or equal odds—that algorithms must satisfy. For example, demographic parity requires that predictions be independent of protected group status, while equal opportunity mandates equal true positive rates across groups. These constraints are then incorporated into the algorithm's training process. Thus, algorithms are regulated directly by altering the types of predictions such algorithms can deliver.

More recently, economists have investigated this issue using standard approaches to devising regulatory outcomes based on decision-making contexts. As Kleinberg et al. (2016) demonstrate, the various computer science–developed fairness criteria are generally incompatible with each other except in trivial cases. More importantly, Rambachan et al. (2020)

Joshua Gans is a professor of strategic management and holder of the Jeffrey S. Skoll Chair of Technical Innovation and Entrepreneurship at the University of Toronto's Rotman School of Management, and a research associate of the National Bureau of Economic Research.

For acknowledgments, sources of research support, and disclosure of the author's material financial relationships, if any, please see https://www.nber.org/books-and-chapters/political-economy-artificial-intelligence/algorithmic-fairness-tale-two-approaches.

show that directly regulating algorithms by removing protected attributes or enforcing fairness constraints can harm disadvantaged groups by reducing prediction accuracy in ways that disproportionately affect them. Thus, instead of regulating prediction outcomes, the economics approach identifies how algorithmic predictions are used. It focuses on the broader decision-making context rather than the algorithms themselves. As articulated by Rambachan et al. (2020), the key insight is that AI predictions should be allowed to use all available information to maximize accuracy, while fairness objectives should be achieved through group-specific decision thresholds. Their theoretical analysis demonstrates that this approach dominates direct algorithmic regulation in terms of both efficiency and equity.

5.2 A Formal Analysis of Approaches

To understand the fundamental difference between computer science and economic approaches to algorithmic fairness, it is helpful to express them formally. Let us consider a setting where a decision-maker must allocate K slots among candidates from two groups ($g \in \{0,1\}$), where group 0 represents a historically disadvantaged group.

The standard computer science approach typically starts with an optimization problem of the form

$$(1) \qquad \min_f \frac{1}{N} \sum L(\omega_i, X_i; f) \text{subject to } f \text{ being ‘fair,’}$$

where f is the algorithm, L is a loss function, ω_i is the true outcome of interest, and X_i represents observable characteristics for each $i \in \{1,\ldots,N\}$. The fairness constraint might take various forms, such as demographic parity:

$$(2) \qquad \Pr[s_i = 1 | g = 1] = \Pr[s_i = 1 | g = 0],$$

where s_i is the algorithm's prediction consistent with being allocated to a slot. This approach directly constrains the algorithm's outputs to achieve fairness goals.

In contrast, the economic approach articulated by Rambachan et al. (2020) formulates the problem as follows:

$$(3) \quad \max_{a(g,x)} \mathbb{E}\left[\sum_{g,x} \phi_g \omega(g,x) a(g,x) F(g,x)\right] \text{subject to} \sum_{g,x} a(g,x) F(g,x) \leq K,$$

where $a(g,x) \in \{0,1\}$ is the allocation decision, ϕ_g represents welfare weights that can differ across groups, and $F(g, x)$ is the distribution of characteristics. Crucially, this formulation separates the prediction problem from the allocation decision, with ϕ_g being a measure of what Agrawal et al. (2018) refer to as *judgment* (in this case, of the regulator or the planner).

The solution takes the form of group-specific thresholds $t^*(g)$, where a candidate is selected if

$$\mathbb{E}[\omega_i(g_i, x_i)] > t^*(g).$$

The economic formulation has several advantages. First, it allows the algorithm f to use all available information to maximize prediction accuracy, which benefits all groups. Second, it explicitly incorporates social preferences through welfare weights ϕ_g rather than through algorithmic constraints. Finally, it recognizes that optimal policy may involve different treatment thresholds across groups even when the underlying predictions are unbiased.

To see why this matters quantitatively, note that

$$s_i = \underbrace{\omega_i}_{\text{Outcome of Interest}} + \underbrace{\Delta_{\omega_i}}_{\text{Measurement Error}}.$$

The difference in the algorithm's estimated predictions, $\mathbb{E}[s_i \mid g = 1] - \mathbb{E}[s_i \mid g = 0]$, is decomposed by Rambachan et al. (2020) as

$$\underbrace{\mathbb{E}[\omega_i \mid g = 1] - \mathbb{E}[\omega_i \mid g = 0]}_{\text{base rate differences}} + \underbrace{\mathbb{E}[\Delta_{\omega_i} \mid g = 1] - \mathbb{E}[\Delta_{\omega_i} \mid g = 0]}_{\text{measurement error differences}},$$

$$+ \underbrace{\hat{\epsilon}(1) - \hat{\epsilon}(0)}_{\text{estimation error differences}}$$

where $\hat{\epsilon}(g) = \mathbb{E}[\theta_i \mid g] - \mathbb{E}[s_i \mid g]$. This shows that there are three broad reasons a signal might differ from the outcome of interest. First, there are estimation errors that arise across groups and may come from differences in data availability or precision. Second, there are measurement errors that arise because there may be model misspecification in the training data or bias in how the training data is collected. Finally, there are base rate differences, which are real differences between groups in terms of expected performance, arising from underlying socioeconomic or other reasons. The important thing to recognize is that while the first two reasons can be corrected by improvements in the algorithm, data, or an understanding of the source of measurement issues, the final reason cannot. Importantly, the computer science approach attempts to eliminate this entire difference through algorithmic constraints. In contrast, the economic approach addresses only the latter two terms through improved prediction while handling base rate differences through decision thresholds.

To concretize these abstract concepts, consider a health-care system deploying an algorithm to identify patients at high risk of developing diabetes for targeted preventive interventions. Historical data show different base rates of diabetes across demographic groups due to social determinants of health, genetic factors, and patterns of access to care. Given limited intervention resources, the algorithm must determine which patients should receive priority.

Under the computer science approach, the algorithm would be constrained to ensure equal selection rates across demographic groups (demographic parity) or equal false positive or negative rates (equal opportunity). This typically involves removing protected attributes or adding constraints that artificially equalize group predictions. While achieving statistical parity, this approach reduces overall prediction accuracy. It can create suboptimal resource allocation: overtreatment of lower-risk individuals alongside undertreatment of higher-risk individuals within specific groups.

In contrast, the economic approach utilizes all available information (including demographic variables) to make the most accurate possible predictions, then applies different risk thresholds for intervention based on welfare weights (ϕ_g), resource constraints, and intervention effectiveness. This approach allows for accurately identifying high-risk individuals while addressing equity through decision rules rather than prediction algorithms. A similar logic applies to other domains such as college admissions, where an AI system predicts student success on the basis of test scores and other factors. Rather than constraining the algorithm to produce equal admission rates, the economic approach would maintain prediction accuracy while potentially setting different admission thresholds for different groups based on broader social welfare considerations.

The intuition favoring the economic approach is straightforward: accurate predictions allow decision-makers to better identify qualified candidates from disadvantaged groups who might otherwise be overlooked. The decision thresholds can then be adjusted to achieve desired representation goals while maintaining the benefits of accurate prediction. This solution recognizes that while measurement and estimation errors can be corrected through algorithm improvement, base rate differences cannot be eliminated through algorithmic constraints alone.

Under reasonable conditions, Rambachan et al. (2020) show that the economic approach weakly dominates any algorithm satisfying typical fairness constraints. An accuracy-maximizing prediction combined with optimal threshold policies can consistently replicate the outcome of a constrained algorithm but may achieve better outcomes by utilizing information more efficiently. Empirical evidence suggests that randomized controlled trials comparing these approaches would show the economic approach correctly identifying more genuinely high-risk patients (or qualified candidates) across all groups. At the same time, the computer science approach misses high-risk individuals in some groups while flagging too many low-risk individuals in others.

The economic framework also better accounts for the reality that decision-makers may have legitimate preferences for diversity or equity that go beyond pure prediction. Rather than conflating these preferences with the prediction task itself, it provides a cleaner separation that allows for more transparent

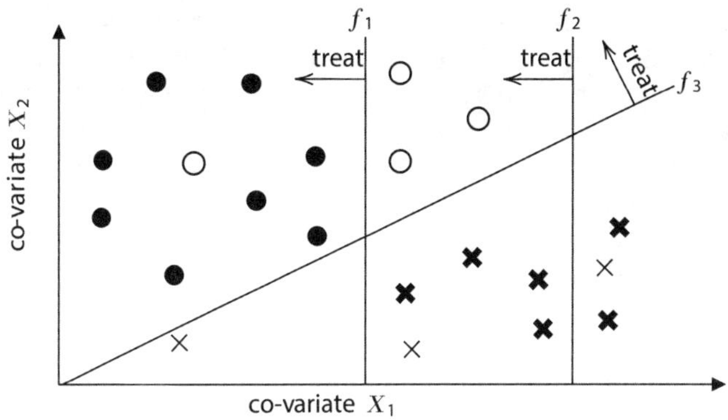

Fig. 5.1 Fairness and accuracy of different algorithms

policy choices. This separation makes the trade-offs explicit and prevents the obfuscation of value judgments within technical algorithmic constraints.

None of this suggests that algorithmic bias is not a serious concern requiring policy intervention. Indeed, the economic approach may ultimately require more active regulation of human decision-makers rather than algorithms.[1] However, it indicates that attempting to solve discrimination through direct algorithmic regulation is likely to be both ineffective and counterproductive, potentially harming the very groups such regulation aims to protect.

5.3 The Fairness Frontier Framework

The foregoing analysis highlights the distinction between regulating prediction algorithms themselves versus regulating how predictions are used. There is another approach to this trade-off that takes the perspective that different algorithms themselves involve a trade-off between accuracy and fairness. The underlying motivation for this approach is that in many regulatory contexts where discrimination or unfairness is regulated, a potential defense is that, in so doing, there would be a cost in terms of accuracy. However, it could also be the case that for a particular algorithm, no such trade-off arises. Identifying such cases, however, requires both understanding the particular fairness criterion applied and understanding the risk preferences of the social planner.

This approach is outlined in Liang et al. (2025). The idea that there is a trade-off between fairness and accuracy is easy to assess. Consider the distribution of outcomes in figure 5.1. There, X comprises two covariates

1. This is discussed in detail in Gans (2025). Chapter 20.

(e.g., random variables), X_1 and X_2, that inform whether a patient should be treated or not. The circular points are helped by the medical treatment, and the crosses are harmed by it. There are various algorithms indicated by demarcation lines, indicating who would be treated or not. Algorithms f_1 and f_2 use only X_1 as an input, while f_3 uses both covariates. It can be seen in f_1 that no red patient is harmed while 4 out of 7 of the blue patients are harmed. Overall, 1 in 21 receives unnecessary treatment while 3 in 21 miss out on the treatment they need. For f_2, the error rates are equalized at a rate of 2/7 for each group, demonstrating a fairness-accuracy trade-off as overall 9 in 21 are harmed, all receiving unnecessary treatment. Notice that if everyone is treated, in this example, the error rates are also equalised at 3/7 for each group. Finally, for f_3, both covariates are available, and there are no errors. Thus, adding a covariate can improve accuracy and fairness, and this covariate could be identifiable as group membership.

Building on our previous formal analysis, the fairness frontier approach developed by Liang et al. (2025) provides a powerful framework for understanding the trade-offs inherent in algorithmic fairness and offers insights into optimal policy design. Let me explain this approach formally and demonstrate why it leads to superior outcomes.

Consider a decision-maker whose utility from algorithm predictions depends on two types of errors for each group g:

$$e_g = (1 - \Pr[s_i = 1 | \omega_i = 1, g])\ell_1 + (1 - \Pr[s_i = 0 | \omega_i = 0, g])\ell_0, \tag{4}$$

where ℓ_1 and ℓ_0 represent the losses from false negatives and false positives, respectively. The fairness frontier can then be characterized in $\{e_0,e_1\}$ space—that is, the error rates for groups 0 and 1.

A key innovation in their framework is the definition of algorithmic dominance. Algorithm f is said to strictly dominate algorithm f' if

$$e_0(f) \leq e_0(f') \text{ and } e_1(f) \leq e_1(f') \tag{5}$$

with at least one strict inequality. This allows us to identify Pareto-optimal algorithms that cannot be improved for one group without harming the other.

The fairness frontier consists of algorithms that minimize a weighted average of group errors:

$$\min_f \lambda e_0(f) + (1 - \lambda)e_1(f) \tag{6}$$

for different values of $\lambda \in [0,1]$. This generates a curve in error space that represents the fundamental trade-offs between accuracy for different groups.

Figure 5.2 provides a graph of the fairness-accuracy frontier on $\{e_1,e_0\}$ space. Two possibilities are depicted. In each, there are three points of interest. The first two are algorithmic choices that result in the best outcomes for members of a particular group g, B_1 and B_0, respectively, minimizing among

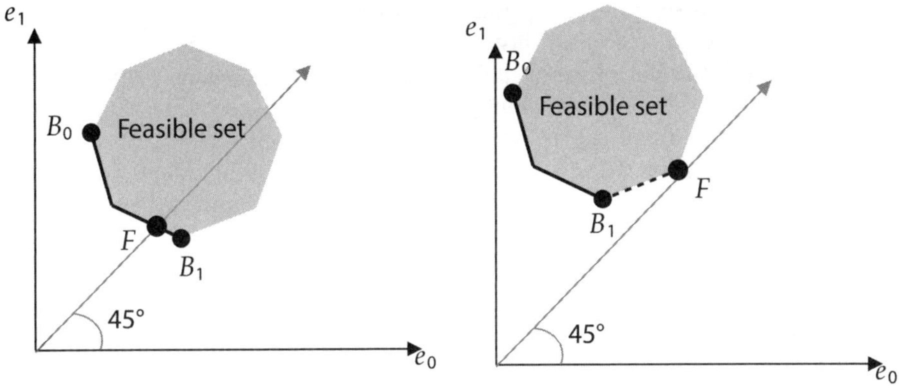

Fig. 5.2 Fairness-accuracy frontier.

feasible outcomes e_1 and e_0, respectively. The final one, F, is the one that is the fairest and minimizes $|e_1 - e_0|$. Note that in both, the accuracy frontier lies on the lower portion of the feasible set between B_1 and B_0. The point that is most fair, F, lies on that frontier in (a) but not in (b). This means that a planner can choose a fair algorithm that does not sacrifice accuracy in (a) but faces a trade-off in (b).

Liang et al. (2025) shows that the difference between the two types of situations depends on the properties of X, the set of observable variables other than group membership that is used to generate predictions. X is group-balanced if an algorithm that is optimal for a group (say, B_1) gives a lower error for $g = 1$ than for $g = 0$. If this condition does not hold, then X is group skewed. In figure 5.2, X is 0 skewed and so has a lower error for group 0 and both B_1 and B_0 than the respective errors at those points for group 1. Group balance arises when X has different implications for each group—for example, a high X implies a high ω for 0 and a lower ω for 1. This could also arise if different dimensions of X are uninformative about ω for each group. Group skewness arises when X is asymmetrically informative. For instance, when medical data is recorded more accurately for high-income patients than low-income patients, making the prediction more dispersed for high-income patients than low-income ones.[2]

This analysis assumes that the planner chooses the algorithm. In some situations, as we have noted earlier, the regulator chooses the inputs that can be used to generate predictions. Liang et al. (2025) show that this makes the problem one of information design where algorithm designers (choosing algorithms for their own goals) use data that is garbled by the regulator (i.e.,

2. Particular special cases can refine this analysis further. For instance, when g is an informative part of the input data, then $B_1 = B_0$ and the fair outcome potentially is Pareto optimal; if $\omega \mid X$ is independent of g, then once you have X you do not have any additional predictive value from g and if there is strong independence in that (X, ω) is independent of g then $B_1 = B_0 = F$.

choosing a coarser partition of the data or leaving out certain variables or introducing an error for, say, privacy reasons). Such garblings can potentially change the feasible set of algorithms and push the agent toward the planner's preferred algorithm. This provides another perspective on whether to, say, ban the use of test scores in admission decisions. Those scores are likely to be decision relevant for both groups. Thus, if group identity, g, is available, excluding test scores will reduce welfare when algorithm designers can garble components of X. By contrast, if g is not available, a fairness-motivated algorithm designer might choose to exclude test scores.

Once again, this framework demonstrates why computer science approaches focusing solely on fairness constraints can be suboptimal. Consider a typical fairness constraint like

$$|e_0 - e_1| \leq \epsilon.$$

This constraint may force the algorithm to operate at point F even when there exist points on the frontier that would improve outcomes for both groups. In contrast, the economic approach allows movement along the frontier to find optimal points based on social welfare weights.

Formally, the optimal policy solves:

$$\max_{f,t_0,t_1} W = \sum_g \phi_g[u(\omega_g, a_g)] \text{subject to } a_g = 1 \text{ if } f(x_g) > t(g), \tag{7}$$

where t_g are group-specific thresholds and ϕ_g are welfare weights.

This formulation allows us to do the following:

1. Choose an algorithm on the efficiency frontier
2. Set thresholds to achieve distributional objectives
3. Explicitly account for social preferences

Using real-world data, Liang et al. (2025) shows that many commonly used fairness constraints force algorithms to operate well inside the frontier, creating unnecessary inefficiency. Their analysis suggests potential Pareto improvements of 10 percent to 30 percent in both accuracy and fairness metrics by moving to frontier-optimal algorithms with appropriate thresholds.

This framework provides a geometric interpretation of the decomposition, $\mathbb{E}[s_i | g = 1] - \mathbb{E}[s_i | g = 0]$ = Base Rate + Measurement + Estimation, we discussed earlier. The shape of the frontier reflects these components, with base rate differences creating fundamental trade-offs while measurement and estimation errors can potentially be eliminated through better algorithm design.

The frontier framework suggests a two-step approach to policy, First, identify the achievable frontier through empirical analysis. Second, choose operating points based on explicit welfare criteria. This approach dominates direct fairness constraints because it maintains maximum predictive accuracy, makes trade-offs explicit, allows for welfare-optimal solutions, and identifies achievable improvements.

The framework thus provides both theoretical justification and practical guidance for favoring economic approaches to algorithmic fairness over computer science constraints. It demonstrates that many apparent accuracy-fairness trade-offs are artificial products of suboptimal regulation rather than fundamental limitations.

5.4 Observable Implications of Alternative Approaches

The theoretical distinctions between computer science and economic approaches to algorithmic fairness lead to several observable implications that can inform real-world policy decisions. These implications span performance metrics, implementation requirements, dynamic effects, and regulatory compatibility.

5.4.1 Measurable Performance Differences

The economic approach demonstrates measurable advantages across several dimensions when implemented in real-world contexts. First, prediction accuracy remains higher across all demographic groups, as algorithms aren't artificially constrained. In empirical studies across domains like lending, hiring, and health care, unconstrained algorithms with group-specific decision thresholds consistently outperform fairness-constrained alternatives in terms of overall accuracy, with improvements ranging from 5 percent to 30 percent depending on the context and constraint type.

Second, resource allocation efficiency significantly improves under the economic approach. For instance, in educational opportunity allocation, unconstrained prediction combined with welfare-weighted thresholds leads to both higher average outcomes and better outcomes for disadvantaged groups compared to constrained alternatives. The economic approach achieves this by directing resources to individuals most likely to benefit, regardless of group membership, while still ensuring equitable distribution through threshold adjustments. Paradoxically, while computer science approaches appear to prioritize fairness, their reduction in prediction accuracy can disproportionately harm disadvantaged groups by misallocating resources that could have benefited them.

5.4.2 Implementation and Transparency Requirements

The economic approach necessitates greater transparency and explicit articulation of social welfare weights and group-specific thresholds. While the computer science approach embeds fairness constraints within the algorithm (often as a "black box"), the economic approach deliberately separates prediction from decision-making, requiring stakeholder engagement in determining how prediction outputs translate into decisions. This separation creates accountability pressures that are often absent in the computer science framework.

Organizations implementing the economic approach must explicitly justify their threshold choices rather than simply claiming their algorithm is "fair by design." This transparency requirement represents both a challenge and an advantage. While it demands more deliberate governance processes, it also creates opportunities for democratic input into fairness determinations and allows for adaptation as societal values evolve. Evidence from institutional implementations suggests that organizations with explicit, transparent decision criteria face less resistance from affected populations compared to those using "black box" fairness-constrained systems, even when outcomes are similar.

5.4.3 Long-Term Dynamic Effects

Perhaps most significant are the long-term implications of each approach. The computer science approach may create perverse incentives—if predictions are artificially constrained, decision-makers might develop workarounds or abandon algorithmic tools altogether. For example, studies of constrained lending algorithms show that loan officers often override algorithmic recommendations more frequently when using fairness-constrained systems, potentially reintroducing human biases the algorithms were meant to eliminate.

The economic approach acknowledges existing disparities while providing a framework for addressing them transparently. Over time, as underlying societal conditions change, the economic approach can adapt through threshold adjustments rather than requiring complete algorithmic redesign. This creates incentives for collecting better data about disadvantaged groups, rather than obscuring group differences through algorithmic constraints. Longitudinal studies of health-care resource allocation systems demonstrate that the economic approach leads to continuous refinement of prediction models for all groups, whereas fairness-constrained systems often stagnate in their predictive quality, particularly for minority populations.

5.4.4 Regulatory and Legal Compatibility

The economic approach aligns better with existing antidiscrimination legal frameworks, which typically focus on disparate treatment rather than disparate impact when there are legitimate business necessities. By making accurate predictions and then applying explicit adjustments for social welfare goals, the economic approach creates a more defensible and adaptable system that can evolve with societal priorities while maintaining optimal prediction accuracy.

Legal analyses of algorithmic fairness cases suggest that systems using the economic approach withstand judicial scrutiny more successfully than those using fairness constraints, particularly in contexts where prediction accuracy directly impacts welfare outcomes. The explicit separation of prediction and decision allows organizations to demonstrate both their commitment to accuracy and their intentional efforts to achieve equitable outcomes. This approach also provides flexibility in responding to regulatory changes without sacrificing the fundamental benefits of algorithmic prediction.

5.5 Conclusion

The economic framework provides both theoretical justification and practical guidance for favoring economic approaches to algorithmic fairness over computer science constraints. It demonstrates that many apparent accuracy-fairness trade-offs are artificial products of suboptimal regulation rather than fundamental limitations.

This perspective aligns with broader economic insights about the importance of getting incentives right rather than trying to control outcomes directly. Just as price controls are generally less effective than targeted subsidies for achieving distributional goals, algorithmic fairness constraints may be less effective than properly structured decision rules and thresholds.

The framework developed here suggests that policies that constrain algorithms may be dominated by policies that focus on the broader institutional context in which algorithms are deployed. Examples of such policies might be requirements for transparency about decision criteria, audits of outcome disparities, and guidelines for appropriate use of group-specific thresholds. These policies could balance the competing goals of accuracy and fairness while avoiding the pitfalls of direct algorithmic regulation.

References

Agrawal, Ajay, Joshua S. Gans, and Avi Goldfarb. 2018. *Prediction Machines: The Simple Economics of Artificial Intelligence*. Harvard Business Review Press.

Barocas, Solon, Moritz Hardt, and Arvind Narayanan. 2023. *Fairness and Machine Learning: Limitations and Opportunities*. MIT Press.

Gans, Joshua S. 2025. *The Microeconomics of Artificial Intelligence*. MIT Press.

Kleinberg, Jon, Sendhil Mullainathan, and Manish Raghavan. 2016. "Inherent Trade-Offs in the Fair Determination of Risk Scores." arXiv preprint arXiv:1609.05807.

Liang, Annie, Jay Lu, Xiaosheng Mu, and Keiji Okumura. 2025. "Algorithm Design: A Fairness-Accuracy Frontier." *Journal of Political Economy*. https://doi.org/10.48550/arXiv.2112.09975.

Rambachan, Ashesh, Jon Kleinberg, Jens Ludwig, and Sendhil Mullainathan. 2020. "An Economic Perspective on Algorithmic Fairness." *AEA Papers and Proceedings* 110: 91–95.

6

Regulating AI
Six Principles and Their Consequences

Jason Furman

Basic research and initial deployments of artificial intelligence have proceeded very rapidly. Workers are rapidly incorporating it into their work (Bick, Blanding, and Deming 2025). So far, however, productivity growth has not increased, and estimates of its impact going forward range from 0.1 percentage point per year to as much as 1 percentage point per year, with the actual number also likely to depend on policymakers' choices (Acemoglu 2024; Filippucci et al. 2024). Applications also have enormous potential in education, health, climate change, and other areas (US Department of Education 2023; World Economic Forum 2024).

The United States is well ahead of Europe in AI development for many reasons, including more flexible and deeper US capital markets and the nature of immigration to the United States (Arnold et al. 2024). An additional factor is that the European Union's more extensive AI rules have slowed progress there (Jin, Wagman, and Jia 2019), in contrast to the more voluntary and disclosure-based approach pursued to date in the United States (White House 2023).

The following regulatory principles would have the consequence of increasing the pace of AI development while also maintaining safety:[1]

Jason Furman is Aetna Professor of the Practice of Economic Policy jointly at the Harvard Kennedy School and the Economics Department at Harvard University, and a nonresident senior fellow at the Peterson Institute for International Economics.

An earlier version of this essay was published in *The Wall Street Journal*. For acknowledgments, sources of research support, and disclosure of the author's material financial relationships, if any, please see https://www.nber.org/books-and-chapters/political-economy-artificial-intelligence/regulating-ai-six-principles-and-their-consequences.

1. See Coglianese (2023) for a broad overview of AI regulation with some overlap but also differences.

1. Balance benefits and risks. The European approach to regulation has been based on the "precautionary principle" that supports delaying AI until it is proved absolutely safe (Guha et al. 2023). An alternative regulatory approach is cost-benefit analysis, which would require regulators to think not only about the risks of AI but also about the risks from slower AI development, such as more cancer deaths because of delayed drug discovery, worse educational outcomes because students lack personalized digital tutors, more car accidents because of delays in self-driving cars, and worsening climate change because of a slowdown in discovering better materials for grid-level battery storage. AI regulation would generate more net benefits, almost by definition, under a benefit-cost framework than the precautionary principle.

2. Compare AI with humans, not to the Almighty. Autonomous cars crash—but how do they compare with human drivers? AI may show biases, but how do these stack up against human prejudices (Kleinberg et al. 2017)? In fact, maximizing social welfare should not require AI to perform at parity with humans, given the dynamic consideration that many AI technologies, like self-driving cars, offer significant convenience and have greater potential for improvement over time than humans do. Recent research suggests that autonomous driving systems have a significantly lower crash rate than human-driven vehicles (Kusano et al., 2024). AI is learning much faster than humans are, and the future gains this learning will generate belong on the benefit side of the ledger.

3. Address how existing regulations are hindering progress. The most obvious are permitting and other obstacles to the expansion of data centers and the power sources they will need; these immediate hurdles delay critical expansions needed to support the growing computational demands of AI (McKinsey and Company 2024). Data centers, which are the backbone of AI infrastructure, face numerous regulatory challenges, often stemming from complex zoning laws, stringent environmental regulations, and local resistance to large-scale infrastructure projects. A potentially more consequential issue over time is the dozens of state laws regulating AI that have already been passed and the hundreds more that have been proposed, creating an unpredictable and fragmented regulatory environment for AI developers (National Conference of State Legislatures 2024). Federal preemption of state rules would have the consequence of ensuring the US remains a digital single market—unlike the fractured EU.

4. Where new regulation is warranted, it would be overseen by existing domain-specific regulators rather than a new superregulator. We don't have a superregulator for all products that use linear regression or electricity; instead, regulators specialize in areas where these are used, such as auto safety, stock trading, and medical devices. Existing regulators, such as the US Food and Drug Administration (FDA) and the Federal Aviation Administration (FAA), can adapt their processes to accommodate AI technologies and should focus on outputs and consequences in their domains, not on inputs and methods—an approach that would minimize regulatory duplication and ensure specialized oversight where it is needed. This may require more AI expertise and flexibility within agencies. For instance, the FDA (2024) has come up with procedures to approve AI-based devices that might fall foul of its standard rules, given the lack of a fixed algorithm with such devices.

5. Avoid setting up regulations that become a moat protecting incumbents. History shows that well-intentioned rules can entrench existing powers, from medieval guilds to hospital certificate-of-need laws (Mitchell 2021). It is possible that regulations in the AI space could follow the same pattern. Centralized licensing bodies could easily become gatekeepers, stifling competition. A superregulator could be captured by big companies. When tech giants enthusiastically promote regulation, it may be a red flag. These types of policies may be inconsistent with a regulatory framework that aims to nurture a competitive AI landscape instead of solidifying the dominance of a few early movers.

6. Not every problem caused by AI can be solved by regulating AI. I hope AI will raise wages without hurting employment, with especially large increases for workers with lower-paying skills, as some expect (Autor 2023). Studies provide some evidence for this, for example, finding that less able writers benefit most from AI-based writing suggestions (Dhillon et al. 2024). But bleak scenarios of swift technological change displacing workers or causing inequality are possible (Acemoglu 2019). It is virtually impossible for regulators to figure out in advance whether each technological advance is job replacing or inequality increasing. Moreover, attempting to shift to a system of permissioned innovation would slow progress and the benefits that AI could bring. Instead, a more effective approach to address any side effects for labor markets would be in more conventional economic policies like training programs that connect people to jobs, wage subsidies, and a more progressive tax and transfer system to ensure that AI's benefits are shared broadly.

To the degree that policymakers want to maximize the net benefits of AI, they should proceed cautiously. Well-intentioned efforts could inadvertently slow progress while falling short of their goals. These six principles would result in an outcome that would help ensure AI lives up to its potential while addressing legitimate concerns around safety and other issues.

References

Acemoglu, D., and P. Restrepo. 2019. "Automation and New Tasks: How Technology Displaces and Reinstates Labor." *Journal of Economic Perspectives* 33 (2): 3–30. https://pubs.aeaweb.org/doi/pdfplus/10.1257/jep.33.2.3.

Acemoglu, D. 2024. "The Simple Macroeconomics of AI." Paper prepared for *Economic Policy*, https://economics.mit.edu/sites/default/files/2024-04/The%20Simple%20Macroeconomics%20of%20AI.pdf.

Arnold, M., S. Fleming, and C. Jones. 2024. "Can Europe's Economy Ever Hope to Rival the US Again?" *Financial Times*, May 13. https://www.ft.com/content/93f88255-787b-4c06-849c- f7722c83e8b6.

Autor, D. 2023. "How AI Could Help Rebuild the Middle Class." *Noema Magazine*, April 19. https://www.noemamag.com/how-ai-could-help-rebuild-the-middle-class/

Bick, Alexander, Adam Blanding, and David Deming. 2025. "The Rapid Adoption of Generative AI." NBER Working Paper 32966.

Coglianese, C. 2023. "Regulating Machine Learning: The Challenge of Heterogeneity." Public Law and Legal Theory Research Paper No. 23–06. University of Pennsylvania Carey Law School. https://papers.ssrn.com/sol3/papers.cfm?abstract_id=4368604.

Dhillon, P. S., S. Molaei, J. Li, M. Golub, S. Zheng, and L. P. Robert. 2024. "Shaping Human-AI Collaboration: Varied Scaffolding Levels in Co-writing with Language Models." In Proceedings of the CHI Conference on Human Factors in Computing Systems, 1–18. https://arxiv.org/abs/2402.11723.

Filippucci, F., P. Gal, C. Jona-Lasinio, A. Leandro, and G. Nicoletti. 2024. "The Impact of Artificial Intelligence on Productivity, Distribution and Growth: Key Mechanisms, Initial Evidence and Policy Challenges." Organisation for Economic Co-operation and Development. https://www.oecd.org/content/dam/oecd/en/publications/reports/2024/04/the-impact-of-artificial-intelligence-on-productivity-distribution-and-growth_d54e2842/8d900037-en.pdf

Guha, N., C. M. Lawrence, L. A. Gailmard, K. T. Rodolfa, F. Surani, R. Bommasani, I. D. Raji, M.-T. Cuéllar, C. Honigsberg, P. Liang, and D. E. Ho. 2023. *The AI Regulatory Alignment Problem*. Stanford Institute for Human-Centered Artificial Intelligence. https://hai.stanford.edu/sites/default/files/2023-11/AI-Regulatory-Alignment.pdf.

Jin, G., L. Wagman, and J. Jia. 2019. "The Short-Run Effects of GDPR on Technology Venture Investment. VoxEU. https://papers.ssrn.com/sol3/papers.cfm?abstract_id=3278912.

Kleinberg, J., H. Lakkaraju, J. Leskovec, J. Ludwig, and S. Mullainathan. 2018. "Human Decisions and Machine Predictions." *The Quarterly Journal of Economics* 133 (1): 237–93. https://sendhil.org/wp-content/uploads/2019/08/Publication-5.pdf.

Kusano, K. D., J. M. Scanlon, Y. H. Chen, T. L. McMurry, R. Chen, T. Gode, and T. Victor. 2024. "Comparison of Waymo Rider-Only Crash Data to Human Benchmarks at 7.1 Million Miles." *Traffic Injury Prevention*: 1–12. https://arxiv.org/pdf/2312.12675.

McKinsey and Company. 2024. *AI Power: Expanding Data Center Capacity to Meet Growing Demand*. October 29. https://www.mckinsey.com/industries/technology-media.-.and-.telecommunications./our.-insights./ai.-power.-expanding.-data.-center.-capacity.-to.-meet.-growing.-demand#/.

Mitchell, M. D. 2021. *Certificate-of-Need Laws: How They Affect Healthcare Access, Quality, and Cost*. Mercatus Center at George Mason University. https://www.mercatus.org/economic-insights/features/certificate-need-laws-how-they-affect-healthcare-access-quality-and-cost.

National Conference of State Legislatures. 2024. Artificial Intelligence 2024 Legislation. September 9. https://www.ncsl.org/technology-and-communication/artificial-intelligence-2024-legislation

White House. 2023. "Voluntary AI Commitments." https://www.whitehouse.gov/wp-content/uploads/2023/09/Voluntary-AI-Commitments-September-2023.pdf.

US Department of Education. 2023. *Artificial Intelligence and the Future of Teaching and Learning: Insights and Recommendations*. May. https://www.ed.gov/sites/ed/files/documents/ai-report/ai-report.pdf.

US Food and Drug Administration. 2024. "Marketing Submission Recommendations for a Predetermined Change Control Plan for Artificial Intelligence." *Machine Learning (AI/ML) Enabled Device Software Functions*. www.fda.gov/media/166704/download.

World Economic Forum. 2024. *How AI Can Combat Climate Change*. https://www.weforum.org/stories/2024/02/ai-combat-climate-change/.

II
AI and Military Power

7

Four Battlegrounds for Artificial Intelligence

Paul Scharre

I want to start by just grounding the discussion in where we are today with artificial intelligence and robotics in warfare. I was in Ukraine earlier this year and had the opportunity to meet with drone developers, drone pilots, and leadership from the Ukrainian government and armed forces.

Drones are heavily used in the Ukraine war by both sides, but most of the drones are remotely piloted (Pettyjohn 2024). This, of course, makes them completely dependent on the communications link to their human operators. Without that communications link, the drone is useless. So both sides have turned to electronic warfare to jam the communications link. There is an enormous amount of jamming on both sides, leading to very high loss rates among drones (*The Economist* 2024). And both sides are desperate to find ways to make the drones more effective in this highly contested electromagnetic environment.

Autonomy is one possible solution. Ukrainian armed forces are working on what they call the "autonomous last-mile solution," or autonomous terminal guidance to guide the drone into its target once the human operator has chosen the target (Hunder 2024).

I got a chance to see this in action. We went to the range, and I saw a Ukrainian drone developer demonstrate this autonomous last-mile solution. They locked onto a target. The drone pilot took his hands off the controls. And the automation did the rest. The automation took over, and the drone zoomed right into the target all on its own and hit it.

What I saw demonstrated was very simple technology. It didn't use any

Paul Scharre is executive vice president at the Center for a New American Security (CNAS).
For acknowledgments, sources of research support, and disclosure of the author's material financial relationships, if any, please see https://www.nber.org/books-and-chapters/political-economy-artificial-intelligence/four-battlegrounds-artificial-intelligence.

sophisticated machine learning. It essentially locked onto some pixels and kept the drone centered on them as it flew toward the target. This wasn't done by an advanced defense company. It was essentially a guy in his garage. That's how widely available this technology is.

The longer that the war in Ukraine drags on, the more likely we are to see innovation on both sides. War is an accelerant of military innovation.

We could be months away from autonomous weapons being used in Ukraine, where the drones, using AI, are carrying out attacks entirely on their own without any human intervention once they're launched. It's possible that it's already happened and we just don't know it yet. In fact, one Ukrainian company has claimed that it has already built and deployed a fully autonomous weapon that has been used in combat (Hambling 2023a, 2023b), although this claim has not been independently verified.

Things are moving fast. And you can see that, in fact, what's happening on the battlefield is still several years behind the state of the art in AI. Machine-learning image classifiers are over 10 years old now (Pinecone n.d.). This is old technology. This doesn't even account for what's happening today in AI.

What I wanted to talk with you about today is where we are headed. Things are moving incredibly fast in the field of AI. We're seeing profound changes underway. And I don't know that anyone can say for certain what kind of progress we'll see in the next 12 months, much less the next decade. Like so many of us, I imagine you are thinking deeply about the changes we're seeing in our world, and you're trying to figure out how to best anticipate the challenges ahead. With that in mind, I want to zoom out and talk about some bigger picture shifts in how artificial intelligence is changing global power.

7.1 The Competition for Global AI Leadership

China's leader Xi Jinping has said, "Science and technology has become the main battleground of global power rivalry." (Feng 2021; Xinhua 2021) Are democratic nations ready for that competition?

Two hundred years ago, we saw during the industrial revolution that nations rose and fell on the global stage on the basis of how rapidly they industrialized (Kennedy 1987, p. 197). At the start of the Industrial Revolution, Russia led Europe in economic power by virtue of its vast size (Kennedy 1987, p. 171). Yet Great Britain and Germany industrialized faster, while Russia fell behind. By the turn of the 20th century, Great Britain and Germany had eclipsed Russia in economic power.

Artificial intelligence has a similar potential to change the global balance of power today. We want to believe that we're Great Britain or Germany. But deep down, our fear is that we might be Russia. And China might be on track to lead the world in AI.

I'm going to tell you a story that, on the surface, sounds like we're Russia. But as you'll see, it's not as bad as it looks. It's about facial recognition and about how China is ahead of the United States and Europe in facial recognition deployment.

China has half the world's one billion surveillance cameras (Lin and Purnell 2019). And they increasingly use AI tools like facial recognition and gait recognition to identify and track individuals (US Department of State 2020). The Chinese Communist Party is building a massive domestic surveillance system. These investments not only fund Chinese AI companies; more importantly, they give Chinese companies data to train their algorithms. And by using their facial recognition systems in the real world, Chinese companies get to improve their algorithms.

Meanwhile, in the United States, it seems like we're totally behind. Facial recognition deployment has stalled out in the United States. There has been a grassroots movement of cities and states banning facial recognition by law enforcement (Fung 2020).

IBM (Denham 2020), Amazon (Amazon 2020), and Microsoft (Greene 2020) have all said they won't sell their facial recognition software to law enforcement.

On the surface, it seems like maybe we're Russia, and China is racing ahead while we're left behind. On the surface, it seems like China is poised to win the AI revolution. But what we may not realize is that the winner of the AI revolution won't be who has the best technology but who finds the best ways of using it. That means using it in every aspect of society—for economic productivity, for social welfare, and for military applications. Yes, Chinese companies will have more data on Chinese faces, but that won't help them train AI fighter pilots. What *is* going to train AI fighter pilots is not facial recognition; it's actually military and civilian scientists working together to find the best ways of using AI for military advantage.

We worry that having an open society can slow us down. China has deployed half a billion cameras while we're still debating the issue (Lin and Purnell 2019). The Chinese Communist Party can simply dictate how Chinese society will adopt a new technology. Meanwhile, in America, there's a messy give-and-take among state, local, and federal authorities, the private sector, civil society, and ordinary citizens (Fung 2020). But that is actually a strength. Because what matters most is finding the best ways of using technology.

The United States and Europe have fundamental strengths in the AI competition that China cannot match—our open societies are a magnet for global talent, and our network of alliances dominates the AI hardware ecosystem. But we have to harness those strengths.

My book, *Four Battlegrounds: Power in the Age of Artificial Intelligence*, outlines what it will take for the United States to win the AI revolution and remain a global leader in artificial intelligence (Scharre 2023). It will require being strategic. We don't need to do everything. We just need to do a few key things right to stay ahead. What I do in the book, and what I want to do with you today, is talk about what actually matters in this competition and outline how the United States and Europe can win.

7.2 The New Metrics of Power in an Age of AI

If we really want to understand how to dominate in AI power, we first need to understand how artificial intelligence is changing global power. So let's go back to the Industrial Revolution.

The Industrial Revolution saw the key metrics of power change. Coal and steel became key inputs of national power (Kennedy 1987, 199–202, 258, 271; Mearsheimer 2014, 64–66). Oil became a geostrategic resource that nations were willing to fight wars over. So what is "the new oil" today?

I want to argue that data, computing hardware, human talent, and institutions are the four key battlegrounds of geopolitical competition in artificial intelligence. The first two, data and computing hardware, are technical inputs into AI. The AI revolution is being driven by dramatic progress in machine learning, in which algorithms are trained on data. Data, algorithms, and computing hardware are the three technical resources needed for machine learning. It's difficult to control the spread of algorithms. The AI research community is incredibly open, with new breakthroughs published online. So any competitive advantage is likely to come from data or computing hardware. The second two battlegrounds of AI competition comprise the social software that enables AI: human talent and institutions—the organizations that shape AI adoption. Whichever companies—and countries—lead in these four areas will lead an AI-driven future.

7.3 Data

Let's talk about data. Data is an essential resource for machine learning. Cutting-edge machine learning models use massive amounts of data. Image recognition models use millions of labeled images (Krizhevsky et al. 2012). Large language models like ChatGPT are trained on trillions of words (Villalobos et al. 2024).

So, does China have a data advantage? In theory, China's alleged authoritarian advantage in data comes from its larger population and massive government surveillance (Zuboff 2019). Both of these things are true, but they don't necessarily add up to a data advantage.

For one, a country's population matters far less than the user base of tech companies. US tech companies have global reach. Facebook and YouTube have over 2 billion users each (Facebook 2020; YouTube n.d.). WeChat, meanwhile, has only 1.2 billion users (Tencent 2020). In fact, except for TikTok, Chinese social media platforms have struggled to succeed outside of China. And while the Chinese Communist Party has built a massive surveillance system for monitoring its citizens, that does not always translate into greater access to data for Chinese companies.

In some areas, like facial recognition, Chinese companies are likely to have an edge over competitors, but that doesn't necessarily translate into an advantage in AI overall. In other areas, like large language models, the Chinese government is regulating AI companies much more heavily than the US government (Creemers and Webster 2021; Das 2021; Dou 2021; He 2021; Thomas et al. 2021). The Chinese Communist Party heavily censors the internet in China and wants to clamp down on what large language models might say online.

And while there are no restrictions in China on government spying, that isn't the case for companies. In fact, the Chinese government has been cracking down on what private companies can do (Creemers and Webster 2021; Das 2021; Dou 2021; He 2021; Thomas et al. 2021). The Chinese Communist Party doesn't want anyone else to have the same spying powers that it has.

Both the US and China have access to ample amounts of data. What will matter more is how they use it. The real data advantage will be those who are successful in building a pipeline for collecting and refining data so that it's ready to be used for machine learning.

The self-driving car company Waymo is an instructive example. It has over 10 million driverless miles (Wilt 2024). But it's also done 20 billion miles in simulations to rack up the data needed to train its models (Waymo 2020). For robotic systems, using synthetic data to augment real-world data can help train more robust systems. Organizations that will have a data advantage are those that can successfully harness data for machine learning.

7.4 Computing Hardware

Machine-learning models are trained on data using hardware. So let's talk about the hardware dimension of this competition—the second battleground of AI competition. If data is overrated, hardware is often underrated as an element of strategic competition.

From the 1950s on, improvements in computing hardware have been governed by Moore's law, a doubling in computing performance about every 24 months (Moore 1998). Now you may have heard that Moore's law is dead, but in fact, what's happening now is way more interesting.

Since 2010, we've seen an explosion in computing hardware for machine learning (Besiroglu et al. 2022). The amount of computing hardware used to train the most advanced AI models is doubling every 6 months (Sevilla and Roldán 2024), much faster than the 24-month doubling rate under Moore's law. And that's a product of two things. First of all, chips continue getting better. The price performance, or performance per dollar, for machine learning GPUs is still doubling every 24 months (Dorner 2021). Plus, tech companies are pouring massive amounts of money into these chips. They're buying more chips and networking them together for massive training runs using tens of thousands of chips. Independent estimates put the cost of the final training run for GPT-4 at around $50 million or so,[1] and the cost for training the most advanced models is doubling around every 10 months (Cottier 2023). That's on top of the fact that the chips themselves are doubling in performance per dollar every 24 months. So you have an exponential on top of an exponential, and you get massive growth in computing hardware.

On top of those trends in chips and spending, you actually get a third exponential, which is algorithmic improvements. Algorithms are improving in their hardware efficiency. That is, algorithms are getting better, allowing you to squeeze more capability out of the same amount of computing power. That's a bit trickier to measure, but research suggests that algorithmic efficiency is doubling about every eight to nine months for large language models (Scharre 2024). So every eight or nine months, you can get twice as much capability with the same amount of computing power.

These three stacked exponentials in chip performance, spending, and algorithmic improvements are what's driving an unbelievable growth rate in computing power for the most advanced AI systems. If current trends continue, by 2030, we will see AI models trained on 1 million times more effective computing power than the current state of the art (Scharre 2024).

I don't know what such systems will be capable of doing—no one does. But this increased computing power will open up new opportunities. We are heading into an era of compute-intensive machine learning in which the largest and most capable models use massive amounts of compute. This means that computing hardware is increasingly a strategic resource that will determine who has access to the most advanced AI capabilities.

We're used to thinking of semiconductors as a foundational technology that empowers all of the digital devices we have, from our phones to factories. But the trends in compute-intensive machine learning suggest something different. Semiconductors are poised to be a strategic global asset, like access to enriched uranium. That divides the world into haves and have-nots. What makes computing hardware so valuable is that it is a physical thing that we can restrict others from using. And in fact, the United States and its allies are already doing so.

Five countries control access to the most advanced chips: Taiwan and South Korea, where the most advanced chips are made (Toews 2023). And the Netherlands, Japan, and the United States, which make the equipment used to manufacture the most advanced chips (Khan and Flynn 2020). The Netherlands and Japan have joined US export controls on advanced AI chipmaking equipment to China (Allen et al. 2023). And the US government

1. Cost estimates for GPT-4 are from https://colab.research.google.com/drive/1O99z9b1I5O66bT78r9ScslE_nOj5irN9#scrollTo=CytB-eruRSGB.

has banned the shipment of advanced chips to China (Shivakumar et al. 2024).

In the near term, China has no alternative way of getting these chips. Without access to the equipment needed to manufacture chips, China will have a steep hill to climb to build a fully indigenous supply chain. Our alliances are a core strength that China cannot compete with if we work together.

7.5 Talent

People are needed to turn the raw inputs of data and computing hardware into useful AI tools. So let's talk about the third battleground, talent.

There is fierce competition for global talent. Freshly minted graduates from AI PhD programs are commanding professional-sports-level salaries from top AI labs (Kahn 2018; Metz 2017). Globally, there is fierce competition among countries as well.

China produces more of the top AI scientists in the world than any other country.[2] But here's the thing—those top Chinese scientists don't stay in China. China's top undergraduates leave China and come to the United States and Europe for graduate school (Mozur and Metz 2020). And they stay outside China (Zwetsloot 2019). Ninety percent of Chinese undergraduates who do their PhD in AI in the United States stay in the US after graduation.

The United States and Europe have a massive advantage in human talent that China cannot match. Yes, there are problems of intellectual property theft and academic espionage. China has an estimated over 200 talent recruitment plans to bring overseas scientific knowledge back to China (US Senate, n.d.). However, overall, the United States and Europe benefit disproportionately from connections to Chinese researchers and the net flow of talent and expertise out of China. If the United States wishes to continue to benefit from the inflow of Chinese talent, the US government will need to work with universities to de-risk these relationships and improve research security. In the competition with China, continued engagement with appropriate guardrails in place is likely to deliver greater net benefits for the United States than complete decoupling.

The United States, Europe, and other democratic allies also need to find better ways to harness the talent we have—to make it easier for our scientists to collaborate with one another. Creating something like a Schengen visa for AI scientists among democratic nations, to make it easier for scientists to travel abroad and do visiting fellowships, could be a smart way to har-

2. "The Global AI Talent Tracker," Macro Polo, https://macropolo.org/digital-projects/the-global-ai-talent-tracker/.

ness our collective strengths. Our open societies and our alliances are core strengths in the global competition for AI talent.

7.6 Institutions

So you've got the data, the computing hardware, the talent—if you want to turn these raw inputs into useful AI applications, you need institutions that can do this. And that's the fourth battleground. The human organizations that are going to develop AI innovations. I want to close with a story that shows how all of this can come together and bring things back to where we started: AI-enabled drone warfare.

Back in 2019, DARPA—the Pentagon's "Department of Mad Scientists"—started the Air Combat Evolution, or ACE, program to train an AI fighter pilot (DARPA 2019). One of its first efforts was an AlphaDogfight challenge, taking a page from AlphaGo. Various companies submitted their AI agents to compete in a simulated aerial combat, and the winning competitor got to go head-to-head against a human pilot. Heron Systems—a company no one had ever heard of—beat defense giant Lockheed Martin in the finals (Scharre 2023, 1). Then it went against an experienced US Air Force fighter pilot. And the AI absolutely crushed the human, 15–0. The human pilot couldn't get a single shot off (Scharre 2023, 1).

Even more amazing, the AI pilot won using a tactic that is essentially impossible for humans, taking head-to-head gunshots when the aircraft are racing at each other at hundreds of miles an hour and there is a split second to get a shot off (Price 2020). This is basically impossible for humans to make a shot like this—in fact, it's banned in training because it's dangerous for humans to even try this when the aircraft are racing toward each other, because of the risk of a collision. But this wasn't a problem for the AI. Even more wild, the AI learned this tactic entirely on its own. It wasn't programmed in.

How did Heron Systems do this? It built a competitive league of 100 AI agents flying against each other in simulations. So it built the data needed. The winning agent had over 30 years of flight time in simulators (Scharre 2023, 221). That gave the company the data.

The company built the computing infrastructure it needed to run these simulations nonstop. In fact, when I visited Heron Systems' offices, I could hear the roar of the computer servers churning away simulations in the server closet.

The company harnessed its talent. One of the company policies was Fun Fridays, in which programmers could work on their own pet projects one day a week. One of their programmers was excited by reinforcement learning, a technique that was showing breakthroughs in AI research, and built a "Doom bot" to play the computer game Doom (Scharre 2023, 221).

And when the company went to pitch DARPA on competing in Alpha-

Dogfight, it was actually the Doom bot playing in the background that piqued the DARPA program manager's interest (Scharre 2023, 221). Because here was an example of reinforcement learning.

None of this would have been possible without an organization like DARPA sponsoring the AlphaDogfight challenge, being willing to take on a hard problem, and creating the space for new start-ups to compete and win.

After winning, Heron Systems was bought by ShieldAI, one of a slew of new defense-oriented AI start-ups (Barnett 2021). And in late 2022, DARPA conducted real-world flights with AI agents on an F-16 fighter jet, moving from simulator to the real world (Marrow 2024).

This isn't just the story of one company. The story of the AI fighter pilot tells us what success looks like and how the United States and its allies will be able to lead in AI by harnessing data, computing hardware, and talent, and by creating the institutions needed to find the best ways of using AI to preserve national advantage. The United States, Europe, and other democratic countries have tremendous strengths in this competition. If we harness them, democratic nations can lead an AI-driven future.

Thank you very much.

References

Allen, Gregory C., Emily Benson, and Margot Putnam. 2023. *Japan and the Netherlands Announce Plans for New Export Controls on Semiconductor Equipment*. Center for Strategic and International Studies, April 10. https://www.csis.org/analysis/japan-and-netherlands-announce-plans-new-export-controls-semiconductor-equipment.

Amazon. 2020. "We Are Implementing a One-Year Moratorium on Police Use of Rekognition." June 10. https://blog.aboutamazon.com/policy/we-are-implementing-a-one-year-moratorium-on police-use-of-rekognition.

Barnett, Jackson. 2021. "Shield AI Buys Company Whose AI Beat a Fighter Pilot in a Dogfight." FedScoop, July 22. https://fedscoop.com/shield-ai-buys-company-whose-ai-beat-a-fighter-pilot-in-dogfight/.

Besiroglu, Tamay, Lennart Heim, and Jaime Sevilla. 2022. "Projecting Compute Trends in Machine Learning." Epoch AI, March 7. https://epochai.org/blog/projecting-compute-trends.

Cottier, Ben. 2023. "Trends in the Dollar Training Cost of Machine Learning Systems." Epoch AI, January 31. https://epochai.org/blog/trends-in-the-dollar-trainingcost-of-machine-learning-systems.

Creemers, Rogier, and Graham Webster. 2021. "Translation: Personal Information Protection Law of the People's Republic of China—Effective Nov. 1, 2021." *DigiChina*, August 20. https://digichina.stanford.edu/work/translation-personal-information-protection-law-of-the-peoples-republic-of-china-effective-nov-1-2021/.

DARPA. 2019. "Training AI to Win a Dogfight." May 8. https://www.darpa.mil/news-events/2019-05-08.

Das, Anjali C. 2021. "China's New Personal Information Protection Law." *National*

Law Review, December 2. https://www.natlawreview.com/article/china-s-new-personal-information-protection-law.
Denham, Hannah. 2020. "IBM's Decision to Abandon Facial Recognition Technology Fueled by Years of Debate." *Washington Post*, June 11. https://www.washingtonpost.com/technology/2020/06/11/ibm-facial-recognition/.
Dorner, Florian E. 2021. "Measuring Progress in Deep Reinforcement Learning Sample Efficiency." arXiv.org, February 9. https://arxiv.org/abs/2102.04881.
Dou, Eva. 2021. "China Built the World's Largest Facial Recognition System. Now, It's Getting Camera-Shy." *Washington Post*, July 30. https://www.washingtonpost.com/world/facial-recognition-china-tech-data/2021/07/30/404c2e96-f049-11eb-81b2-9b7061a582d8_story.html.
The Economist. 2024. "Many Ukrainian Drones Have Been Disabled by Russian Jamming." May 29. https://www.economist.com/science-and-technology/2024/05/29/many-ukrainian-drones-have-been-disabled-by-russian-jamming.
Facebook. 2020. "Facebook Reports Third Quarter 2020 Results." News release, October 29. https://investor.fb.com/investor-news/press-release-details/2020/Facebook-Reports-Third-Quarter-2020-Results/default.aspx.
Feng, Coco. 2021. "Chinese President Xi Jinping Seeks to Rally Country's Scientists for 'Unprecedented' Contest." *South China Morning Post*, May 29. https://www.scmp.com/news/china/politics/article/3135328/chinese-president-xi-jinping-seeks-rally-countrys-scientists.
Fung, Brian. 2020. "Tech Companies Push for Nationwide Facial Recognition Law: Now Comes the Hard Part." *Philadelphia Tribune*, June 15. https://www.phillytrib.com/news/business/tech-companies-push-for-nationwide-facial-recognition-law-now-comes-the-hard-part/article_fe78e04e-e8be-5aab-9402-00203a44510f.html.
Greene, Jay. 2020. "Microsoft Won't Sell Police Its Facial-Recognition Technology, Following Similar Moves by Amazon and IBM." *Washington Post*, June 11. https://www.washingtonpost.com/technology/2020/06/11/microsoft-facial-recognition/.
Hambling, David. 2023a. "Ukrainian AI Attack Drones May Be Killing Without Human Oversight." *New Scientist*, October 13. https://www.newscientist.com/article/2397389-ukrainian-ai-attack-drones-may-be-killing-without-human-oversight/.
Hambling, David. 2023b. "Ukraine's AI Drones Seek and Attack Russian Forces Without Human Oversight." *Forbes*, October 17. https://www.forbes.com/sites/davidhambling/2023/10/17/ukraines-ai-drones-seek-and-attack-russian-forces-without-human-oversight/.
He, Laura. 2021. "China Is Raising the Alarm over Corporate Surveillance: But It's Got a Massive Network of Its Own." *CNN Business*, March 19. https://edition.cnn.com/2021/03/19/tech/china-consumer-rights-surveillance-intl-hnk/index.html.
Hunder, Max. 2024. "Ukraine Rushes to Create AI-Enabled War Drones." Reuters, July 18. https://www.reuters.com/technology/artificial-intelligence/ukraine-rushes-create-ai-enabled-war-drones-2024-07-18/.
Kahn, Jeremy. 2018. "Sky-High Salaries Are the Weapons in the AI Talent War." *Bloomberg Businessweek*, February 13. https://www.bloomberg.com/news/articles/2018-02-13/in-the-war-for-ai-talent-sky-high-salaries-are-the-weapons.
Kennedy, Paul. 1987. *The Rise and Fall of the Great Powers*. Random House.
Khan, Saif M., and Carrick Flynn. 2020. *Maintaining China's Dependence on Democracies for Advanced Computer Chips*. Brookings Institution, April. https://www.brookings.edu/wp-content/uploads/2020/04/FP_20200427_computer_chips_khan_flynn.pdf.
Krizhevsky, Alex, Ilya Sutskever, Geoffrey E. Hinton. 2012. "ImageNet Classifica-

tion with Deep Convolutional Neural Networks." In *Advances in Neural Information Processing Systems 25 (NIPS 25)*, edited by F. Pereira, C. J. Burges, L. Bottou, and K. Q. Weinberger. https://proceedings.neurips.cc/paper_files/paper/2012/file/c399862d3b9d6b76c8436e924a68c45b-Paper.pdf.

Lin, Liza, and Newley Purnell. 2019. "A World with a Billion Cameras Watching You Is Just Around the Corner." *Wall Street Journal*, December 6. https://www.wsj.com/articles/a-billion-surveillance-cameras-forecast-to-be-watching-within-two-years-11575565402.

Marrow, Michael. 2024. "In a 'World First,' DARPA Project Demonstrates AI Dogfighting in Real Jet." *Breaking Defense*, April 19. https://breakingdefense.com/2024/04/in-a-world-first-darpa-project-demonstrates-ai-dogfighting-in-real-jet/.

Mearsheimer, John J. 2014. *The Tragedy of Great Power Politics*. W. W. Norton and Co.

Metz, Cade. 2017. "Tech Giants Are Paying Huge Salaries for Scarce A.I. Talent." *New York Times*, October 22. https://www.nytimes.com/2017/10/22/technology/artificial-intelligence-experts-salaries.html.

Moore, Gordon E. 1998. "Cramming More Components onto Integrated Circuits." *Proceedings of the IEEE* 86 (1): 82–85. https://www.cs.utexas.edu/~fussell/courses/cs352h/papers/moore.pdf.

Mozur, Paul, and Cade Metz. 2020. "A US Secret Weapon in A.I.: Chinese Talent." *New York Times*, June 9. https://www.nytimes.com/2020/06/09/technology/china-ai-research-education.html.

Pettyjohn, Stacie L. 2024. "Drones Are Transforming the Battlefield in Ukraine but in an Evolutionary Fashion." *War on the Rocks*, March 5. https://warontherocks.com/2024/03/drones-are-transforming-the-battlefield-in-ukraine-but-in-an-evolutionary-fashion/.

Pinecone. N.d. "AlexNet and ImageNet: The Birth of Deep Learning." https://www.pinecone.io/learn/series/image-search/imagenet/.

Price, Colin "Farva." 2020. "Navy F/A-18 Squadron Commander's Take on AI Repeatedly Beating Real Pilot In Dogfight." *The Drive*, August 24. https://www.thedrive.com/the-war-zone/35947/navy-f-a-18-squadron-commanders-take-on-ai-repeatedly-beating-real-pilot-in-dogfight.

Scharre, Paul. 2023. *Four Battlegrounds: Power in the Age of Artificial Intelligence*. W. W. Norton and Co.

Scharre, Paul. 2024. *Future-Proofing Frontier AI Regulation: Projecting Future Compute for Frontier AI Models*. Center for a New American Security, March. https://s3.us-east-1.amazonaws.com/files.cnas.org/documents/CNAS-Report AI-Trends FinalC.pdf.

Sevilla, Jaime, and Edu Roldán. 2024. "Training Compute of Frontier AI Models Grows by 4–5x per Year." Epoch AI, May 28. https://epochai.org/blog/training-compute-of-frontier-ai-models-grows-by-4-5x-per-year.

Shivakumar, Sujai, Charles Wessner, and Thomas Howell. 2024. *Balancing the Ledger: Export Controls on U.S. Chip Technology to China*. Center for Strategic and International Studies, February 21. https://www.csis.org/analysis/balancing-ledger-export-controls-us-chip-technology-china.

Tencent. 2020. "Tencent Announces 2020 Third Quarter Results." News release, November 12. Hong Kong. https://static.www.tencent.com/uploads/2020/11/12/4c2090d5f6f00fd90ddc9bbd9a1415d1.pdf.

Thomas, Liisa M., Julia K. Kadish, and Kari M. Rollins. 2021. "Update on the State of Privacy Law in China." *National Law Review*, September 20. https://www.natlawreview.com/article/update-state-privacy-law-china.

Toews, Rob. 2023. "The Geopolitics of AI Chips will Define the Future of AI."

Forbes, May 7. https://www.forbes.com/sites/robtoews/2023/05/07/the-geopolitics-of-ai-chips-will-define-the-future-of-ai/.

US Department of State. 2020. *Risks and Considerations for Businesses with Supply Chain Exposure to Entities Engaged in Forced Labor and Other Human Rights Abuses in Xinjiang*. July 1. https://www.state.gov/wp-content/uploads/2020/07/Xinjiang-Supply-Chain-Business-Advisory_FINAL_For-508-8.pdf.

US Senate. N.d. *Threats to the U.S. Research Enterprise: China's Talent Recruitment Plans*. Staff report, Permanent Subcommittee on Investigations, Committee on Homeland Security and Governmental Affairs. https://www.hsgac.senate.gov/wp-content/uploads/imo/media/doc/2019-11-18%20PSI%20Staff%20Report%20-%20China's%20Talent%20Recruitment%20Plans%20Updated2.pdf.

Villalobos, Pablo, Anson Ho, Jaime Sevilla, Tamay Besiroglu, Lennart Heim, and Marius Hobbhahn. 2024. "Will We Run Out of Data? Limits of LLM Scaling Based on Human-Generated Data." Epoch AI, June 6. https://epochai.org/blog/will-we-run-out-of-data-limits-of-llm-scaling-based-on-human-generated-data.

Waymo. 2020. "Waymo Raises First External Investment Round." March 2. https://blog.waymo.com/2020/03/waymo-raises-first-external-investment.html.

Wilt Brian. 2024. (@brianwilt) "When I Posted This Last February, I Wasn't Expecting That It Would Take Less Than a Year to Pass 10M Driverless Miles." X, January 30. https://x.com/brianwilt/status/1752457616897478881

Xinhua. 2021.（受权发布）习近平：在中国科学院第二十次院士大会、中国工程院第十五次院士大会、中国科协第十次全国代表大会上的讲话 [(Authorized Release) Xi Jinping: Speech at the 20th Academician Conference of the Chinese Academy of Sciences, the 15th Academician Conference of the Chinese Academy of Engineering, and the 10th National Congress of the Chinese Association for Science and Technology]." *Xinhua*, May 28. http://www.xinhuanet.com/politics/2021-05/28/c_1127505377.htm.

YouTube. N.d. "YouTube for Press." YouTube Official Blog. https://blog.youtube/press/.

Zuboff, Shoshana. 2019. *The Age of Surveillance Capitalism: The Fight for a Human Future at the New Frontier of Power*. PublicAffairs.

Zwetsloot, Remco. 2019. *Keeping Top AI Talent in the United States*. Center for Security and Emerging Technology, December 10. https://cset.georgetown.edu/wp-content/uploads/Keeping-Top-AI-Talent-in-the-United-States.pdf.

Comment Daniel P. Gross

There is a growing view that we are racing into a future where wars are fought and won with autonomous, AI-driven weapons across all domains—land, sea, air, space, and cyber.

Daniel P. Gross is an associate professor in the Strategy area at Duke University's Fuqua School of Business and a faculty research fellow of the National Bureau of Economic Research.

I am grateful for helpful comments from participants in the Fall 2024 NBER Economics of Artificial Intelligence conference and coeditor Avi Goldfarb. All errors are my own. For acknowledgments, sources of research support, and disclosure of the author's material financial relationships, if any, please see https://www.nber.org/books-and-chapters/political-economy-artificial-intelligence/comment-four-battlegrounds-artificial-intelligence-gross.

Proponents of this view point to recent and active conflicts and to military innovation pipelines (e.g., Brose 2020; Scharre 2018). Autonomy has been a prominent theme in military technology for decades—with a history tracing through automatic machine guns, automatic gun-laying radar, heat-seeking missiles, unmanned aerial vehicles, and more. The meaning of autonomy has itself expanded over time, from mechanization (a mechanical layer between human operators and machine operation) to electronic control (a software layer) to cybernetics (self-regulation through feedback loops, such as autopilot). All three are now prevalent in military hardware, including vehicles and weapons.

In all these cases, however, a human sits at the top of the kill chain, using judgment and discretion to identify targets and make the choice to engage them. Artificial intelligence (AI) has the potential to automate this, too, opening up new possibilities and fears about the future of war—or even civilization—when control is delegated to algorithms and humans are taken out of the loop.

Are we on the precipice of a new era of warfare: the age of AI? If so, what will determine the military advantage of nations in the era of drone swarms and clone wars?

Artificial Intelligence at War

According to Scharre's (2023) *Four Battlegrounds: Power in the Age of Artificial Intelligence*, this future has arrived—and the critical question is who is poised to win.

Getting a handle on this question requires, first, a better understanding of what functions AI can serve in combat settings. These cases might be usefully reduced to two categories:

1. *Automating routine tasks.* Complement high-skill humans, who remain in the loop but can focus their time and attention on non-routine cases requiring judgment. For example, target identification.
2. *Undertaking complex tasks.* Substitute for humans—with the goal of opening new frontiers for military strategy. For example, coordinated operation of massive numbers of attritable units.

The central thesis of Scharre (2023) is that military advantage this century will hinge on four critical AI assets: data, compute, talent, and institutions. One might think of this as a framework—a "resource-based view" of military performance—paralleling the resource-based view (RBV) of firm strategy (Wernerfelt 1984), which argues that firms' internal resources and capabilities are their primary source of competitive advantage. Control over AI resources, according to Scharre, constitutes the "four battlegrounds" where the future will be won or lost. Although one might contend that it is not enough to simply control resources; Porter (1996) and others have argued that effective strategies must also integrate these resources, making them work together such that the whole is more than the sum of the parts.

Scharre (2023) uses much of his book to discuss opportunities, challenges, and especially geopolitical competition for each of these resources, focused on the US and China. At the present moment, it is hard to think about military AI without this competition being a central focus. By and large, most observers—including some participants of this conference—argue that China is outcompeting (some might even say dominating) the US and NATO allies in these battlegrounds. Arguments often point to the size of China's population, the power of the state, the level of AI technology development, and the size of the industrial base as sources of advantage across the four battlegrounds. Yet it is not clear that all these resources are general purpose enough to confer broad or insurmountable advantages (e.g., data are typically domain-specific, frontier AI requires frontier chips and chip-making equipment). Where there are gaps, history suggests these can also potentially be closed quickly: At the dawn of World War II, Germany led the military technology frontier, but by the end of the war, the US did. This reversal of fortunes was made possible by existing investments that created a platform of science, talent, and industrial capacity that could be mobilized for war and rapidly progressed.

How Close Are We to the Clone Wars?

Is it time to panic?

At the time of writing, ongoing hot wars around the world suggest we are still awaiting the AI revolution in combat. The war in Ukraine is more or less a conventional war, fought with major weapons systems, heavy artillery, and human attrition. The war in Gaza is more or less a guerrilla war being fought in dense urban war zones. Each mode of war has historical precedents—such as World War II or Vietnam. Where AI is being used in combat, it appears to be in more tactical applications. Scharre (2023), for example, describes Ukrainian development of autonomous "last mile" solutions for drone attacks, where remote pilots may lose contact or visibility and delegate operation to the machine.

Changing how wars are fought, however, is a systems problem—and systems problems are hard (Agarwal et al. 2022). In the past 15 years, more than one US military service effort to develop modern "systems of systems" for combat has collapsed under the weight of its own complexity—like the Army's Future Combat Systems (FCS) program and the Coast Guard's Deepwater program.

One source of inertia is organizational dynamics. A sizable literature in economics, management, and associated fields has documented the challenges large organizations face in incorporating and adapting to new technology (e.g., Milgrom and Roberts 1990). The US Department of Defense (DoD) is the second-largest organization in the world by headcount (behind the Indian Ministry of Defense and ahead of the Chinese People's Liberation Army) and undertakes a wider range of activities than even the largest private firms. Human-centric military strategy and organizational routines have been refined over centuries, with significant interdependencies in and across combat and noncombat operations. Competing interests, information silos, bureaucracy, and existing technology also tend to slow change. As the world's dominant superpower for the past three to four decades, the US military in particular has been less incentivized to upend itself (Arrow 1962)—although this is changing with geopolitical competition from China.

The R&D problem is also complex. AI-driven systems are fundamentally software-driven systems, and these have been growing in complexity for decades: compared to the Apollo Guidance Computer that took humans to the moon, a modern F-35 Joint Strike Fighter has over 50 times as many lines of code (about 8 million vs. less than 150,000; McCandless 2015), with its concomitant interdependencies too. Beyond software, coordinated, AI-powered weapons systems will likely also require networks of tens of thousands of sensors providing real-time data feeds, and powerful computers supporting autonomous decisions in microseconds while withstanding the rigors of a battlefield. Each of Scharre's (2023) four battlegrounds represents an essential ingredient. But these pieces also need to come together in a coordinated system, which it appears will require a fundamentally different military-technological architecture (in the spirit of Henderson and Clark 1990). Here, too, AI introduces new weaknesses for military use: Security vulnerabilities, power requirements, and potential countermeasures may limit its value, at least in the short run, as a basis for systemic change in the nature and conduct of war.

Although one cannot fully rule out that some undisclosed new capabilities are already in place—frontier military technology is often classified (Gross 2023)—experience and economic logic suggest that there are reasons to believe changes in how wars are fought will take some time.

AI Transformation Behind the Scenes?

However, weapons of war are only one of many use cases for AI in large militaries. The applications that create the most value may be elsewhere—and might be implemented well before large drone swarms. Recruiting, screening, and training tens of thousands of warriors; predictive maintenance on billions of dollars of equipment; and the review of millions of hours of surveillance video or digital communications are all activities that consume significant resources on an ongoing basis, where AI might provide large productivity gains. Even in war, history has shown that noncombat problems like military supply logistics may benefit from AI: A 1980s AI decision-support tool for optimizing the routing of supplies and personnel, originally funded by DARPA as an experimental system, was deployed in the Gulf War and achieved a level of savings that was claimed to be the monetary equivalent of all funding DARPA had directed to AI research for the prior 30 years combined (Hedberg 2002, 81).

Critical Questions at the Intersection of the Economics of AI and National Security

Important questions nevertheless remain in Scharre's (2023) four battlegrounds. These are profoundly important opportunities for further work. I offer a few examples. On data: Are the marginal returns to data in AI innovation increasing or decreasing? When do data have dual-use value? How important are human-specified models as a complement to (or substitute for) machine learning in problems where data are intrinsically scarce, such as certain mobilization and combat functions? On compute: How well are policies to advance frontier chip R&D, onshore supply chain, and limit foreign access working? To what degree does export control motivate catch-up R&D by adversaries? On talent: What are the effects of education and immigration policy—the weapons in this battleground—on AI talent acquisition and retention? What attracts top AI talent to the defense sector? On institutions: What policies foster a defense AI industrial base—and what keeps firms from participating? What are the organizational impediments to adopting AI in military settings, and what are the effects of specific AI systems on performance?

The biggest question, however, is not what but when: Is an "AI revolution" in warfare imminent? It is useful to remember that AI research has been underway for over 60 years—and most of that time, DoD was its leading patron. Autonomy broadly, and AI specifically, are not new to the military, but the present moment is increasingly seen as an inflection point vis-à-vis AI's technological potential.

Yet in the battlefield, as in business, we are still waiting for transformative change. The innovation problem is complex. The organizational one is possibly even more. This kind of systemic change may wait until a crisis forces a scaled-up R&D effort and an accelerated organizational evolution that puts it into practice. Ruttan (2006) argues that "a major war, or the threat of major war, [is] necessary to mobilize the scientific, technical, and financial resources" needed to make progress. My own work (e.g., Gross and Roche 2024; Gross and Sampat 2021, 2023), which has studied past conflagrations, reinforces this view. The high cost of failure can motivate not only a deluge of public funding but also a willingness to take more risk than usual, including parallel attempts that otherwise look wasteful. It can also inspire new approaches to innovation, including large, coordinated, cross-sectoral attacks on complex technological problems. Past examples, like radar or the atomic bomb in World War II, or even COVID-19 vaccines, have engaged the full value chain, from research to mass production and deployment—overcoming coordination failures that in ordinary times make it hard for complex technologies to progress. Importantly, however, in these examples, the response drew from (and depended on) existing science, research talent, and domestic manufacturing capabilities.

Historical experience thus suggests that stocking the arsenal of Scharre's four battlegrounds now will prepare them to be put to work when the next great power conflict arises.

References

Agarwal, Ajay, Joshua Gans, and Avi Goldfarb. 2022. *Power and Prediction: The Disruptive Economics of Artificial Intelligence*. Harvard Business Press.

Arrow, Kenneth J. 1962. "Economic Welfare and the Allocation of Resources for Invention." In *The Rate and Direction of Inventive Activity: Economic and Social Factors*, edited by Richard Nelson, 609–26. Princeton University Press.

Brose, Christian. 2020. *The Kill Chain: Defending America in the Future of High-Tech Warfare*. Hachette Books.

Gross, Daniel P. 2023. "The Hidden Costs of Securing Innovation." *Management Science* 69 (4): 2318–38.

Gross, Daniel P., and Maria P. Roche. 2024. "Coordinated R&D Programs and the Creation of New Industries." Working paper.

Gross, Daniel P., and Bhaven N. Sampat. 2021. "The Economics of Crisis Innovation Policy: A Historical Perspective." *AEA Papers & Proceedings* 111: 346–50.

Gross, Daniel P., and Bhaven N. Sampat. 2023. "America, Jump-Started: World War II R&D and the Takeoff of the US Innovation System?" *American Economic Review* 113 (12): 3323–56.

Hedberg, Sara Reese. 2002. "DART: Revolutionizing Logistics Planning." *IEEE Intelligent Systems*, May/June. https://gwern.net/doc/ai/2002-hedberg.pdf.

Henderson, Rebecca M., and Kim B. Clark. 1990. "Architectural Innovation: The Reconfiguration of Existing Product Technologies and the Failure of Established Firms." *Administrative Science Quarterly* 35 (1): 9–30.

McCandless, David. 2015. "Million Lines of Code." *Information Is Beautiful*. https://informationisbeautiful.net/visualizations/million-lines-of-code/.

Milgrom, Paul, and John Roberts. 1990. "The Economics of Modern Manufacturing: Technology, Strategy, and Organization." *American Economic Review* 80 (3): 511–28.

Porter, Michael E. 1996. "What Is Strategy?" *Harvard Business Review* 74 (6): 61–78.

Ruttan, Vernon W. 2006. *Is War Necessary for Economic Growth? Military Procurement and Technology Development*. Oxford University Press.

Scharre, Paul. 2018. *Army of None: Autonomous Weapons and the Future of War*. W. W. Norton & Co.

Scharre, Paul. 2023. *Four Battlegrounds: Power in the Age of Artificial Intelligence*. W. W. Norton & Co.

Wernerfelt, Birger. 1984. "A Resource-Based View of the Firm." *Strategic Management Journal* 5 (2): 171–80.

8

The More Dismal Science
Perspectives from International Relations on Military Automation

Jon R. Lindsay

Major powers like China and the United States are investing heavily in military automation. Professional military journals are filled with articles about how automation and drones are already changing battlefield operations in Ukraine and the Levant. The AI revolution thus seems poised to reinvent war as much as the advent of rifles and warplanes.

But the gunpowder and aviation revolutions required major systemic transformations in military doctrine and defense industries (Roland 2016). Not every nation was successful in implementing these transformations, and those that were did not always win their wars. Political actors with great military strength may not be willing or able to use it. Actors weak in military power may be strong in resolve. The failure of the highly advanced US military to win decisively in Vietnam, Afghanistan, and Iraq should give pause to anyone who expects advances in AI to deliver victory. Improvements in tactics do not necessarily improve strategy.

Yet popular accounts of military AI betray an expectation that dramatic results will follow from improvement in technical inputs such as data, computing power, and algorithms. Technical AI expertise and governance institutions are often seen as important supplements as well (Scharre 2023). Improvements in these inputs are assumed to improve military power. Autonomous drone swarms and targeting intelligence systems, therefore, will enhance the speed, scope, scale, precision, and lethality of battlefield

Jon R. Lindsay is an associate professor at the School of Cybersecurity and Privacy and the Sam Nunn School of International Affairs at the Georgia Institute of Technology.

For acknowledgments, sources of research support, and disclosure of the author's material financial relationships, if any, please see https://www.nber.org/books-and-chapters/political-economy-artificial-intelligence/more-dismal-science-perspectives-international-relations-military-automation.

operations (Scharre 2018; Singer 2009). Nations that best harness AI inputs, from this perspective, will gain a major competitive advantage in great power politics (Milley and Schmidt 2024; Schmidt 2023). It is a short jump to the conclusion that China is on the cusp of gaining a major military advantage, unless its AI inputs can be controlled.

This view is plausible but incomplete. Military power is not a simple production function. AI may improve the technical efficiency of prediction, but this does not simply translate into improvements in military effectiveness. AI systems and concepts developed in the commercial world may not perform as well in the very different "business" of warfare (Lindsay 2023), because peaceful commerce relies on institutionalized currencies, contracts, and courts, while anarchic warfare is a realm of uncertainty, coercion, and violence.

Put simply, the economics of AI must consider the politics of war. There is a large body of literature in international relations on the relationship between emerging military technology and political behavior (Horowitz 2020). An overarching theme in this literature is that military-technical factors do not uniquely determine the onset, escalation, or termination of war. Advanced weaponry by itself does not determine military outcomes (Biddle 2004; Grauer 2016; Lindsay 2020; Talmadge 2015), except perhaps in the very general sense of encouraging more complex arms races over time (Dafoe 2015). War is not just a military contest but a political process. Therefore, it is important to understand how AI both affects and is affected by this process. The technical inputs of AI have ambiguous or indeterminate implications for political behavior.

The Prussian strategist Carl von Clausewitz gives three distinct definitions of war in the first book of *On War*. He begins by likening war to a duel in which each side tries to disarm the other or compel surrender. This is a pure military contest of strength. The input theory of military AI often stops here: Better AI provides more power to win this contest, often conceived as a set-piece battle or a war game. But why might an actor be motivated to fight any given battle or start a war in the first place? Clausewitz (1976, 87) goes on to make his famous observation that war is "a continuation of political intercourse, carried on with other means." Actors use war to pursue their interests, and different interests lead to different types of war. While the duel tends toward large-scale violence ("absolute war"), politics and operations create limits in practice ("real war"). The input theory of AI says little about how the AI means of war achieve their political object, let alone how the absolute advantages of AI at scale might be limited by strategic realities. Clausewitz then concludes by redefining war as a "paradoxical trinity" that combines a government's political strategy, a military's management of violence, and a nation's unpredictable passions (Clausewitz 1976, 89). Information technologies like AI are more likely to be determined by this chaotic interaction than vice versa (Beyerchen 1992).

The Clausewitzian intuition that war is politics by other means is captured in mainstream international relations by the bargaining model of war (Blainey 1988; Fearon 1995; Powell 2002). In its simplest version, two actors bargain over a contested resource like territory. Each has the outside option of going to war, but war is costly in blood and treasure, which destroys some of the bargaining surplus. Actors who are rational and well informed, therefore, even if they are nominally more powerful, should always prefer a peaceful deal over a costly war. Yet because each wants to capture more of the surplus in the bargaining range, actors have incentives to misrepresent their strength in peacetime to gain a coercive bargaining advantage and, for the same reason, to suspect that threats are just cheap talk. The root cause of war in this model is uncertainty about the true balance of power, costs of war, or willingness to commit to an agreement (Gartzke 1999; Ramsay 2017).[1] Actors can attempt to resolve uncertainty and improve credibility through costly signaling, for instance, by tying hands (e.g., tripwires) or sinking costs (e.g., mobilizations) (Fearon 1997; Jervis 1970; Schelling 2008).

Assume for now the input theory of military AI that better automation produces better fighting as well as the rationalist foundations of the bargaining model. Both assumptions are suspect in practice due to the messy realities of organizing political violence and human decision-making. But we do not even have to relax these assumptions to discover political problems in military AI. The simplest bargaining model of war has just four main components: the *power* to win a war, the *costs* of war, the bargaining *demand*, and *uncertainty* about any of these factors. To ask how AI might affect the politics of war is therefore to ask how AI might affect any of these factors. It turns out that AI can affect them all, in different ways and to different degrees. Let us take each in turn.

By stipulation, AI might improve military power. AI systems might improve the efficiency of administration and logistics, the collection and analysis of intelligence, the planning and coordination of forces, and the employment of lethal autonomous weapon systems. In principle, the improvement of military power can shift the bargaining range so that more favorable out comes are mutually desirable in lieu of war. A rational actor facing an AI-enabled military, all things being equal, should then be more willing to make concessions than go to war, in effect making war less likely while making coercive revision more likely.

But this assumes that there is mutual knowledge about the shift in power. Many concepts of operations for using military AI depend on speed, stealth, maneuver, and surprise. Military capabilities that depend on secrecy for war-fighting efficacy cannot easily be revealed for credible coercion (or deterrence), because the very act of communicating the threat enables an actor

1. Indivisible stakes are also a rational cause of war but are often offset by side payments in practice.

to take countermeasures to disarm it (Gartzke and Lindsay 2018; Green and Long 2020). This is one reason deterrence is not very useful in cyber operations, which rely on hidden exploits. If the adoption of AI improves power without reducing uncertainty, then deterrence failure and miscalculation become more likely. Indeed, interactions and outcomes with automated forces are likely to be highly chaotic and uncertain, which makes it difficult to deliver credible deterrence (Horowitz 2019; Johnson 2020).

AI might also shift the costs of war. Most obviously, AI reduces exposure for friendly forces by automating the pointy end of the spear. If AI reduces costs for both sides, the bargaining range must shrink as war becomes less costly and potentially more attractive. Yet AI also increases the ability to impose costs by efficiently destroying enemy forces. In principle, this could open up the bargaining range and create credible options for coercion through punishment that is asymmetrically costly for the target and costless for the punisher (Zegart 2018).

But credible coercion is as much about displaying a willingness to pay costs as to inflict them. Automated forces literally have no skin in the game. Low-cost punishment thus introduces another information problem. The target cannot tell if the punisher is relying on AI because automated weapons are the most effective way to impose costs or because the punisher is averse to suffering any costs itself. Because AI-enabled forces pool with low-resolve actors, the target has reason to doubt the resolve of the punisher and seek out more informative strategies. Instead of fighting back against robots, therefore, a target might opt to draw blood from civilians to test the punisher's resolve. Sadly, there is empirical evidence consistent with this mechanism that militants subjected to drone attacks tend to conduct more terrorist attacks against civilians (Gartzke and Walsh 2022).

In practice, it is very unlikely that AI-enabled warfare will be costless. The war in Ukraine demonstrates that both sides of a war can use semiautomated drones in attrition warfare, exacerbating rather than relieving contests of pain and endurance. Better prediction and information do not necessarily substitute for mass but can rather require greater reliance on massed effects in protracted conflicts (Horowitz 2024). Furthermore, military AI is making human beings more important, not less. As cheaper prediction increases the value of data and judgment—the complements of AI—military institutions and operations tend to become more complex (Goldfarb and Lindsay 2022). This is part of a larger historical trend whereby increasing exposure to technological lethality encourages greater dispersion of forces and more complex force employment doctrine (Biddle 2004). Combined arms coordination in conditions of extreme fog and friction is very difficult, and AI is likely to amplify rather than reduce coordination problems—an important disanalogy from well-controlled business or war-gaming cases.

The pinnacle of judgment in national security strategy is deciding what is worth killing and dying for and how much risk to accept in coercive diplomacy. These are hard judgments that AI cannot make, even as AI might help to evaluate intelligence and scenarios to support strategic decision-making. Actors who want more influence over the status quo will likely have to accept greater risk of war. Actors who prize strategic stability will likely have to cede some influence in order to reassure and accommodate allies and adversaries alike.

Yet AI also has the potential to exacerbate judgment problems by expanding the number of things to bargain over. If AI inputs improve military power, then influencing those inputs (e.g., access to chips, data, talent) becomes important. Key nodes in the AI supply chain (e.g., Taiwan's TSMC) might even change the stakes of the conflict (by making Taiwan more important to the United States). In the bargaining model of war, judgment determines the demands.

In even the simple bargaining model of war, prior to relaxing problematic assumptions about implementation and rationality, there is already tremendous complexity. Each actor wants to increase its expected gain, but there are many ways to do this, by maximizing power, minimizing costs, maximizing influence, or minimizing uncertainty. These goals cannot be achieved at the same time or to the same degree. Preferences about which to prioritize, moreover, are exogenous to the model. Judgments about whether to prioritize power, efficiency, influence, or stability affect in turn the attractiveness of strategies of warfare, deception, coercion, or accommodation (Gartzke and Lindsay 2024; Lindsay and Gartzke 2022).

The impact of AI on national security is profoundly indeterminant because AI, as we have seen, can affect power, costs, demands, and uncertainty in different ways, and different actors may make different judgments about how and why to do so. AI is not simply an input to politics, furthermore; politics also shapes the inputs to AI. Precisely because AI has implications for important political factors like power, costs, and strategic stability, the technical inputs of AI, like data, computing infrastructure, algorithms, and even personnel, must become contested as well.

Simple scenarios of AI robot wars or Chinese military dominance can probably be discounted. The future of humanity will probably still look a lot like its past: full of violence, exploitation, manipulation, and confusion. If the economics of AI is a dismal science, then, the politics of AI is even more dismal.

References

Beyerchen, Alan. 1992. "Clausewitz, Nonlinearity, and the Unpredictability of War." *International Security* 17 (3): 59–90.

Biddle, Stephen D. 2004. *Military Power: Explaining Victory and Defeat in Modern Battle*. Princeton University Press.
Blainey, Geoffrey. 1988. *Causes of War.* 3rd ed. Simon and Schuster.
Clausewitz, Carl von. 1976. *On War*. Translated by Michael Howard and Peter Paret. Princeton University Press.
Dafoe, Allan. 2015. "On Technological Determinism: A Typology, Scope Conditions, and a Mechanism." *Science, Technology, & Human Values* 40 (6): 1047–76.
Fearon, James D. 1995. "Rationalist Explanations for War." *International Organization* 49 (3): 379–414.
Fearon, James D. 1997. "Signaling Foreign Policy Interests: Tying Hands Versus Sinking Costs." *The Journal of Conflict Resolution* 41 (1): 68–90.
Gartzke, Erik. 1999. "War Is in the Error Term." *International Organization* 53 (3): 567–87.
Gartzke, Erik, and Jon R. Lindsay. 2018. "The Cyber Commitment Problem and the Destabilization of Nuclear Deterrence." In *Bytes, Bombs, and Spies: The Strategic Dimensions of Offensive Cyber Operations*, edited by Herbert S. Lin and Amy B. Zegart, 195–234. Brookings Institution Press.
Gartzke, Erik, and Jon R. Lindsay. 2024. *Elements of Deterrence: Strategy, Technology, and Complexity in Global Politics*. Oxford University Press.
Gartzke, Erik, and James Igoe Walsh. 2022. "The Drawbacks of Drones: The Effects of UAVs on Militant Violence in Pakistan." *Journal of Peace Research* 59 (4): 463–77.
Goldfarb, Avi, and Jon R. Lindsay. 2022. "Prediction and Judgment: Why Artificial Intelligence Increases the Importance of Humans in War." *International Security* 46 (3): 7–50.
Grauer, Ryan. 2016. *Commanding Military Power: Organizing for Victory and Defeat on the Battlefield.* Cambridge University Press.
Green, Brendan Rittenhouse, and Austin Long. 2020. "Conceal or Reveal? Managing Clandestine Military Capabilities in Peacetime Competition." *International Security* 44 (3): 48–83.
Horowitz, Michael C. 2019. "When Speed Kills: Lethal Autonomous Weapon Systems, Deterrence and Stability." *Journal of Strategic Studies* 42 (6): 764–88.
Horowitz, Michael C. 2020. "Do Emerging Military Technologies Matter for International Politics?" *Annual Review of Political Science* 23 (1): 385–400.
Horowitz, Michael C. 2024. "Battles of Precise Mass: Technology Is Remaking War—and America Must Adapt." *Foreign Affairs*, October 22. https://www.foreignaffairs.com/world/battles-precise-mass-technology-war-horowitz.
Jervis, Robert. 1970. *The Logic of Images in International Relations*. Princeton University Press.
Johnson, James. 2020. "Delegating Strategic Decision-Making to Machines: Dr. Strangelove Redux?" *Journal of Strategic Studies* 45 (3): 439–77.
Lindsay, Jon R. 2020. *Information Technology and Military Power*. Cornell University Press.
Lindsay, Jon R. 2023. "War Is from Mars, AI Is from Venus: Rediscovering the Institutional Context of Military Automation." *Texas National Security Review* 7 (1): https://tnsr.org/2023/11/war-is-from-mars-ai-is-from-venus-rediscovering-the-institutional-context-of-military-automation/.
Lindsay, Jon R., and Erik Gartzke. 2022. "Politics by Many Other Means: The Comparative Strategic Advantages of Operational Domains." *Journal of Strategic Studies* 45 (5): 743–76.
Milley, Mark A., and Eric Schmidt. 2024. "America Isn't Ready for the Wars of the Future: And They're Already Here." *Foreign Affairs*, August 5. https://www

.foreignaffairs.com/united-states/ai-america-ready-wars-future-ukraine-israel-mark-milley-eric-schmidt.

Powell, Robert. 2002. "Bargaining Theory and International Conflict." *Annual Review of Political Science* 5 (1): 1–30.

Ramsay, Kristopher W. 2017. "Information, Uncertainty, and War." *Annual Review of Political Science* 20 (1).

Roland, Alex. 2016. *War and Technology: A Very Short Introduction*. Oxford University Press.

Scharre, Paul. 2018. *Army of None: Autonomous Weapons and the Future of War*. W. W. Norton & Co.

Scharre, Paul. 2023. *Four Battlegrounds: Power in the Age of Artificial Intelligence*. W. W. Norton & Co.

Schelling, Thomas C. 2008. *Arms and Influence: With a New Preface and Afterword*. Yale University Press.

Schmidt, Eric. 2023. "Innovation Power: Why Technology Will Define the Future of Geopolitics." *Foreign Affairs*, February 28. https://www.foreignaffairs.com/united-states/eric-schmidt-innovation-power-technology-geopolitics.

Singer, Peter W. 2009. *Wired for War: The Robotics Revolution and Conflict in the Twenty-First Century*. Penguin.

Talmadge, Caitlin. 2015. *The Dictator's Army: Battlefield Effectiveness in Authoritarian Regimes*. Cornell University Press.

Zegart, Amy. 2018. "Cheap Fights, Credible Threats: The Future of Armed Drones and Coercion." *Journal of Strategic Studies* 43 (1): 6–46.

III

AI and Political Identity

9 Nation Building and AI

Vasiliki Fouka and Bryony Reich

9.1 Introduction

For centuries, governments have intervened to forge national identities and national cohesion. At the unification of modern Italy in 1860, Massimo d'Azeglio famously remarked, "Italy has been made; now it remains to make Italians." Italian elites then implemented a range of policies to create a national identity, including enforcing a national language (Tuscan was chosen) and introducing compulsory schooling.[1] Government policies to form national identities and create national cohesion have ranged from the introduction of compulsory schooling, like in Italy, to the orchestrated integration of different groups, to repression and persecution of those who fall outside the desired identity.

We refer to policies that aim to form citizens' national identities to shape the polity as "nation building" policies. Within political economy, an active literature has emerged to examine the role of such policies (Rohner and Zhuravskaya 2023, 2025). This chapter considers the impact of artificial intelligence (AI) on the policies of nation building.

While nation-building policies are implemented through various chan-

Vasiliki Fouka is Bing Professor of Human Biology and associate professor of political science at Stanford University, a senior fellow at the Stanford Institute for Economic Policy Research, and a faculty research fellow of the National Bureau of Economic Research.

Bryony Reich is an assistant professor of strategy at the Kellogg School of Management at Northwestern University.

For acknowledgments, sources of research support, and disclosure of the authors' material financial relationships, if any, please see https://www.nber.org/books-and-chapters/political-economy-artificial-intelligence/nation-building-and-ai.

1. The author of the 1877 Italian compulsory schooling reform stated that the aim of compulsory schooling was to "create a population . . . devoted to the fatherland and the king" (Duggan 2007).

nels, to constrain the remit of this chapter, we focus on nation building via education. Education is considered perhaps the most powerful tool for nation building. Napoleon I articulated the importance of state-controlled education in shaping the views and identity of children and, through this, the cohesion of a nation: "There cannot be a firmly established political state unless there is a teaching body with definitely recognized principles. If the child is not taught from infancy that he ought to be a republican or a monarchist, a Catholic or a free-thinker, the state will not constitute a nation."[2] A second reason to focus on AI and nation building in education is that, in the current context of AI, there is already a lot to say about AI in education, which will allow us to be more concrete in this chapter.

The chapter proceeds as follows. We first provide a brief introduction to the nation-building literature in economics. We discuss how states nation build through education and provide examples of nation-building policies from the literature. We discuss evidence on when nation-building policies work (or fail). We then consider and speculate on the role of AI in nation building. We first discuss how AI will impact nation building technologies. Putting to one side the incentives of policymakers and citizens, we consider how AI will make nation-building technologies more productive. If AI makes nation-building technologies more productive, to what extent will this translate into more nation building? We discuss the role of AI in overcoming opposition to nation building by states, and finally, we consider the impact of AI on education more generally. We conclude the chapter by asking how AI will change the type of nation building that states wish to implement. We highlight the importance of research on government incentives and constraints to nation build.

To be clear, this is not an exhaustive discussion of AI and nation building. We will focus on nation building through education. We will not consider other natural channels of nation building, such as via social media. Even within education, we limit ourselves to direct rather than indirect impacts of AI on nation building, such as through political change.

9.2 How Do States Nation Build Through Education?

Education forms a major part of nation-building policies. For Tilly (1975, 43–44), "Almost all European governments eventually took steps which homogenized their populations: . . . institution of a national language, eventually the organization of mass public instruction." Alesina et al. (2021) argue that nation building was a significant motivating factor in the development of state intervention in schooling and compulsory education. Hobsbawm (1990, 91) describes how "states would use the increasingly powerful machinery for communicating with their inhabitants, above all

2. Quote from Ramirez and Boli (1987).

the primary schools, to spread the image and heritage of the 'nation' and to inculcate attachment to it."

We distinguish between three ways in which governments use education to nation build: by directly inculcating national identity, by shaping the values and preferences of students to create a homogeneous population, and by engineering contact across diverse groups in the school context. A growing body of papers in economics examines government education policies in these three broad categories. Here we illustrate with just a small fraction of the examples from this active literature.[3]

9.2.1 Building Common Identity

Governments use education to directly shape perceptions of belonging to a common nation and instill identification with that nation (Alesina et al. 2021). One means of achieving that is through curriculum content. Most countries introduced courses on national history, geography, and literature in their curricula as they began to roll out public education in the 19th and early 20th century (Del Río et al. 2023). Throughout the 20th century and still in many countries today, part of the curriculum is explicitly dedicated to nation building and is referred to as "civic education." National narratives still occupy a place in the modern educational systems of most countries.

A study by Ben Krause, Michael Kremer, Eduardo Rivera, and Enrique Seira provides evidence for the success of such narratives in instilling national identity. In their project "The Influence of Historical Narrative on Individual and National Identity," the authors examine the impact of teaching the government narrative of Mexican history on national identity and community participation. The Mexican government espouses a historical narrative, created after the Mexican Revolution, that Mexico is a place where cultures and races mix without becoming extinct, and that interaction is what defines Mexican identity. The authors ask whether school activities can foster national identity and civic participation among marginalized groups.

The authors study a government program that takes secondary school students from marginalized secondary schools in the city of Puebla to historical museums and sites. Treatment was a five-hour tour of museums and monuments. The tour script was "developed from textbooks, national curricula, and sites of Puebla" with the aim of providing a narrative of "mixed national identity of Mexico, of shared history, and national pride." It included statements like "Those with indigenous origins are great and are Mexican," "Mexicans have built great things," and "Indigenous men and women have defended Mexico" (Krause et al. 2024). Krause et al. (2024) find that treated students were more likely to identify with an identity based on Mexican culture, more likely to report as indigenous, self-report a darker skin color, and more likely to volunteer in a club to clean streets and parks.

3. For an expansive review see Rohner and Zhuravskaya (Forthcoming).

Perhaps the most commonly employed means of nation-building in education is the use of a national language as a medium of instruction. By controlling the language of education, states both enabled communication across people of diverse dialects and cultural backgrounds and shaped those people's perceptions of belonging to the same group. A study by Blanc and Kubo (2024) examined the most well-known case of national language dissemination in early compulsory education, that of France in the early nineteenth century. Using a detailed linguistic atlas and applying a regression discontinuity design that exploited the state-mandated construction of schools and teaching in the national language in municipalities with above 500 inhabitants, the authors show that the 1833 "Guizot laws" introducing mass primary public schooling led to significant linguistic homogenization and effects on national identification that persisted all the way into the second half of the twentieth century. This evidence complements findings of earlier studies on the role of language in national identity. Most prominently, Clots-Figueras and Masella (2013) found that the 1983 introduction of Catalan in Catalonia's education system, which had previously been Spanish only, strengthened Catalan identity among affected cohorts of students.

More broadly, the study by Blanc and Kubo (2024) identified the effect of a bundled treatment and pointed to an impact of education on national identity formation beyond the role of curriculum and language use. Compulsory education implies that the population undergoes a common standardized experience of schooling for a long period of time during childhood and adolescence. This very process, regardless of curriculum content and medium of instruction, instills in students shared knowledge and a common view of the world, which contributes to the perception that they are members of the same community and to the internalization of a common identity.

9.2.2 Shaping Preferences and Ideology

Besides shaping educational content to directly build a common identity, governments also use schooling to instill a range of other preferences and values or shape ideologies and beliefs. The values and beliefs transmitted through educational systems are those that align with the state's ideology and goals (Alesina et al. 2021; Dewey 1916; Freire 1970; Paglayan 2024). Such interventions in schooling have the effect of generating homogeneity among the schooled population, albeit homogeneity in the direction of the state's goals, and contribute to the shaping of the polity.

We next describe two economics papers that examine changes in curricula (in China and Finland, respectively) with the aim of instilling in students a certain set of ideological beliefs.

Davide Cantoni, Yuyu Chen, David Yang, Noam Yuchtman, and Jane Zhang, in their paper "Curriculum and Ideology," examine the causal impact of a curriculum reform in China on students' views on government, political institutions, and economic institutions (among other things). The paper studies a textbook reform for senior high school students that was part of China's Eighth Education Reform. An explicit aim of the reform was to shape students' values and ideology. The substantially revised textbooks were introduced in different provinces between 2004 and 2010. The revisions included new material on government authority, to teach that the government is subject to the rule of law and should not abuse its powers. New material was included to promote and develop student understanding of a "socialist democracy." New sections on this topic were titled "The choice of election methods and its basis," "Various ways of participating in democratic decision-making," and "Orderly and disorderly political participation." New material on the economy aimed to teach students about the "socialist market economy," with new sections in the textbook including "Limitations of Market Allocation of Resources" and "Basic Characteristics of the Socialist Market Economy."

Cantoni et al. (2017) surveyed students at Peking University, finding that students exposed to the new curriculum show views in line with many of the goals of the changed curriculum; they "have greater trust in government officials, view government officials as more civic minded, see China as more democratic, are more skeptical of unconstrained democracy, and express more skeptical views of unconstrained free markets."

Jaakko Meriläinen and Matti Mitrunen, in their paper "Long-Run Consequences of Propaganda in the Classroom," examine the impact of a "rogue" experiment in Finland from 1973 to 1975. This experiment exposed fifth-grade children in one municipality to a new history and social studies curriculum based on Soviet and Marxist-Leninist ideology. The experiment was implemented to study how schools can shape a "functioning worldview." Fifth-grade history and social studies learning was based on a new student handout and an accompanying teacher handout. The handouts described world history as a Marxist class struggle in which the highest form of society was a socialist one achieved by workers' efforts and revolution (Meriläinen and Mitrunen 2024). They described the Soviet Union as a place with no unemployment and citizens as equals. The handouts emphasized class struggle and class hatred and asked students to "use these lectures to ponder how some became rich and others poor and how some of the population did all the hard work while others only enjoyed themselves."

Meriläinen and Mitrunen (2024) find that students exposed to this experiment had substantially lower incomes compared to nonexposed cohorts. These students work fewer hours, select into occupations considered more civic minded, like teaching and nursing, and are less likely to select into upper management.

In the same way, a curriculum might aim to teach children to use math in daily life, curricula also typically aim to build national identity to form a citizen who contributes to a cohesive polity. This is also the case in democratic regimes. For example, the UK national curriculum has a statutory citizenship program of study. The "purpose of study" states that it "should foster pupils' keen awareness and understanding of democracy, government and how laws are made and upheld" and should "prepare pupils to take their place in society as responsible citizens."[4]

9.2.3 Engineering Contact

Finally, education achieves a nation-building function simply by engineering contact in the classroom. By bringing together people from different backgrounds, compulsory schooling may increase cohesion and trust across diverse groups, fostering a cohesive society. Schooling is likely to have this effect because it often satisfies the conditions—such as equal status and common goals—identified by the psychologist Gordon Allport (1954) as requirements for positive contact across groups. Instances of nation-building through education that fosters contact across groups can be identified in a wide range of contexts, from 19th-century United States to contemporary Africa. Bandiera et al. (2019) show that US states adopted compulsory education in response to large-scale immigration from Europe. Besides instilling American civic values in immigrants coming from countries without broad public schooling, US compulsory schooling laws plausibly also contributed to nation building by increasing contact and interactions across diverse immigrant groups and the local population. In Tanzania, Carlitz et al. (2022) studied the effects of a program that created planned ethnically diverse villages in which children received education that emphasized the nation-state over tribal identities. Carlitz et al. (2022) found that the reform boosted national identity and intermarriage across ethnic lines. Though the distinct contribution of intergroup contact in the classroom has not yet, to our knowledge, been isolated by empirical studies relative to other components of educational reforms, these papers point to its likely relevance for nation building through education.

9.3 When Does Nation Building Through Education Work?

To understand how AI may affect nation building through education, it is useful to first briefly take stock of what we know in terms of when education successfully constructs common identity and when it fails to do so.

Key to understanding when nation-building education works is the incentives of governments to undertake nation building and their objectives, as well as the incentives and constraints faced by citizens in following nation building policies or resisting. There remains much still to understand about these questions.

4. The statutory requirements for the citizenship programs of study, published 11 September 2013, https://www.gov.uk/government/publications/national-curriculum-in-england-citizenship-programmes-of-study/national-curriculum-in-england-citizenship-programmes-of-study-for-key-stages-3-and-4.

Alesina et al. (2021) study the incentives of states to nation build. The authors show that incentives and constraints are very different under democratic versus nondemocratic regimes. Nondemocratic regimes have more latitude in their choice of nation building policies, while democracies need to consider the views of the population to a greater degree when implementing nation building. Since nation-building policies under a democracy are closer to the preferred policies of the population as a whole, democratic nation building may face less opposition. In contrast, nation-building policies under a nondemocratic regime may be unwanted and far from the preferred policies of the population.

Interventions to shape identity and preferences can face resistance and even backfire. Groups and communities have resisted attempts to change their identities since the earliest nation-building interventions (Weber 1976), and citizens may oppose the state's efforts to control ideology in education today. For example, in Hong Kong, protesters turned out in 2012 against the proposed introduction of "Moral and National Education," accusing the government of aiming to indoctrinate students with pro-Chinese government propaganda in schools. The proposals were then shelved.

The strongest reaction originates from parents, who may not only oppose government intervention in their children's schooling but also actively substitute into activities that mitigate or compensate for the state content of nation-building policies. Fouka (2020) studied the case of German-language bans that were implemented, due to anti-German sentiment, in some US states after World War I and found backlash as a response. Children of German immigrants exposed to the ban were more likely to marry within their own ethnic group, choose more "German" names for their children (e.g., Franz instead of Daniel), and were less likely to volunteer in World War II. German Americans placed importance on preserving German culture and language. Evidence suggests that parents whose children were subject to the ban substituted by investing more into children's cultural identity: The effects were stronger for children with two German parents, stronger in communities with a higher share of Lutheran Church members (using German in schools and churches), and Lutheran Sunday pupil attendance increased after the ban. In Turkey, Sakalli (2019) identifies similar dynamics in terms of stronger religious identities for children of religious parents who were exposed to a secularization reform. Carvalho et al. (2024) generalized these empirical findings to show that, in theory, when education transmits identities that do not accord with those of parents, groups may respond in a variety of ways that include "dropping out," "tuning out," or "turning out" to oppose state content.

Fouka (2023) reviewed recent empirical literature, identifying three factors that affect the success of nation building efforts through education. First, as evidenced in Fouka (2020) and Sakalli (2019), backlash is more likely with strong identities or a greater degree of distance of individuals' and groups' preferences from those the state attempts to instill through education. Second, the severity of penalties for those who resist nation building also matters, with backlash being observed in cases where enforcement of educational policies is less strict. Stricter enforcement may work through incentives for teachers and local elites to pass the government narrative to students. Blanc and Kubo (2024) show that the impact of state-sponsored education was greater when there was a greater concentration of local elites. These elites were involved in administration, supervision of schools and teaching, and funding. They also find a larger impact of state-sponsored education in places where most of the clergymen had sworn an oath of allegiance to the secular state.

Finally, backlash is least likely when educational reforms are combined with strong incentives to acquire education or to acquire the national identity espoused by the state. In 19th-century France, as state education was rolled out, there were expansive opportunities for upward mobility via employment in state administration for those who spoke French and were educated by the state-sponsored system. Blanc and Kubo (2024) argue that in 19th-century France, the impact of state-provided schooling in teaching children French was larger in localities where the benefits of schooling were highest. They proxy for the benefit of education using a measure of demand (children choosing to attend school) and the pace of technological progress (adoption of the steam engine) in different localities.

Incentives for acquiring education may also be provided indirectly, when minority groups (often the target of nation building efforts) face lower discrimination and fewer barriers to their full incorporation in society should they receive education. In a recent example from Germany, which faces rising diversity from immigration, Felfe et al. (2021) found that trust and cooperation in the classroom increase for immigrant students who were subject to a legal reform granting them birthright citizenship. By increasing those students' opportunities and chances of future inclusion, this policy increased social cohesion, enhancing any effect of schooling through intergroup contact.

9.4 The Role of AI in Nation-Building Education

9.4.1 An Increase in the Productivity of the Nation-Building Technology

AI has the potential to put a more powerful nation-building technology in the hands of states. It is important to consider the implications of this. In this subsection, we discuss how AI could increase productivity in nation-building education.

On the impact of AI on education, Acemoglu and Restrepo (2020) write, "The potential improvements in terms of educational productivity could be quite large (we just do not know)." In this subsection, we highlight three ways in which AI productivity improvements in education could translate to nation-building education. First, AI may help to provide an effective and efficient way to embed nation-building narratives throughout the curriculum. Second, AI can facilitate more personalized nation building in schools. Third, AI can be used to learn what works in nation-building education. Echoing Acemoglu and Restrepo (2020), the potential increase in productivity in nation-building education could be quite large.

We also discuss where AI productivity improvements in education do not translate to nation-building education. In contrast to subjects such as mathematics, it is more difficult to access convincing nation-building "outcomes" that can feasibly measure the amount of nation building that is "learned." This may limit technological gains to nation-building education.

9.4.1.1 *Efficient and Enhanced Resources*

AI can be used to generate resources more efficiently. For example, AI can assist teachers with project ideas, grading, and quiz creation (for various examples of prompts to generate teaching assistance, see Mollick and Mollick 2024). In the context of nation-building education, AI could more efficiently embed nation-building information, ideology, and propaganda into other aspects of the curriculum. To give an example, in the context of the Finnish experiment studied in Meriläinen and Mitrunen (2024), AI could embed ideas on class struggle and inequality into math learning, examples, and quizzes.

AI is also used to create enhanced resources such as experiential resources, role-playing scenarios, negotiation simulations, interactions with historical, fictional, or political characters, and even immersive virtual environments (for some current examples, see Mollick and Mollick 2023). Meriläinen and Mitrunen (2024) describe how in the school experiment in Finland, children were split into groups called "rich" and "poor"; the poor were served worse food at lunch and had to build slum housing at recess. Students also organized a protest against Finnish capitalist society. This illustrates experiential exercises being used for nation building without AI. AI has the potential to provide states with novel and more efficient ways to generate experiential nation-building exercises.

Many of the resources discussed here are feasible without AI but would require high levels of teacher time, expertise, and financing, beyond what is typically available in school settings. AI has the ability to embed nation building in standard and experiential resources much more cheaply and at scale, especially if the resources are put together by a centralized government department with strong expertise.

9.4.1.2 *Personalized Learning*

AI is already in use to personalize student learning. Henkel and Lee (2024) studied the impact of additional mathematics instruction through an AI tutor available on WhatsApp that is personalized to the student's level and pace. Students in Ghana who were given access to the AI tutor saw significantly higher growth in math scores. Learning can also be personalized by adapting to student engagement and preferred ways of learning.

Personalization in nation-building education can be applied in the same way as other subjects. Historically, and still today, learning a common national language comprises an important element of nation building (see, e.g., Clots-Figueras and Masella 2013). This is of particular relevance for ethnically diverse countries, as well as for countries that experience an increase in linguistic heterogeneity through migration. AI makes it cheaper and easier to personalize language learning. Similarly, learning facts and details about government institutions, the legal system, and how to participate in democracy can be personalized to the student's level and knowledge, in a similar way to mathematics education. Such personalization can be particularly useful for enhancing learning in civic education when students come from a wide range of origin countries with different institutions and political regimes.

Nation-building education often aims to transmit a particular ideology, values, or sense of belonging to the nation. States may seek to use AI to personalize this aspect of nation building toward a group or individual. The government program studied by Krause et al. (2024) in the city of Puebla, takes students on tours of major historical sites in the city. This program targets potentially marginalized students to build up feelings of Mexican identity and belonging. Since AI facilitates personalization, states could use it to offer distinct educational content and messages to minority versus majority groups or different education approaches that facilitate inclusion in different ways for different groups.

States could also seek to use AI to target students who the state determines are "lacking" certain ideologies or values. Targeting of groups in this way is a feature of historical nation-building policies; for example, US states targeted mainly German immigrants with language bans post–World War I (Fouka 2020). Alternatively, governments might seek to target areas of ideology or values that a student is more open to adopting. Empirical studies on the effects of nation-building policies in education find heterogeneity in their effects, with success being lower for more culturally or linguistically distant groups or stronger prior identities (Fouka 2020; Sakalli 2019). States may choose to target those more amenable to a reform or, instead, those who are, at baseline, least likely to respond to it. This kind of targeting requires identifying personalized messages for different students, and we discuss this in the next subsection.

9.4.1.3 Learning About Teaching Methodology

An exciting prospect of AI is the potential for learning about which teaching methods and content work well and engage students, and for which kinds of student (Acemoglu and Restrepo 2020). AI could even be used in the discovery of new teaching methods and learning patterns. Here we discuss how the ability of AI to learn about the effectiveness of different educational approaches applies to nation-building education.

Empirical analyses of nation building often examine "broad brush" policies, in part because many nation-building policies within education are relatively broad (e.g., the introduction of new curricula or changes in textbooks and exams). In terms of understanding the details of what kind of nation-building education works, there is a lot to learn. Does learning the institutional details of governance have a nation-building impact? Does effective nation building require persuasive text and language? Does nation building require repeat exposure to ideas and ideologies or exposure through multiple channels? Is trust and cohesion facilitated by diverse students simply being in a class together, or can it be enhanced by students working on certain projects together?

Learning about the effectiveness of educational content and methods requires large data sets on teaching methods, content, and student outcomes. For example, a large dataset on math teaching, content, approach, and students' answers to questions and engagement with the material could allow AI learning about which approaches work best and for which students. The immediate difficulty in translating this into nation-building education is the question of student outcomes. If nation-building outcomes are simply knowledge, for example, about national history or governance and institutions, then these outcomes can be measured in the same way as other standard material. But nation-building outcomes also include whether certain identity, values, beliefs, ideology, or feelings of belonging are held. These outcomes are harder to test than knowledge is.

There are, however, economics papers that seek to test for outcomes on identity, values, and ideology. Krause et al. (2024) examine the nation-building impact of the tours of Puebla using survey questions about feelings on identity and skin color, participation in student volunteering, and the choice to spend monetary winnings to buy Mexican art. Blouin and Mukand (2019) examine the salience of Hutu and Tutsi identity in Rwanda using a "salience of identity" test that captures subconscious or conscious categorizing of others on the basis of their ethnicity. They also examine the choice of who to engage with in a cooperative task and outcomes of a trust game. If it is difficult for states to feasibly acquire these kinds of measures of student outcomes, however, this will limit the states' ability to learn about nation building using AI.

9.4.2 AI in Overcoming Opposition to Nation Building

AI may make nation-building technologies much more effective. Yet, as discussed, technological constraints are not the only constraints to nation building. Political constraints and resistance can impact both the implementation and the effectiveness of nation-building policies. Here we discuss how AI may play a role in reducing resistance to nation building within education.

Nation building typically requires teachers to transmit nation-building policies into the classroom. Blanc and Kubo (2024) show that nation building was more effective in localities in 19th-century France with greater concentrations of elites responsible for overseeing local teachers and their lessons, suggesting that teacher compliance was important to the success of nation building. Meriläinen and Mitrunen (2024) explain how the experiment to inculcate children with Marxist-Leninist views in Finland was also intended for ninth graders (as well as fifth graders); however, teacher opposition and resistance prevented the material from being taught to the ninth graders. To the extent that AI can facilitate the efficient creation of resources, including enhanced experiential resources and personalized lessons, at a centralized level, this reduces the reliance on teachers as a transmission channel for nation building.

An additional, indirect way AI may enhance nation-building is by increasing the appeal of education, counteracting any reasons that students or their parents have to resist or "tune out" in response to educational content. For instance, as explained in Section 9.3, resistance to nation-building interventions in education is greater when returns to schooling are perceived as limited. Parents who may oppose the ideological content of education will still send their children to school if they expect that education will benefit them later in life. By the same token, increasing engagement with education and the learning process in the classroom may work as a counterforce to any resistance on the part of parents. AI deployment in educational settings has been particularly successful in increasing student motivation to learn and engagement with class content (Ruan et al. 2021; Wu and Yu 2024). The use of AI in enhancing the attractiveness of education for students and parents can thus work against any opposition to nation-building content.

AI may also be able to optimize team composition, informing how best to create diverse teams of students for various activities that will tend to promote integration and belonging rather than division and opposition.

9.4.3 AI-Driven Impacts on Education with Nation-Building Implications

The biggest impact of AI on nation building through education is likely to work indirectly through AI's impact on education more broadly. All the ways of improving the productivity of nation-building education just discussed—efficient and enhanced resources, personalized learning, and learning about teaching methodology—will apply all the more to the improvement of productivity of education writ large. Because nation building through schooling is achieved through a variety of means, some of which pertain to every aspect of the educational experience, such as sharing a classroom and common content over several years (Section 9.2), a general-purpose technology that increases efficiency in education will increase the level of nation building achieved at any given level of education. For this reason, the effects of extensive AI use in education on nation building will likely be larger in those countries where educational technology and the quality of the educational system are currently worse.

One of the most important ways AI may facilitate nation building without being used directly to transmit national identity or ideology is by reducing educational inequalities. In many countries, persistent religious, ethnic, or other identity cleavages are perpetuated through accompanying educational and socioeconomic differences across identity groups (Alesina et al. 2016). Enhanced resources and advances in personalized learning through AI have the potential to improve educational outcomes to a greater extent among students of marginalized backgrounds or those who belong to minority groups. One concrete example is personalized language learning. Laitin and Ramachandran (2022) show that indigenous language instruction in Africa significantly increases literacy and that human capital is lower in linguistically diverse countries that rely on colonial languages as a medium of instruction in primary education. Personalized language learning through AI in education has the capacity to increase education and human capital overall but also to close educational gaps and enhance cohesion in societies where the language of the dominant ethnic group is imposed on members of other ethnicities (see also Ramachandran 2017).

In addition to language, recent research in economics demonstrates the capacity of targeted educational interventions to improve outcomes for students of disadvantaged backgrounds. Carlana et al. (2022) found that tutoring and career counseling offered to high-ability immigrant students in Italy closed the gap in grade retention for male students, who displayed the largest gap in performance pre-intervention. AI may allow for a more cost-effective implementation of similar interventions at scale. Alesina et al. (2024) show that the immigrant-native gap in grades in Italian schools was reduced when teachers were made aware of their own biases (as reflected in an implicit association test) prior to assigning grades. The potential of AI technology for identifying such biases provides an additional opportunity to address educational gaps at scale. For example, AI may be used to analyze a large amount of teacher-generated data, including natural language from classroom interactions, to identify and remedy biases in instruction that may have adverse effects on students of disadvantaged backgrounds (Tan and Demszky 2023).

By reducing persistent educational inequalities, AI may indirectly contribute to weakening the identity cleavages that map onto those inequalities and increasing social cohesion. This could be a more "benign" use of AI in nation building education, than applications that focus on direct transmission of values and beliefs.

Although the effects of enhanced resources and personalization on social cohesion through the aforementioned channels are likely to be large, extensive use of AI may also undermine some aspects of education that contribute to nation building. As discussed in Section 9.2, the standardization of experience for youth in the schooling system is a major part of what contributes to common identity formation. Personalization of classroom experiences works against this homogenizing function of education and differentiation of teaching methods, content, and approach for students of different backgrounds may to some extent highlight, rather than bridge their differences.

Finally, there is no doubt that AI will change education as we know it in fundamental ways. Modern education systems were introduced by states in the nineteenth century, in part, to standardize the population's skills and values in response to democratization and industrialization (Alesina et al. 2021; Gellner 2008), and they achieved their nation-building function through such standardization. It is hard to predict how education will respond to the challenges of the information revolution, but it is likely that its overall goal will be much less targeted toward homogenization and standardization of skills and preferences.

9.5 Conclusion

This chapter speculates on the role of AI in nation building. We could instead have speculated on exactly the inverse: the role of nation building in a world with AI. Nation building has been ubiquitous since the French Revolution and remains so today. As AI becomes more and more relevant, nation building will continue to be an important government policy. What kind of nation building should we expect governments to implement in a world with AI?

AI may shift the direction in which governments wish to shape preferences, values, and ideology. Predictions on the implications of AI for jobs, inequality, and the role of work range from the possibility that jobs will be obsolete and the role of work will be radically altered to the alternative that AI will simply continue the march of automation and resulting inequality (for further discussion, see Acemoglu 2024; Autor 2024). The analysis of the Finnish experiment in Meriläinen and Mitrunen (2024) suggests that nation building can influence how citizens value and choose different forms of employment and their role as workers in society. Perhaps nation building will be used to shape future workers, albeit to a different shape from that of today.

To understand how states will nation build in response to AI and the changes AI brings, we need a firm understanding of the incentives and objectives of states in implementing nation-building policies, as well as the constraints they face. Should we expect democracies to limit nation building to creating cohesive communities and fostering knowledge of democratic processes and institutions? Do nondemocratic regimes have the same objectives and the same restraints when it comes to nation building? Should we expect nondemocratic regimes to respond more nimbly to AI because they have more latitude when it comes to means of nation building?

While there is growing work on when nation-building policies are successful, there is relatively little work on political decision-making (Giuliano et al. 2023) and the constraints that bind (Fouka 2023). This chapter calls for more research on political decision-making and the incentives of those who make nation building policies.

References

Acemoglu, Daron. 2024. "The Simple Macroeconomics of AI." NBER Working Paper No. 32487. National Bureau of Economic Research.

Acemoglu, Daron, and Pascual Restrepo. 2020. "The Wrong Kind of AI? Artificial Intelligence and the Future of Labour Demand." *Cambridge Journal of Regions, Economy and Society* 13 (1): 25–35.

Alesina, Alberto, Michela Carlana, Eliana La Ferrara, and Paolo Pinotti. 2024. "Revealing Stereotypes: Evidence from Immigrants in Schools." *American Economic Review* 114 (7): 1916–48.

Alesina, Alberto, Paola Giuliano, and Bryony Reich. 2021. "Nation-Building and Education." *The Economic Journal* 131 (638): 2273–2303.

Alesina, Alberto, Stelios Michalopoulos, and Elias Papaioannou. 2016. "Ethnic Inequality." *Journal of Political Economy* 124 (2): 428–88.

Allport, Gordon W. 1954. *The Nature of Prejudice*. Doubleday & Co.

Autor, David. 2024. "Applying AI to Rebuild Middle Class Jobs." NBER Working Paper No. 32140. National Bureau of Economic Research.

Bandiera, Oriana, Myra Mohnen, Imran Rasul, and Martina Viarengo. 2019. "Nation-Building Through Compulsory Schooling During the Age of Mass Migration." *The Economic Journal* 129 (617): 62–109.

Blanc, Guillaume, and Masahiro Kubo. 2024. "French." Working paper. https://papers.ssrn.com/sol3/papers.cfm?abstract_id=4636225.

Blouin, Arthur, and Sharun W. Mukand. 2019. "Erasing Ethnicity? Propaganda, Nation Building, and Identity in Rwanda." *Journal of Political Economy* 127 (3): 1008–62.

Cantoni, Davide, Yuyu Chen, David Y. Yang, Noam Yuchtman, and Y. Jane Zhang. 2017. "Curriculum and Ideology." *Journal of Political Economy* 125 (2): 338–92.

Carlana, Michela, Eliana La Ferrara, and Paolo Pinotti. 2022. "Goals and Gaps: Educational Careers of Immigrant Children." *Econometrica* 90 (1): 1–29.

Carlitz, Ruth, Ameet Morjaria, and Joris M. Mueller. 2022. "State-Building in a Diverse Society." NBER Working Paper No. 30731. National Bureau of Economic Research.

Carvalho, Jean-Paul, Mark Koyama, and Cole Williams. 2024. "Resisting Education." *Journal of the European Economic Association*, jvae008.

Clots-Figueras, Irma, and Paolo Masella. 2013. "Education, Language and Identity." *The Economic Journal* 123 (570): F332–57.

Del Río, Adrián, Carl Henrik Knutsen, and Philipp M. Lutscher. 2023. "Education Policies and Systems Across Modern History: A Global Dataset." *Comparative Political Studies*, 00104140241252075.

Dewey, John. 1916. *Democracy and Education: An Introduction to the Philosophy of Education*. Macmillan.

Duggan, C. 2007. *The Force of Destiny: A History of Italy Since 1796*. Penguin Books.

Felfe, Christina, Martin G. Kocher, Helmut Rainer, Judith Saurer, and Thomas Siedler. 2021. "More Opportunity, More Cooperation? The Behavioral Effects of Birthright Citizenship on Immigrant Youth." *Journal of Public Economics* 200: 104448.

Fouka, Vasiliki. 2020. "Backlash: The Unintended Effects of Language Prohibition in U.S. Schools After World War I." *The Review of Economic Studies* 87 (1): 204–39.

Fouka, Vasiliki. 2023. "Language Policies in Education and the Possibility of Identity Backlash." In *Nation-Building: Big Lessons from Successes and Failures*, edited by Dominic Rohner and Ekaterina Zhuravskaya. CEPR.

Freire, Paulo. 1970. *Pedagogy of the Oppressed*. Continuum.

Gellner, Ernest. 2008. *Nations and Nationalism*: Cornell University Press.

Giuliano, Paola, Bryony Reich, and Alessandro Riboni. 2023. "What Motivates Leaders to Invest in Nation-Building?" In *Nation-Building: Big Lessons from Successes and Failures*, edited by Dominic Rohner and Ekaterina Zhuravskaya. CEPR.

Henkel, Owen, Nessie Kozhakhmetova, Hannah Horne-Robinson, and Amanda Lee. 2024. "Effective and Scalable Math Support: Experimental Evidence on the Impact of an AI-Math Tutor in Ghana." Working paper.

Hobsbawm, E. J. 1990. *Nations and Nationalism Since 1780: Programme, Myth, Reality*. Cambridge University Press.

Krause, Ben, Michael Kremer, Eduardo Rivera, and Enrique Seira. 2024. "The Influence of Historical Narrative on Individual and National Identity." Slides.

Laitin, David D., and Rajesh Ramachandran. 2022. "Linguistic Diversity, Official Language Choice and Human Capital," *Journal of Development Economics* 156: 102811.

Meriläinen, Jaakko, and Matti Mitrunen. 2024. "Long-Run Consequences of Propaganda in the Classroom." Working paper.

Mollick, Ethan R., and Lilach Mollick. 2023. "Assigning AI: Seven Approaches for Students, with Prompts." Research paper. Wharton School.

Mollick, Ethan R., and Lilach Mollick. 2024. "Instructors as Innovators: A Future-Focused Approach to New AI Learning Opportunities, with Prompt." Research paper. Wharton School

Paglayan, Agustina. 2024. *Raised to Obey: The Rise and Spread of Mass Education*. Princeton University Press.

Ramachandran, Rajesh. 2017. "Language Use in Education and Human Capital Formation: Evidence from the Ethiopian Educational Reform." *World Development* 98: 195–213.

Ramirez, F. O., and J. Boli. 1987. "The Political Construction of Mass Schooling: European Origins and Worldwide Institutionalization." *Sociology of Education* 60 (1): 2–17.

Rohner, Dominic, and Ekaterina Zhuravskaya. 2023. *Nation Building: Big Lessons from Successes and Failures*. CEPR Press.

Rohner, Dominic, and Ekaterina Zhuravskaya. 2025. "The Economics of Nation-Building: Methodological Tool Kit and Policy Lessons." *Annual Review of Economics*.17 (August 2025): 453–478. https://doi.org/10.1146/annurev-economics-081224-103104

Ruan, Sherry, Liwei Jiang, Qianyao Xu, Zhiyuan Liu, Glenn M. Davis, Emma

Brunskill, and James A. Landay. 2021. "EnglishBot: An AI-Powered Conversational System for Second Language Learning." In *Proceedings of the 26th International Conference on Intelligent User Interfaces* (IUI '21), April 14–17, College Station, TX. ACM, 2021. https://doi.org/10.1145/3397481.3450648.

Sakalli, Seyhun Orcan. 2019. "Secularization and Religious Backlash: Evidence from Turkey." Working paper.

Tan, Mei, and Dorottya Demszky. 2023. "Sit Down Now: How Teachers' Language Reveals the Dynamics of Classroom Management Practices."

Tilly, C. 1975. "Reflections on the History of European State-Making." In *The Formation of National States in Western Europe*, edited by C. Tilly. Princeton University Press.

Weber, Eugen. 1976. *Peasants into Frenchmen: The Modernization of Rural France, 1870–1914*. Stanford University Press.

Wu, Rong, and Zhonggen Yu. 2024. "Do AI Chatbots Improve Students Learning Outcomes? Evidence from a Meta-Analysis." *British Journal of Educational Technology* 55 (1): 10–33.

10

Robotization and the Political Response of Politicians

Maria Petrova, Gregor Schubert, Bledi Taska, and Pinar Yildirim

10.1 Introduction

Technology is a powerful force shaping individuals' experiences in the labor market, significantly impacting both their short- and long-term economic outcomes (Acemoglu and Restrepo 2018). Among recent technological shifts, the rapid rise in robotization has arguably had the most profound effect on the workforce over the past two decades. According to the Inter-

Maria Petrova is a professor of economics and ICREA Research Professor at the Universitat Pompeu Fabra, research professor at Barcelona School of Economics, and a researcher at the Barcelona Institute for Political Economy and Governance (IPEG).

Gregor Schubert is an assistant professor of finance at the UCLA Anderson School of Management.

Bledi Taska is chief data and analytics officer at TalentNeuron.

Pinar Yildirim is an associate professor of marketing at the Wharton School and an associate professor by courtesy in the Department of Economics at the University of Pennsylvania, and a faculty research fellow of the National Bureau of Economic Research.

Authors are listed alphabetically. This chapter was initially part of the working paper titled "Automation, Career Values and Political Preferences" by the same authors. We are grateful to Burning Glass Technologies for providing the data used in the analyses. We thank Daron Acemoglu, Christian Dustmann, John Friedman, Sergei Guriev, Rafael Lalive, Guy Michaels, Joan Monras, Giacomo Ponzetto, Piero Stanig, Daniel Sturm, Marco Tabellini, Ekaterina Zhuravskaya, the audiences at Aarhus, Berkeley, Berlin, Bologna, Carlos III, CEPR Labour Symposium 2024, CREI, Dortmund, Hamburg, Harvard, HEC, LISER, Northwestern, Padua, Paris School of Economics, Pompeu Fabra, Schwartz Reisman Institute, Sciences Po, Stanford, Autònoma Barcelona, UCL, and "Studying Critical Junctions" Conference in Munich and Resek Conference at UIUC for their extremely valuable feedback. We thank Felipe Barbieri, Nikita Belyi, Fedor Boboshin, Felipe Brugues, Mario Carillo, Sebastian Ellingsen, Gregori Galofre-Vila, Adilzhan Ismailov, Shreya Mathur, Elisa Mougin, Milan Quentel, Gianluca Russo, Juan Andres Russy, Nikita Varyoshkin, Yihao Yuan, and Georgii Zherebilov for excellent research assistance. Maria Petrova thanks funding from the European Research Council (ERC) under the European Union Horizon 2020 research and innovation program (Grant Agreement 803506), the Plan Nacional project PID2020–120118GBI0, and the Severo Ochoa

national Federation of Robotics, the number of robots installed annually more than doubled between 2013 and 2023, increasing from 13,000 to over 44,000 per year.[1] As of September 2024, there were over four million robots operating worldwide.

Parallel to the growth in robotization, numerous studies have documented its negative impact on labor markets. Acemoglu and Restrepo (2019) found that robots have led to job displacement and loss in the short term. Within individual firms, wage effects have been mixed: higher-skilled workers have seen wage increases, while lower-skilled workers have experienced declines (Acemoglu and Restrepo 2024). This wage inequality extends beyond individual firms, with studies reporting increased aggregate wage disparity in the US due to higher levels of robotization (Acemoglu and Restrepo 2022).

Income declines resulting from job loss and wage reductions have been documented as significant sources of economic shocks, which, in turn, shape individuals' political responses (Guriev and Papaioannou 2022; Panunzi et al. 2024). Politicians who understand how their constituents react to these economic shocks may seek to leverage these fluctuations to their advantage. However, the literature has yet to fully explore or document how politicians respond to labor market changes driven by automation and the resulting waves of unemployment.

In this paper, we examine the supply-side political response to robotization, focusing specifically on how politicians respond to increasing automation. To achieve this, we conduct an analysis using data from the International Federation of Robotics, examining how robotization evolved in the US between 2000 and 2016. We investigate various political responses, such as the campaign visits of presidential candidates in the 2016 elections and the policy positions of elected officials, inferred from their roll-call votes.

Robot adoption affects both people's electoral preferences and, in response, politicians' behavior in multiple ways. Research indicates that robotization has contributed to rising unemployment, greater inequality (Acemoglu and Restrepo 2022), and diminished opportunities for upward mobility (Petrova et al. 2024). In theory, such negative economic shocks can drive support for politicians on both extremes of the political spectrum (Margalit 2019). Studies suggest that recent economic transformations, especially skill-biased technological change and globalization, have led to future income losses and, consequently, increased support for right-wing

Programme for Centres of Excellence in R&D (Barcelona School of Economics CEX2019–000915-S), funded by MCIN/AEI/10.13039/501100011033. Yildirim thanks the Mack Institute and the Dean's Research Fund at the Wharton School for their research support. For acknowledgments, sources of research support, and disclosure of the authors' material financial relationships, if any, please see https://www.nber.org/books-and-chapters/political-economy-artificial-intelligence/robotization-and-political-response-politicians.

1. "U.S. Companies Invest Heavily in Robots—IFR Preliminary Results," International Federation of Robotics Press Release, April 20, 2024, https://ifr.org/ifr-press-releases/news/u.s-companies-invest-heavily-in-robots

and populist politicians. Frey et al. (2018) and Petrova et al. (2024) suggest that in the United States, robot adoption has bolstered electoral support for Donald Trump, who is viewed as the most populist of recent Republican presidential nominees. Additionally, Anelli et al. (2021) and Gallego et al. (2022) argue that robot adoption and digitalization have pushed individuals further toward right-leaning political preferences.

There are theoretical foundations for these effects. Guiso et al. (2017) and Di Tella and Rotemberg (2018) argue that income loss and feelings of betrayal can foster anti-elite sentiments. Similarly, Panunzi et al. (2024) present a theory in which income dissatisfaction resulting from economic loss makes disillusioned voters more risk tolerant in their political choices, ultimately increasing support for populist candidates.

We construct a dataset using preexisting industry shares weighted by the US robot adoption rates within corresponding industries. We examine how robot exposure in commuting zones—geographic areas where people are likely to work—affects certain political behaviors. Specifically, we analyze campaign visits during the 2016 presidential election, distinguishing between all campaign visits and those that are late in the campaign, in October and November. To account for potential endogeneity, we use robot adoption in select EU countries (Denmark, Italy, Sweden, Finland, France, Germany, and the UK) as an instrument for the robot adoption in the US, following the approach of Acemoglu and Restrepo (2020) and Faber et al. (2022).

We find that the Republican presidential candidate, Donald Trump, was more likely to visit areas with higher robot exposure, particularly in October (on average) and in November, within the high-manufacturing commuting zones (those with manufacturing employment above the median). Our findings indicate that each additional robot per 1,000 workers increased campaign visits by an average of 1.03 visits in October and 0.7 visits in November. We do not observe a similar effect for the Democratic presidential candidate in 2016, Hillary Clinton.

We also examine the effect of robot adoption on the policy positions of congressional representatives, as inferred from their roll call votes. Specifically, we utilize NOMINATE scores from Poole and Rosenthal (2011) and McCarty et al. (2006), along with similar roll-call-based scores from Nokken and Poole (2004). Our findings indicate that in areas with greater exposure to robots, politicians were more likely to shift their policy preferences to the right.

Our results suggest that the effects of labor-displacing technologies, such as robot adoption, extend beyond shifts in electoral preferences; they also lead politicians to adjust their behavior. Specifically, our findings show that politicians modify both their campaign strategies and their roll-call voting patterns once elected.

The chapter is organized as follows: Section 10.2 provides a summary of the data and outlines the methodology, Section 10.3 presents the empirical results, and Section 10.4 concludes.

10.2 Empirical Strategy

10.2.1 Data

We use several data sources in this chapter, which we detail here before we describe the empirical specification. We aggregate all data at the level of commuting zones based on 1990 boundaries.

Robot stock data. To measure exposure to robots, we follow the literature and gather data from the International Federation of Robotics (IFR), an association that reports annual statistics on the number of robots installed and in operation for a number of North American and European countries (Acemoglu and Restrepo 2019). The dataset contains data from various industries, codified according to the International Standard Industrial Classification (ISIC) code. We map these codes to the North American Industrial Classification to be able to map the labor market shares to relevant industries. IFR's historical data provides information about nearly 50 countries and dates to 1993, and it is claimed to cover roughly 90 percent of the robot market. However, it is only after 2004 that the data contain a mapping between the robot data and the industries. For more details on this data set, please see Petrova et al. (2024).

Campaign visit data. Data on campaign visits come from Devine (2019). Devine collects and reports data for the campaign visits of the 2016 presidential candidates, and we aggregate it to the commuting zone level. We were not able to obtain similar campaign visit datasets for the 2008 and 2012 elections.

From an anecdotal perspective, looking at data on the content of campaign speeches demonstrates that it is not unusual for political candidates to directly address job losses, often with specific examples from the manufacturing industry. Anecdotally, speeches tend to put the blame on "Capitol Hill" or elite politicians, who forgot about the working class. For instance, on June 28, 2016, during a campaign visit in Monessen, PA, presidential candidate Donald Trump made a stop at Alumisource, a metals recycling facility, and made the following speech:

> Our politicians have aggressively pursued a policy of globalization—moving our jobs, our wealth and our factories to Mexico and overseas. Globalization has made the financial elite who donate to politicians very wealthy. But it has left millions of our workers with nothing but poverty and heartache. For years, they watched on the sidelines as our jobs vanished and our communities were plunged into depression-level unemployment. Our politicians took away from the people their means of making a living and supporting their families. Skilled craftsmen and tradespeople

and factory workers have seen the jobs they loved shipped thousands of miles away. Many Pennsylvania towns once thriving and humming are now in a state despair.[2]

Political ideology of politicians. We measure political ideologies by using NOMINATE and Nokken and Poole scores for the US House of Representatives for the year 2016, available via Voteview (voteview.com).

Demographic characteristics of a region. We also use several Census-based variables, primarily as commuting-zone-level controls, including population, share of females, age characteristicssuch as share of population older than 65 years, education characteristics like shares of population with no college, some college, college and professional degrees, and masters and doctoral degrees; as well as racial characteristics like shares of Whites, Blacks, Hispanics, and Asians in a commuting zone. We use data from the 2000 Census in the US.

Labor market characteristics of a region. We also control for the general labor market characteristics by including share of employment in manufacturing, share of female employment in manufacturing, and share of employment in light manufacturing (e.g., textile industry and the paper, publishing, and printing industry).

10.2.2 Empirical Estimation

We are interested in establishing a causal relationship between robotization and the response of politicians to the changes that followed robotization. The overall empirical strategy in this chapter is detailed in Petrova et al. (2024), and we refer the readers to this study. More specifically, we run regressions of the following form:

$$(1) \quad Political\_Reponse_{c,t} = \beta_1 + \beta_2 Exposure\_to\_robots_{c,(t_0,t_1)} + \beta X_c + \varepsilon^{\ell}_{c,t},$$

where $Political\_Reponse_{c,t_1}$ is the observed political response by a politician at time t in a commuting zone (CZ) c. This response is triggered by the economic and labor market outcomes that come as a result of labor market exposure to robotization in CZ c over period (t_0,t_1), $Exposure\_to\_robots_{c,(t_0,t_1)}$.

To address potential confounders at the level of commuting zones, we include a rich set of control variables that are common in the robotization literature (e.g., Acemoglu and Restrepo 2019; Faber et al. 2019; Petrova et al. 2024) and use an instrumental variables approach explained in detail subsequently. More specifically, X_c includes the controls for region c from 1990, including log of population, share of females (in total population), share of population older than 65 years, share of population with high school, some college, college and postgraduate education, share of Whites,

2. Politico Staff, "Full Transcript: Donald Trump NYC Speech on Jobs," *Politico*, June 28, 2016, https://www.politico.com/story/2016/06/full-transcript-trump-job-plan-speech-224891.

African Americans, Hispanics, and Asians (in total population), share of employment in manufacturing, share of female employment in manufacturing, share in light manufacturing (textile industry and the paper, publishing, and printing industry), share of employment in routine occupations, using data from the American Community Survey and County Business Patterns. This specification follows Petrova et al. (2024), which builds on Acemoglu and Restrepo (2020). For the analysis, we focus on the period 2000–2016, for which we have detailed outcome data.

The right-hand-side variable is measured as the exposure to robots introduced in a commuting zone CZ c in period (t_0,t_1), $Exposure\_to\_robots_{c,(t_0,t_1)}$, as in Acemoglu and Restrepo (2019), Faber et al. (2019), and Petrova et al. (2024). This measure combines an exposure due to local industry employment shares with a "shifter" in the form of a change in the robot stock impacting a particular industry code. Specifically, exposure to robots in commuting zone c over the period (t_0,t_1), denoted as $Exposure\_to\_robots_{c,(t_0,t_1)}$, is calculated as the product of the local industry employment share and the average of the change in robot stock within a given industry, following the approach of Acemoglu and Restrepo (2019) and Faber et al. (2019):

$$Exposure\_to\_robots_{c,(t_0,t_1)} = \sum_{i \in \iota} l_{ci} \Delta APR_{i,(t_0,t_1)},$$

where $\Delta APR_{i,(t_0,t_1)}$ represents the change in adjusted robot penetration in industry i between t_0, and t_1, and l_{ci} is the share of industry i employment in total employment in CZ c.

The above specification is subject to endogeneity concerns. Local labor market shares may be influenced by unobserved factors that simultaneously drive both employment patterns and the adoption of robots, introducing potential bias in the estimates. To address this issue, we adopt an instrumental variables (IV) approach, consistent with Acemoglu and Restrepo (2019) and Petrova et al. (2024). Specifically, we instrument robot adoption in the US using data on robots installed in a subset of European countries (Denmark, Italy, Sweden, Finland, France, Germany, and UK). This strategy exploits variation in robot adoption driven by industry-level dynamics in Europe while minimizing the influence of local US labor market conditions, providing a more robust estimate of the causal impact of robot exposure.

10.3 Results

In this section, we report whether the economic shocks generated through robotization demand for populism, as identified in the previous literature, Guriev and Papaioannou (2022); Panunzi et al. (2024), triggered some changes in the behavior of politicians. To illustrate the deliberate campaigning patterns of presidential candidates, figure 10.1, sourced from the website

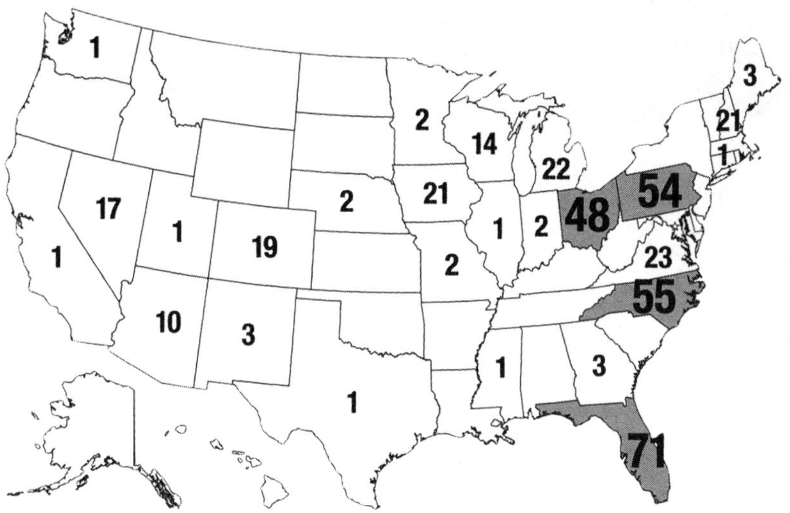

Fig. 10.1 Number of campaign visits by Donald Trump to each state, 2016 presidential campaign

Note: The figure is reprinted from NationalVote.com.

NationalVote.com, shows the number of campaign visits by Donald Trump to each state when he was a presidential candidate in 2016. The figure demonstrates that Trump's campaign visits were more heavily concentrated on the East Coast of the United States. More than half of these visits are in states considered part of the Rust Belt: Illinois, Indiana, Michigan, Missouri, New York, Ohio, Pennsylvania, West Virginia, and Wisconsin.

In table 10.1, we check if the automation exposure of a CZ is correlated with the number of campaign visits to that location, looking separately at the visits by the Republican and Democratic presidential candidates while campaigning for the 2016 presidential election. We find no significant evidence of Democratic candidates' more frequent campaign visits to CZs with higher automation exposure. Still, we find a positive association for the Republican candidate. One standard deviation increase in robot exposure is associated with 0.83 additional visits to a CZ for the Republican candidate in October 2016 and 0.45 additional visits in November. When we split the commuting zones as high-manufacturing and low-manufacturing based on the median share of labor force in manufacturing occupations, Panel B shows that this increase is guided exclusively by a significant increase in the number of visits of the Republican candidate in the high-manufacturing CZs, and that this effect is concentrated in the last months of the campaign (columns 1 and 4 include visits from July to November 2016). Panel C indicates no significant association between campaign visits and robot exposure in areas with a

Table 10.1. Robot adoption and campaign visits, 2016

	Republicans			Democrats		
	All (1)	November 2016 (2)	October 2016 (3)	All (4)	November 2016 (5)	October 2016 (6)
Panel A: All CZs						
US robot exposure '04–'16	1.216	0.454**	0.835*	–0.693	–0.470	–0.214
	(1.105)	(0.206)	(0.457)	(1.677)	(0.379)	(0.715)
Mean of DV	1.924	0.293	0.823	1.708	0.334	0.655
KP *F*-stat.	1327	1327	1327	1327	1327	1327
Observations	722	722	722	722	722	722
Panel B: High-manufacturing CZs						
US robot exposure '04–'16	0.918	0.617***	0.532	–0.818	–0.647	–0.068
	(1.257)	(0.137)	(0.561)	(1.852)	(0.572)	(0.752)
Mean of DV	2.767	0.329	1.283	2.221	0.454	0.857
KP *F*-stat.	615	615	615	615	615	615
Observations	362	362	362	362	362	362
Panel C: Low-manufacturing CZs						
US robot exposure '04–'16	1.774	4.495	0.803	24.006	4.822	11.784
	(15.029)	(8.150)	(2.222)	(44.375)	(6.923)	(19.910)
Mean of DV	1.076	0.257	0.361	1.193	0.213	0.452
KP *F*-stat.	9	9	9	9	9	9
Observations	360	360	360	360	360	360
Census Division FE	Yes	Yes	Yes	Yes	Yes	Yes
Controls	Yes	Yes	Yes	Yes	Yes	Yes

Notes: Robust standard errors are in brackets and clustered by state. All columns include census division dummies as well as controls for demographic characteristics of commuting zones in 1990 identical to those in Acemoglu and Restrepo (2020) (log population; the share of females; share of population older than 65 years; share of population with no college, some college, college and professional degrees, and master's and doctoral degrees; the shares of Whites, Blacks, Hispanics, and Asians; the share of employment in manufacturing; the share of female employment in manufacturing; the share of employment in light manufacturing, namely, textile industry and the paper, publishing, and printing industry; the share of employment in routine occupations using data from the American Community Survey and County Business Patterns). US robot exposure is instrumented using robot exposure in Denmark, Italy, Sweden, Finland, France, Germany, and UK in the same periods. Observations are weighted by commuting zone population.

***$p < .01$. **$p < .05$. *$p < .10$.

low proportion of manufacturing, although this finding comes with wide confidence intervals because the instrument is weaker for this subgroup of geographies, as indicated by the F-statistics.

We also ask whether exposure to automation and robotization translated into differential policies. Table 10.2 presents roll-call votes by politicians as well as the Nokken and Poole (2004) scores for the US House of Representatives for the year 2016 (Lewis et al. 2023). Here, a score of −1 indicates a far-left ideology, a score of 1 indicates a far-right ideology, and near 0 represents moderate ideologies. Panel A in the table finds no correlation on average between a CZ's robot exposure and the score of the candidates representing it in the House of Representatives. Panels B and C break down the CZs by high- and low-manufacturing labor shares. In columns 1 and 2, we see that in CZs with higher manufacturing intensity, greater exposure to automation is associated with a more conservative record of the politician representing the CZ, whereas there is no statistically significant relationship in low-manufacturing-intensity regions. Specifically, in high-manufacturing areas, a one-unit increase in automation exposure of labor is associated with a 0.030-percentage-point increase in the roll-call score, controlling for the score in 2012. This implies a more conservative roll-call voting behavior.

In columns 3, 4, 7, and 8, we consider the effect on absolute changes in ideology scores and find that exposure to robotization is related to an increase in the absolute level of scores. This suggests a rise in extreme political views. This effect is evident in both high- and low-manufacturing CZs, with the largest effect observed in low-manufacturing areas. Together with the smaller and statistically not significant change in the average political bias of local politicians' votes, this implies that some politicians in low-manufacturing CZs became more left leaning in ideology, even as others may have moved to the right. This change in absolute levels of ideology is consistent with the perception of increasing polarization in the country, and it may indicate that the differential effects of automation exposure could be one of its drivers.

10.4 Conclusion

In this study, we have reported a few key findings regarding the political response to automation. While a number of studies document the demand side of political response to robotization (Petrova et al. 2024), how politicians' rhetoric changes in response to growing robotization has been underdocumented.

Our findings demonstrate that increased exposure to robots in high-manufacturing areas is associated with politicians' campaign strategies and likely contributed to the observable shifts in the policy positions of elected officials. Specifically, the analysis of the 2016 presidential election reveals that the Republican candidate, Donald Trump, targeted regions with high robot adoption in his campaign visits during the critical months of October and November, and in commuting zones with a higher share of manufacturing workers. This campaign focus is likely to capitalize on the economic concerns and sense of disenfranchisement among voters in these areas (Guriev and Papaioannou 2022), where income loss and economic insecurity heighten anti-elite and populist sentiments (Rodrik 2021).

Table 10.2. **Automation and roll-call votes**

	Nominate scores (House of Representatives)				Nokken Poole (House of Representatives)			
	2016 score (1)	2016 score (2)	2016 Abs score (3)	2016 Abs score (4)	2016 score (5)	2016 score (6)	2016 Abs score (7)	2016 Abs score (8)
Panel A: All CZs								
US robot exposure '04–'16	0.016	0.014	0.011	0.011	0.012	0.010	0.008	0.007
	(0.025)	(0.024)	(0.014)	(0.014)	(0.027)	(0.026)	(0.016)	(0.015)
Ideology '12		–0.091		–0.052		–0.096		–0.099
		(0.127)		(0.106)		(0.131)		(0.113)
Mean of DV	0.311	0.313	0.351	0.353	0.317	0.319	0.359	0.362
SD of DV	0.240	0.240	0.176	0.175	0.253	0.253	0.188	0.187
F-stat.	1325	1209	1325	1249	1325	1216	1325	1245
Observations	719	714	719	714	719	714	719	714
Panel B: High-manufacturing CZs								
US robot exposure '04–'16	0.034*	0.030*	0.027**	0.026**	0.032	0.027	0.026**	0.025**
	(0.018)	(0.016)	(0.011)	(0.011)	(0.020)	(0.018)	(0.013)	(0.012)
Ideology '12		–0.271*		–0.129		–0.295*		–0.182
		(0.157)		(0.118)		(0.162)		(0.124)

Mean of DV	0.287	0.288	0.334	0.335	0.291	0.292	0.342	0.343
SD of DV	0.243	0.243	0.173	0.172	0.256	0.256	0.183	0.182
F-stat.	615	672	615	630	615	658	615	618
Observations	362	361	362	361	362	361	362	361
Panel C: Low-manufacturing CZs								
US robot exposure '04–'16	–0.267	–0.225	0.362*	0.386**	–0.337	–0.304	0.331*	0.370**
	(0.227)	(0.235)	(0.192)	(0.181)	(0.233)	(0.235)	(0.200)	(0.189)
Ideology '12		0.007		0.226		–0.014		0.225
		(0.097)		(0.184)		(0.094)		(0.196)
Mean of DV	0.336	0.338	0.369	0.372	0.342	0.346	0.377	0.381
SD of DV	0.235	0.235	0.178	0.176	0.248	0.247	0.191	0.189
F-stat.	10	8	10	9	10	7	10	9
Observations	357	353	357	353	357	353	357	353
Census Division FE	Yes	Yes	Yes	Yes	Yes	Yes	Yes	Yes
Controls	Yes	Yes	Yes	Yes	Yes	Yes	Yes	Yes

Notes: Robust standard errors are in brackets and clustered by state. All columns include census division dummies as well as controls for demographic characteristics of commuting zones in 1990 identical to those in Acemoglu and Restrepo (2020) (log population; the share of females; the share of population above 65 years; the share of population with no college, some college, college and professional degrees, and master's and doctoral degrees; the shares of Whites, Blacks, Hispanics, and Asians; the share of employment in manufacturing; the share of female employment in manufacturing; and the share of employment in light manufacturing, namely, textile industry and the paper, publishing, and printing industry; the share of employment in routine occupations using data from the American Community Survey and County Business Patterns). We also control for the scores from 2012 in columns 2, 4, 6, and 8. US robot exposure is instrumented using robot exposure in Denmark, Italy, Sweden, Finland, France, Germany and UK in the same time periods. Observations are weighted by commuting zone population.

***$p < .01$. **$p < .05$. *$p < .10$.

Moreover, the effects of robotization and politicians' responses extend beyond the electoral period to longer-term effects, including the congressional representatives' voting behaviors. We observe a rightward shift in policy preferences in response to robotization, as measured by the NOMINATE and Nokken and Poole (2004) scores. Therefore, it is possible that the economic concerns of the electorate, influenced by robotization, reflect on the political attitudes and decision-making among legislators. This trend might be partly because the profile and the party of the elected representatives change as robotization alters the political preferences of the electorate (Petrova et al. 2024), or because the politicians themselves start to take different policy positions in response.

Our findings highlight the impact of automation penetrating the political arena. Robotization has repercussions of political shifts, and a potential for increased polarization, which puts pressure on representatives to adopt positions that resonate with the impacted constituencies. Overall, our research points to the need for studies addressing the economic and political challenges posed by automation and the consequences of labor market disruptions on policymakers.

References

Acemoglu, D., and P. Restrepo. 2018. "The Race Between Man and Machine: Implications of Technology for Growth, Factor Shares, and Employment." *American Economic Review* 108 (6): 1488–1542.

Acemoglu, D., and P. Restrepo. 2019. "Automation and New Tasks: How Technology Displaces and Reinstates Labor." *Journal of Economic Perspectives* 33 (2): 3–30.

Acemoglu, D., and P. Restrepo. 2020. "Robots and Jobs: Evidence from US Labor Markets." *Journal of Political Economy* 128 (6): 2188–2244.

Acemoglu, D., and P. Restrepo. 2022. "Tasks, Automation, and the Rise in US Wage Inequality." *Econometrica* 90 (5): 1973–2016.

Acemoglu, D., and P. Restrepo. 2024. "Automation and Rent Dissipation: Implications for Wages, Inequality, and Productivity." Technical report, National Bureau of Economic Research.

Anelli, M., I. Colantone, and P. Stanig. 2021. "Individual Vulnerability to Industrial Robot Adoption Increases Support for the Radical Right." *Proceedings of the National Academy of Sciences* 118 (47): e2111611118.

Devine, C. J. 2019. "Voter Mobilization 101: Presidential Campaign Visits to Colleges and Universities in the 2016 Election." *PS: Political Science & Politics* 52 (2): 261–66.

Di Tella, R., and J. J. Rotemberg. 2018. "Populism and the Return of the 'Paranoid Style': Some Evidence and a Simple Model of Demand for Incompetence as Insurance Against Elite Betrayal." *Journal of Comparative Economics* 46 (4): 988–1005.

Faber, M., A. Sarto, and M. Tabellini. 2019. "The Impact of Technology and Trade on Migration: Evidence from the US." BGIE Unit Working Paper (20–071), Harvard Business School.

Faber, M., A. P. Sarto, and M. Tabellini. 2022. "Local Shocks and Internal Migration: The Disparate Effects of Robots and Chinese Imports in the US." NBER Working Paper No. 30048. National Bureau of Economic Research.
Frey, C. B., T. Berger, and C. Chen. 2018. "Political Machinery: Did Robots Swing the 2016 US Presidential Election?" *Oxford Review of Economic Policy* 34 (3): 418–42.
Gallego, A., T. Kurer, and N. Schöll. 2022. "Neither Left Behind nor Superstar: Ordinary Winners of Digitalization at the Ballot Box." *The Journal of Politics* 84 (1): 418–36.
Guiso, L., H. Herrera, M. Morelli, T. Sonno, et al. 2017. "Demand and Supply of Populism." Centre for Economic Policy Research.
Guriev, S., and E. Papaioannou. 2022. "The Political Economy of Populism." *Journal of Economic Literature* 60 (3): 753–832.
Lewis, J. B., K. Poole, H. Rosenthal, A. Boche, A. Rudkin, and L. Sonnet. 2023. "Voteview: Congressional Roll-Call Votes Database." https://voteview.com.
Margalit, Y. 2019. "Political Responses to Economic Shocks." *Annual Review of Political Science* 22 (1): 277–95.
McCarty, N., K. Poole, and H. Rosenthal. 2006. *Polarized America: The Dance of Ideology and Unequal Riches*. Walras-Pareto Lectures. MIT Press.
Nokken, T. P., and K. T. Poole. 2004. "Congressional Party Defection in American History." *Legislative Studies Quarterly* 29 (4): 545–68.
Panunzi, F., N. Pavoni, and G. Tabellini. 2024. "Economic Shocks and Populism." *The Economic Journal* 134 (663): 3047–61.
Petrova, M., G. Schubert, B. Taska, and P. Yildirim. 2024. "Automation, Career Values, and Political Preferences." https://ssrn.com/abstract=4728005.
Poole, K., and H. Rosenthal. 2011. *Ideology and Congress*. American Studies. Transaction Publishers.
Rodrik, D. 2021. "Why Does Globalization Fuel Populism? Economics, Culture, and the Rise of Right-Wing Populism." *Annual Review of Economics* 13 (1): 133–70.

Comment

Italo Colantone

I was delighted to have the opportunity to act as a discussant for this paper at the NBER Economics of Artificial Intelligence Conference, held in Toronto in September 2024.

Based on rich individual-level data, the authors estimate the career value of occupations, combining information on the likelihood of transitions across occupations with the earning potential of these occupations. The paper documents a downward trend in the growth of career values in the

Italo Colantone is an associate professor of economic policy at Bocconi University, the director of the GREEN Research Centre, and a research fellow of the BAFFI Research Centre, CESifo, IEP, and FEEM.

For acknowledgments, sources of research support, and disclosure of the author's material financial relationships, if any, please see https://www.nber.org/books-and-chapters/political-economy-artificial-intelligence/comment-robotization-and-political-response-politicians-colantone.

US between 2000 and 2016. This is mostly driven by reduced upward occupational mobility. At the level of commuting zones, higher exposure to robot adoption lowers average career values. The effect is more pronounced for low-skilled individuals. Lower career values, in turn, are related to lower investment in schooling and housing, and to higher electoral support for candidate Trump in the 2016 presidential elections.

I find the focus on career values very interesting, as they provide an important summary indicator of labor market dynamics. Overall, I think the analysis is rich and carefully executed. I also appreciate that the study spans beyond labor-market dynamics, although perhaps at the risk of some loss in focus. In my discussion, I have made some comments about the instrumental variables (IV) strategies adopted in the paper and about the way some of the results are interpreted. I summarize my points in what follows.

In the spirit of Acemoglu and Restrepo (2020), the authors instrument robot adoption in the US using robot adoption in European countries. The intuition behind this approach is that of exploiting technological trajectories that are (1) relevant for automation, (2) common across countries, and (3) exogenous to local conditions across US labor markets. I am sympathetic with this approach, which I have employed in my own work joint with Massimo Anelli and Piero Stanig (Anelli et al. 2019, 2021). However, there may be a problem with the exclusion restriction, given the presence of demand and supply shocks that are correlated across countries. This limitation is particularly evident if one thinks of the automotive industry, where the largest share of robots is adopted. Here we have that the same companies are often producing both in the US and in Europe (e.g., Ford, FCA), leading to decisions about robot adoption in these two geographical contexts that are ultimately under the control of the same management. The role of correlated shocks seems to be actually relevant for the results. For instance, the power of the instrument is much lower in the period after the financial crisis of 2008, which is when the business cycles of the US and Europe diverge.

Having faced this problem in my own work, I have suggested a possible alternative instrumental variables approach, as introduced in an updated version of Anelli et al. (2019) and later in Anelli et al. (2021). In particular, in our cross-country European analysis, we define the following:

$$(1) \quad IV \text{ Regional Exposure}_{crt} = \sum_j \frac{L_{crj}^{pre-sample}}{L_{cr}^{pre-sample}} * Rep_j * \Delta Index_{t-1,t-n},$$

where c indexes countries, r regions, and t years. $(L_{crj}^{pre-sample} / L_{cr}^{pre-sample})$ is the pre-sample share of each industry out of the total employment of each region. Rep_j is an industry-level replaceability index—that is, the share of hours worked within industry j in occupations replaceable by robots—as computed by Graetz and Michaels (2018) based on US Census data of 1980. $\Delta Index_{t-1,t-n}$ is the change in either average unit price of industrial robots sold in the US (IFR); producer index of computer prices (Fred); or one of two indexes of advances in computing, specifically single-thread performance and number of transistors per microprocessor. The idea behind this approach is to capture more directly global technological shifts in robots and computing that matter for automation, with heterogeneity across industries driven by their *ex ante* replaceability score. While the first two indexes may be problematic in this context, given the focus on the US, the other indexes may prove useful for an alternative IV approach.

In table 4 of the version of the paper presented at the conference, the power of the instrument seems to vary substantially across columns. In particular, the result in column 1 seems rather weak. Similar considerations apply elsewhere in the paper. I was wondering whether this is an implication of the IV Lasso approach. As a baseline, I think it would be better to exploit the same identifying variation across different regressions, especially when the comparison of magnitudes across specifications is so important.

When focusing on the effect of career value changes at the level of commuting zones, the authors introduce a new instrument. Specifically, they instrument the average career value of a commuting zone using the career values of sufficiently similar but distant communities. These are identified as commuting zones in states outside a 100-mile radius around the commuting zone of interest. The motivation behind this approach is not spelled out, and I am wondering where the power of this instrument comes from. If it comes from macro dynamics that are common across different areas of the US, then again there could be a problem with the exclusion restriction. As an alternative, one could select for the instrument commuting zones that are similar according to pre-sample characteristics, for instance, in terms of the composition of employment across industries.

I have a more general comment about the way results are interpreted in the analysis of the effects of career values. The authors interpret the effect of career value changes as an effect of long-run expectations held by individuals. However, career values also embody current income, which is likely to be relevant for housing, schooling, and voting decisions. This could be more openly acknowledged. If the authors want to disentangle the role of expectations from the role of current conditions, then they should find a way to separate the two pieces of information in the analysis.

As concluding remarks, I would suggest enriching and clarifying the discussion of mechanisms, especially concerning changes in consumption. I am wondering that consumer responses may be seen more as an outcome rather than a mechanism. I would also suggest providing more information on how occupational mobility is evaluated. In particular, upward versus downward mobility based on wages is clear, while other measures are less obvious. For instance, a transition from production to architecture or engineering seems constrained by education or qualifications. This is something that could be discussed more. Finally, the analysis spans the period of the Great Financial Crisis of 2007–8, but the possible implications for the results are not discussed. I would recommend that the authors engage with this.

Overall, I think there is a lot of value in this work. I hope my comments can be useful for improving it further.

References

Acemoglu, D., and P. Restrepo. 2020. "Robots and Jobs: Evidence from US Labor Markets." *Journal of Political Economy* 128 (6): 2188–2244.

Anelli, M., I. Colantone, and P. Stanig. 2019. "We Were the Robots: Automation and Voting Behavior in Western Europe." Research Paper, 2019–115. BAFFI CAREFIN Centre.

Anelli, M., I. Colantone, and P. Stanig. 2021. "Individual Vulnerability to Industrial Robot Adoption Increases Support for the Radical Right." *Proceedings of the National Academy of Sciences* 118 (47): e2111611118.

Graetz, G., and G. Michaels. 2018. "Robots at Work." *Review of Economics and Statistics* 100 (5): 753–68.

11

Political Preferences and Support for Artificial Intelligence

Jordan Mansell, Alexander Beyer, Ori Freiman,
John McAndrews, and Clifton van der Linden

Studies of technology show that the best predictors of support for AI are measures of technological optimism, defined as attitudes or beliefs that technologies will produce positive societal outcomes (Clark et al. 2016; Edison and Geissler 2003; Königs 2022). Unfortunately, because technology optimism measures are tautological, explaining support for AI technology with positive sentiments about technology, they provide little insight into the causes of attitude variation about AI, such as why some people are optimistic (Hochschild et al. 2012; Kelley et al. 2021). While this problem is recognized by researchers, there remains limited research into the source of these variations (Hochschild and Sen 2015; Kerschner and Ehlers 2016; for exceptions, see Chen and Wen 2021; Cruz-Cárdenas et al. 2019; Danaher 2022; Kleizen et al. 2023; Kreps et al. 2023).

Petrova et al. (2024) document that local exposure to factory robotics decreased employment and increased support for Trump in 2016, suggesting a connection between technology and political preferences. This discussion examines support for AI by political affiliation, as measured in a 2023 survey of residents of Toronto, Canada's largest city. The results suggest that

Jordan Mansell is an instructor in public policy at McMaster University and an adjunct professor of political science at Western University.

Alexander Beyer served as a postdoctoral fellow in the Department of Political Science and the Digital Society Lab at McMaster University.

Ori Freiman is a postdoctoral fellow in the Digital Society Lab at McMaster University.

John McAndrews is an adjunct assistant professor of political science and managing director of the Digital Society Lab at McMaster University.

Clifton van der Linden is an associate professor of political science and director of the Digital Society Lab at McMaster University.

For acknowledgments, sources of research support, and disclosure of the authors' material financial relationships, if any, please see https://www.nber.org/books-and-chapters/political-economy-artificial-intelligence/political-preferences-and-support-artificial-intelligence.

support for AI varies with party identification and that it positively and significantly correlates with conservative orientation.

11.1 Methods

11.1.1 Sample

We use the Vox Pop Labs Toronto Post Election Study (PES) dataset. The PES is a nonprobability survey of public attitudes and opinions administered June 26–July 13, 2023, following a Toronto mayoral election. Participants received no monetary compensation for their participation in the PES study. As the survey allows participants to skip questions, the number of observations in statistical models changes slightly with adjustment of our independent or control variables. Given our large sample size, small changes in the number of observations are unlikely to meaningfully affect the outcomes. Consequently, we do not standardize the number of observations in our dataset. Approximately 5,434 individuals completed the PES study. The number of observations ranges from 4,911 to 619. The reduction in sample size occurs because not all questions are asked of all participants. Ethics approval for this study was obtained from McMaster University #6571.

11.1.2 Politics in Canada

Canada operates using a federal system of parliamentary government. Multiple political parties compete within this system; however, the five parties with the most popular support in the province of Ontario are the New Democratic Party (NDP), the Green Party (GPC), the Liberal Party of Canada (LPC), the Conservative Party of Canada (CPC), and the People's Party of Canada (PPC). Ideologically, this party list is arranged from left to right, with the NDP being the most ideologically left and the People's Party the most ideologically right. The Liberal Party is currently the governing party of Canada. In the 2021 election, parties received the following share of the popular vote: NDP (17.8 percent), Green (2.3 percent), Liberal (32.6 percent), CPC (33.7 percent), PPC (4.9 percent) (Elections Canada 2024). Figure 11.1 visually represents these parties according to social and economic issues.

In terms of policies, the NDP, Green, and Liberal Parties all favor progressive social and economic policies. While the three parties are ideologically similar, the NDP distinguishes itself as the most vocal advocate for social justice and policies to support the economically least well-off Canadians (Goodyear-Grant 2013; Olive 2015). The Green Party is the strongest advocate for environmental policies and protections (Olive 2015). The Liberal Party is often described as a "big tent" party, practicing brokerage policies that attempt to balance progressive policies with responsible economic stew-

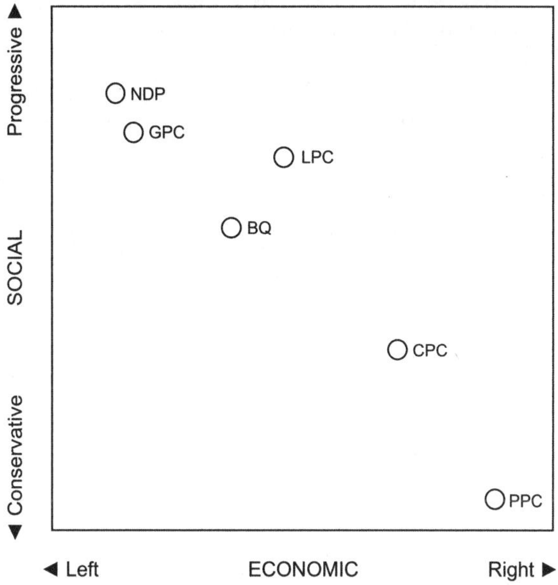

Fig. 11.1 Visual representation of the ideological positions of Canadian political parties in the 2021 election

Source: Vote Compass, https://votecompass.com.

Note: BQ refers to the Bloc Québécois, which runs candidates only in Quebec and therefore was not part of the Toronto post-election study.

ardship (Bittner and Koop 2013; Carty 2015). On the ideological right, the Conservative Party advocates for both socially and economically conservative policies (Gagnon and Tanguay 2017; Johnson 2016; Lewis and Everitt 2017; Smith 2014). In comparison, the People's Party of Canada is often described in the media as conservative with some right-wing populist and libertarian policies (Lévesque 2023; Vastal 2018).

11.1.3 Analysis

The analysis uses ordinary-least-squares (OLS) regression models with 95 percent confidence intervals. Attitudes toward AI are assessed using two separate dependent variables: Do you support or oppose the use of artificial intelligence in general? And, Should the use of artificial intelligence in general be encouraged or restricted? The response categories are described in table 11.1. Both outcomes were first recoded so that higher values denote more positive responses and that "don't know" responses are at the scale midpoint (as indicated in table 11.1); then, both outcomes were standardized to have a mean of 0 and a standard deviation of 1. All models include controls for political interest, knowledge and familiarity with AI, frequency

Table 11.1. **Scales and distributions of the separate dependent variables measure support and encouragement for use of AI**

Likert Scale	Support	Likert Scale	Encourage
Strongly oppose (1)	199 (3.6%)	Strongly restricted (1)	619 (11.3%)
Somewhat oppose (2)	958 (17.5%)	Somewhat restricted (2)	1,944 (35.67%)
Neither (3)	830 (15.2%)	Neither (3)	666 (12.2)
Don't know (3)	139 (2.5%)	Don't know (3)	175 (3.2%)
Somewhat support (4)	2,783 (50.9%)	Somewhat encouraged (4)	1,690 (30.9%)
Strongly support (5)	555 (10.2)	Strongly encouraged (5)	368 (6.7%)
Total	5464		5462

Table 11.2. **Scales and distributions of party vote in 2021 Canadian federal election and symbolic ideology**

Scale	Frequency	Scale	Frequency
NDP	1,525 (28.1%)	Left—0	397 (7.8%)
Greens	310 (5.7%)	1	494 (9.7%)
Liberal	2,804 (51.6%)	2	1,049 (20.7%)
CPC	536 (9.9%)	3	1,269 (25.0%)
PPC	76 (1.4%)	4	770 (15.2%)
Other	33 (0.6%)	5	246 (4.9%)
Spoiled	24 (0.4%)	6	370 (7.3%)
Didn't vote	126 (2.3%)	7	258 (5.1%)
		8	142 (2.8%)
		9	36 (0.7%)
		Right—10	42 (0.8%)
Total	5,434	Total	5,073

of internet use, as well as age, education, employment, income, and gender. The question wordings are provided in appendix D (https://osf.io/sequn/?view_only=803d430607d749ca8e7e16820278afdd).

Political preferences are assessed using two measures: party vote in the 2021 Canadian federal election and self-reported symbolic ideology. On the first independent variable, party vote, response options listed the five largest federal parties in the province of Ontario—New Democratic Party of Canada, Green Party of Canada, Liberal Party of Canada, Conservative Party of Canada, People's Party of Canada—as well as the alternative response options of "other party," "spoiled ballot," and "did not vote." The second independent variable, symbolic ideology, is assessed on an 11-point sliding scale: "In politics, people sometimes talk of left and right. Where would you place yourself on the scale below, where 0 is left and 10 is right?"

We report on three groups of statistical models. Model 1 examines how

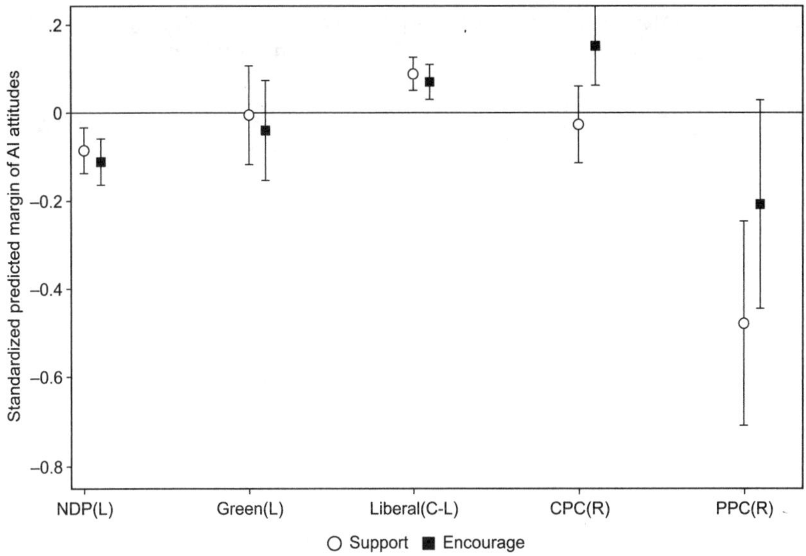

Fig. 11.2 The effect of party vote on support and encouragement for AI as estimated in Model 1

Note: For clarity we omitted values from respondents who stated their party vote as "other," who spoiled their ballot, or who did not vote. Each party's left (L), center-left (C-L), and right (R) ideological orientation is listed in brackets. The figure displays the predicted marginal means.

political preferences predict attitudes toward AI. Model 2 examines whether the relationship between political preferences and attitudes toward AI is independently mediated by four variables: openness to experience, future optimism, technology optimism, and AI optimism. Openness to experience is included because past studies demonstrate that it is a significant predictor of attitudes toward technology (Park and Woo 2022). Openness to experience is assessed using scale items from Gosling et al. (2003). The three measures of optimism are assessed using a 5-point Likert scale and the following question: "In general, I am optimistic about [the future, technology, artificial intelligence]." Participants were randomly assigned to answer one of the three optimism measures. Model 3 examines the correlations between political preferences and the four mediating variables.

11.2 Results

The results of model 1 are summarized in figure 11.2 and table 11.3. We report the postestimation standardized predicted marginal means for each party vote category; for ideology, which is treated as continuous, we simply

Table 11.3. **Model 1 summary statistics: Separate correlations between party vote in the 2021 federal election or symbolic ideology on support or encouragement of AI**

Dependent variables	(A) Support for AI use	(B) Support for AI use	(C) Belief that AI should be encouraged	(D) Belief that AI should be encouraged
Predicted marginal means				
NDP (L)	–0.084**		–0.110**	
	0.026		0.027	
Greens (L)	–0.006		–0.040	
	0.057		0.058	
Liberal (C-L)	0.088**		0.070**	
	0.019		0.020	
CPC (R)	–0.027		0.152**	
	0.044		0.045	
PPC (R)	–0.476**		–0.207	
	0.117		0.119	
Other party	–0.496*		–0.373*	
	0.176		0.180	
Spoiled ballot	–0.295		–0.401	
	0.203		0.207	
Didn't vote	0.135		0.151	
	0.090		0.092	
Linear regressions				
Ideology		0.039*		0.079**
		0.015		0.015
F	23.34	25.85	15.95	18.66
Adj. R^2	0.095	0.084	0.066	0.061
N	4,911	4,589	4,910	4,588

Notes: Table 11.3 lists the summary statistics from Model 1 regressions, tables 1–6, in appendix A. Columns A and C display the standardized predictive marginal means of vote choice in the 2021 Canadian federal election. Columns B and D show the linear effect of symbolic ideology. The dependent variables are support for the use of AI (Columns A and B) and the belief that the use of AI should be encouraged. Both dependent variables and the measure of symbolic ideology are standardized.
$*p < 0.050$. $**p < 0.001$.

report the coefficient from the standard OLS regression. We find that voting NDP, PPC, or other party is negatively and significantly associated with support for AI, while voting Liberal is positively and significantly associated with support for AI. Voting for the NDP or other party is negatively and significantly associated with encouragement of AI use, while voting for Liberal and CPC is positively and significantly associated with encouragement. Looking at symbolic ideology, there is a positive and significant correlation between conservative orientation and support for AI and encouragement of AI.

In model 2, we find that future optimism, technology optimism, and AI optimism mediate the effect of party vote and symbolic ideology on AI

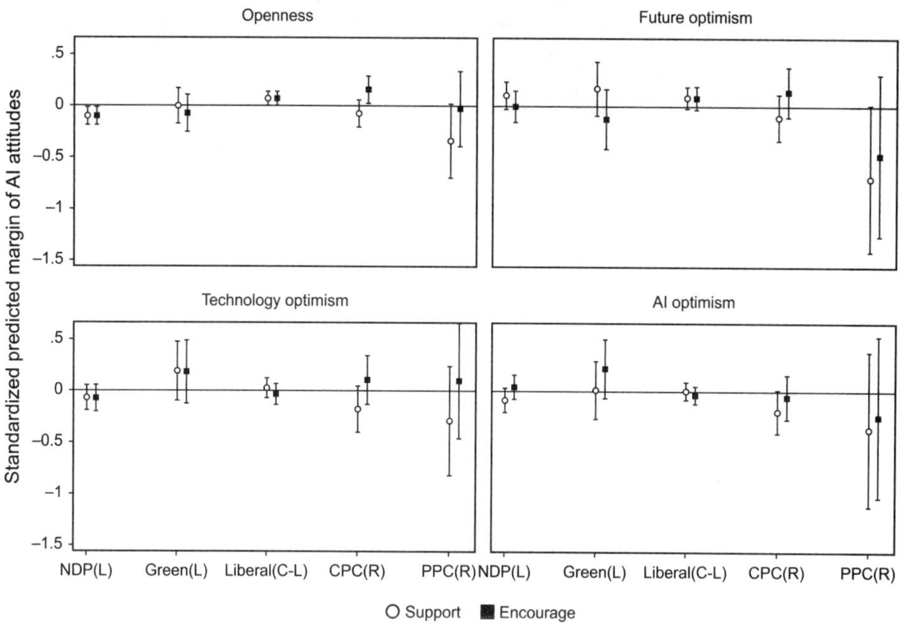

Fig. 11.3 The mediated effect of party vote on support and encouragement of AI
Note. Mediators: Openness, Future, Technology, and AI Optimism in Model 2. The left (L) and right (R) ideological orientation of parties are listed in brackets. The figure displays the predicted marginal means.

support and encouragement. After controlling for openness to experience, however, the predicted margin of voting for the NDP, Liberal, or other party remains significant for AI support and encouragement as well as for the CPC for AI encouragement. After controlling for openness to experience, symbolic ideology also significantly correlates with attitudes for AI encouragement, but not AI support. The results are summarized in figure 11.3; the full results are available in appendix B, tables 7–30.

In model 3, as summarized in figure 11.4 and table 11.4, voting for the ideologically left NDP positively correlates with openness, while voting for the ideologically right CPC negatively correlates with openness. Symbolic ideology also negatively correlates with openness. This is consistent with the psychological literature about ideological behavior (Fatke 2017). Looking at the measures of optimism, neither party vote nor symbolic ideology correlates with future optimism. Technology optimism negatively and significantly correlates with voting for the NDP or spoiling the ballot, but positively and significantly correlates with voting Liberal. AI optimism negatively and significantly correlates with voting NDP but positively and significantly correlates with voting Liberal and with voting for other party.

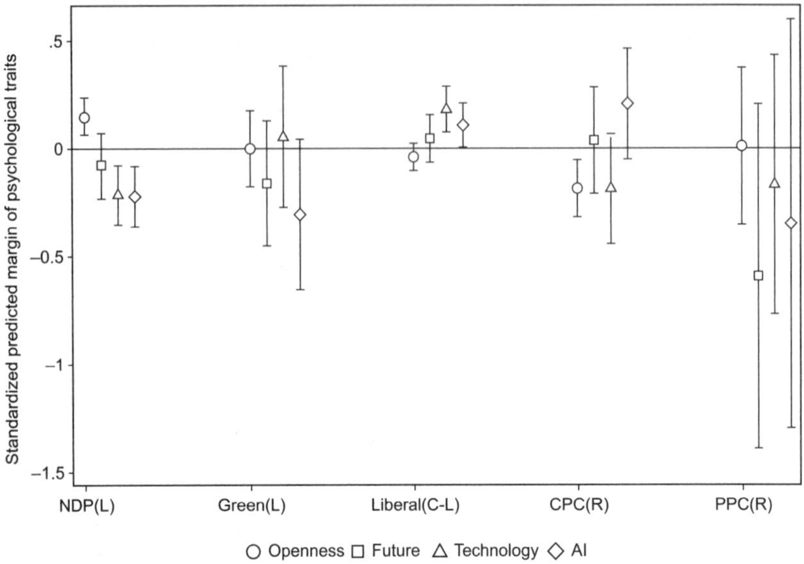

Fig. 11.4 The effect of party vote on the four mediating traits in Model 3

Note: For clarity we omitted values from respondents who voted for another party, spoiled a ballot, or did not vote. The left (L) and right (R) ideological orientation of parties is listed in brackets. The figure displays the predicted marginal means.

AI optimism also positively and significantly correlates with symbolic ideology, indicating that a more conservative ideological orientation is generally associated with more favorable views of artificial intelligence.

11.3 Discussion

Contrary to stereotypes that ideologically left-leaning individuals are more progressive and accepting of change, we find—in the Canadian context—that AI attitudes tend to be less favorable, particularly so when captured in terms of AI encouragement, among both the populist left (NDP) and the populist right (PPC) compared to the more established left (Liberal) and right (CPC) parties, though the small sample size of the PPC makes its estimates more uncertain. This result adds important nuance to Petrova et al. (2024), which finds—in the American context—that support for automation is lower among Trump supporters.

While the current study cannot explain this pattern, one possible explanation is that left- and right-leaning populist voters are more concerned about job loss from automation. Such an explanation is consistent with studies in Europe that find an association between workers' self-assessed vulnerability to automation and support for left-leaning parties as well as increases in

Table 11.4. **Model 3 summary statistics: Separate correlations between party vote in the 2021 federal election or symbolic ideology and four dependent variables assess openness to experience and optimism**

Dependent variables	(A) Openness	(B) Future optimism	(C) Technology optimism	(D) AI optimism
Predicted marginal means				
NDP (L)	0.149**	–0.079	–0.214*	–0.222*
	0.043	0.077	0.069	0.070
Greens (L)	–0.003	–0.161	0.054	–0.305
	0.090	0.148	0.167	0.177
Liberal (C-L)	–0.039	0.044	0.181**	0.109*
	0.031	0.056	0.054	0.051
CPC (R)	–0.186*	0.037	–0.187	0.207
	0.067	0.126	0.129	0.132
PPC (R)	0.011	–0.591	–0.168	–0.348
	0.185	0.405	0.306	0.482
Other party	0.195	–0.902	–0.616	1.234*
	0.294	0.985	0.393	0.556
Spoiled ballot	–0.614	–0.299	–1.169**	–0.359
	0.310	0.712	0.568	0.441
Didn't vote	0.189	0.411	0.357	0.115
	0.166	0.243	0.262	0.236
F	8.04	1.77	4.06	3.78
Adj. R^2	0.076	0.028	0.096	0.088
N	1,965	623	666	665
Linear model				
Ideology	–0.161**	0.071	0.016	0.158**
	0.023	0.046	0.042	0.043
F	11.95	2.03	3.77	4.01
Adj. R^2	0.092	0.030	0.070	0.077
N	1846	577	631	619

Notes: Table 11.4 lists the summary statistics from Model 3 regressions, tables 31–42, in appendix C. The table summarizes the predicted marginal means of vote choice in the 2021 Canadian federal election and the effect of ideology on four dependent variables: openness to experience, future optimism, technology optimism, and AI optimism. Ideology and each of the four dependent variables are standardized.

$*p < 0.050$. $**p < 0.001$.

business digitization and support for right-leaning populism (Borwein et al. 2023; Güvercin 2022; Milner 2021).

Additionally, studies by Magistro et al. (2024) demonstrate that, while voters' preferences on automation policies are stable, they are open to political messages about worker protection from candidates across the political spectrum. This suggests that owning the political issue of protecting workers from automation may depend on parties' messages and strategies to court voters (Borwein et al. 2024). Accordingly, the results of Petrova et al. (2024) may be explained by public perceptions of Trump's positions on the protection of American jobs (Lamont et al., 2017). Consequently, we believe that researchers should pay closer attention to the effects of party and candidate messaging and strategies regarding technology issues, particularly in multiparty political systems, as this may significantly impact future economic policies about artificial intelligence or automation.

11.4 Conclusion

Using data from a postelection study in Toronto, we investigated the relationship between political preferences and attitudes toward artificial intelligence. We find several significant correlations between vote choice and symbolic ideology, on the one hand, and support and encouragement for the use of AI, on the other. We further find that these same political preferences significantly correlate with measures of technological optimism, some of the best-known predictors of attitudes toward AI.

References

Bittner, A., and R. Koop, eds. 2013. *Parties, Elections, and the Future of Canadian Politics*. UBC Press.

Borwein, S., B. Bonikowski, P. J. Loewen, B. Lee-Whiting, and B. Magistro. 2023. "Perceived Technological Threat and Vote Choice: Evidence from 15 European Democracies." *West European Politics*: 1–28.

Borwein, S., B. Bonikowski, P. Loewen, B. Magistro, and B. Lee-Whiting. 2024. "Who Can Assert Ownership over Automation? Workplace Technological Change, Populist and Ethno-Nationalist Rhetoric, and Candidate Support." *Political Behavior*: 1–24.

Carty, R. K. 2015. *Big Tent Politics: The Liberal Party's Long Mastery of Canada's Public Life*. UBC Press.

Chen, Y. N. K., and C. H. R. Wen. 2021. "Impacts of Attitudes Toward Government and Corporations on Public Trust in Artificial Intelligence." *Communication Studies* 72 (1): 115–31.

Clark, B. B., C. Robert, and S. A. Hampton. 2016. "The Technology Effect: How Perceptions of Technology Drive Excessive Optimism." *Journal of Business and Psychology* 31: 87–102.

Cruz-Cárdenas, J., E. Zabelina, O. Deyneka, J. Guadalupe-Lanas, and M. Velín-Fárez. 2019. "Role of Demographic Factors, Attitudes Toward Technology, and Cultural Values in the Prediction of Technology-Based Consumer Behaviors: A Study in Developing and Emerging Countries." *Technological Forecasting and Social Change* 149: 119768.

Danaher, J. 2022. "Techno-optimism: An Analysis, an Evaluation and a Modest Defence." *Philosophy and Technology* 35 (2): 54.

Edison, S. W., and G. L. Geissler. 2003. "Measuring Attitudes Towards General

Technology: Antecedents, Hypotheses and Scale Development." *Journal of Targeting, Measurement and Analysis for Marketing* 12: 137–56.

Elections Canada. 2024. December 4. https://elections.ca/res/rep/off/ovr2021app/53/table8E.html.

Fatke, M. 2017. "Personality Traits and Political Ideology: A First Global Assessment." *Political Psychology* 38 (5): 881–99.

Gagnon, A. G., and A. B. Tanguay, eds. 2017. *Canadian Parties in Transition*. University of Toronto Press.

Goodyear-Grant, E. 2013. *Gendered News: Media Coverage and Electoral Politics in Canada*. UBC Press.

Gosling, S. D., P. J. Rentfrow, and W. B. Swann Jr. 2003. "A Very Brief Measure of the Big-Five Personality Domains." *Journal of Research in Personality* 37 (6): 504–28.

Güvercin, D. 2022. "Digitalization and Populism: Cross-Country Evidence." *Technology in Society* 68: 101802.

Hochschild, J., A. Crabill, and M. Sen. 2012. "Technology Optimism or Pessimism: How Trust in Science Shapes Policy Attitudes Toward Genomic Science." *Issue in Technology Innovation at Brookings* 21.

Hochschild, J., and M. Sen. 2015. "Genetic Determinism, Technology Optimism, and Race: Views of the American Public." *The Annals of the American Academy of Political and Social Science* 661 (1): 160–80.

Johnson, D. 2016. *Thinking Government: Public Administration and Politics in Canada*. University of Toronto Press.

Kelley, P. G., Y. Yang, C. Heldreth, C. Moessner, A. Sedley, A. Kramm, D. T. Newman, and A. Woodruff. 2021. "Exciting, Useful, Worrying, Futuristic: Public Perception of Artificial Intelligence in 8 Countries." In *Proceedings of the 2021 AAAI/ACM Conference on AI, Ethics, and Society*, 627–37. July.

Kerschner, C., and M. H. Ehlers. 2016. "A Framework of Attitudes Towards Technology in Theory and Practice." *Ecological Economics* 126: 139–51.

Kleizen, B., W. Van Dooren, K. Verhoest, and E. Tan. 2023. "Do Citizens Trust Trustworthy Artificial Intelligence? Experimental Evidence on the Limits of Ethical AI Measures in Government." *Government Information Quarterly* 40 (4): 101834.

Königs, P. 2022. "What Is Techno-optimism?" *Philosophy and Technology* 35 (3): 63.

Kreps, S., J. George, P. Lushenko, and A. Rao. 2023. "Exploring the Artificial Intelligence 'Trust Paradox': Evidence from a Survey Experiment in the United States." *PLOS One* 18 (7): e0288109.

Lamont, M., B. Y. Park, and E. Ayala-Hurtado. 2017. "Trump's Electoral Speeches and His Appeal to the American White Working Class." *The British Journal of Sociology* 68: S153–80.

Lévesque, Catherine. 2023. "Bernier Accuses Tories of Veering Left as He Launches Byelection Campaign in Manitoba." *National Post*, May 12. https://nationalpost.com/news/politics/maxime-bernier-lashes-out-at-conservative-party.

Lewis, J. P., and J. Everitt, eds. 2017. *The Blueprint: Conservative Parties and Their Impact on Canadian Politics*. University of Toronto Press.

Magistro, B., P. Loewen, B. Bonikowski, S. Borwein, and B. Lee-Whiting. 2024. "Attitudes Toward Automation and the Demand for Policies Addressing Job Loss: The Effects of Information About Trade-Offs." *Political Science Research and Methods* 1–16.

Milner, H. V. 2021. "Voting for Populism in Europe: Globalization, Technological Change, and the Extreme Right." *Comparative Political Studies* 54 (13): 2286–2320.

Olive, A. 2015. *The Canadian Environment in Political Context*. University of Toronto Press.

Park, J., and S. E. Woo. 2022. "Who Likes Artificial Intelligence? Personality Predictors of Attitudes Toward Artificial Intelligence." *The Journal of Psychology* 156 (1): 68–94.

Petrova, M., G. Schubert, B. Taska, and P. Yildirim. 2024. "Robotization and the Political Response of Politicians." In *The Political Economy of Artificial Intelligence*, edited by Ajay Agrawal, Joshua Gans, Avi Goldfarb, and Catherine E. Tucker. University of Chicago Press.

Smith, M., ed. 2014. *Group Politics and Social Movements in Canada*. University of Toronto Press.

Trump, D. J. 2017. *Presidential Executive Order on Assessing and Strengthening the Manufacturing and Defense Industrial Base and Supply Chain Resiliency of the United States.* https://trumpwhitehouse.archives.gov/presidential-actions/presidential-executive-order-assessing-strengthening-manufacturing-defense-industrial-base-supply-chain-resiliency-united-states/.

Vastal, Marie. 2018. "Maxime Bernier on Next Steps for The People's Party of Canada." Interview, *Le Devoir*, September 15. https://www.ledevoir.com/politique/canada/536810/maxime-bernier-lance-son-parti-populaire-du-canada.

12

AI and Social Media
A Political Economy Perspective

Daron Acemoglu, Asuman Ozdaglar, and James Siderius

12.1 Introduction

Artificial Intelligence (AI) is reshaping almost every aspect of our social lives. Many of its far-ranging consequences are poorly understood and understudied. Its potential impacts on politics are no exception. There are myriad ways in which AI can change both autocracies and democracies. Although there is no conclusive evidence, many commentators suggest that these effects are already visible. Several works (Beraja et al. 2023; Beraja, Yang, and Yuchtman 2023; Zeng 2020) show how AI-driven surveillance has transformed authoritarian, and especially Chinese, politics. In the meantime, we are witnessing both high levels of misinformation and disinformation and much greater levels of polarization in democracies (Feezell, Wagner, and Conroy 2021; Pew Research Center 2014). There is also some suggestive evidence that online platforms are playing a major role in promot-

Daron Acemoglu is an Institute Professor in the Department of Economics at the Massachusetts Institute of Technology, a research fellow of the Centre for Economic Policy Research, and a research associate of the National Bureau of Economic Research.

Asuman Ozdaglar is MathWorks Professor of Electrical Engineering and Computer Science and head of the Electrical Engineering and Computer Science Department at the Massachusetts Institute of Technology.

James Siderius is an assistant professor of business administration and Wei-Chung Bradford Hu T'89 Faculty Fellow at the Tuck School of Business at Dartmouth College.

This book chapter is inspired by the work in Acemoglu, Huttenlocher, et al. (2024) and Acemoglu, Ozdaglar, and Siderius (2024), with a special thanks to Daniel Huttenlocher for his contributions to the former. We would also like to thank numerous participants from the Economics of AI Conference 2024, Johns Hopkins Social & Political Economy Conference, and the International Monetary Fund internal seminar series for their feedback. For acknowledgments, sources of research support, and disclosure of the authors' material financial relationships, if any, please see https://www.nber.org/books-and-chapters/political-economy-artificial-intelligence/ai-and-social-media-political-economy-perspective.

ing polarization and the spread of divisive (and often misinforming) content (see, e.g., Nayak et al. 2021; Rathje et al. 2024).

This paper is a first attempt to develop a formal model of some of AI's impacts on democratic politics. We study the effects of AI-powered business models of online platforms on the polarization of voters and parties. This choice is motivated by several considerations. An increasing fraction of the population in democracies receives their news and political information from social media. For example, 18 percent of Americans list social media as their main source of political and election information, while over 50 percent receive at least some news from social media sources (Associated Press 2024; Pew Research Center 2020, 2024). The amount of time that people spend on online platforms for other reasons, including entertainment, shopping, and other forms of communication, is even larger, and the average American is estimated to spend two to eight hours a day on online digital platforms (Hruska and Maresova 2020; Kemp 2020; Statista Research Department 2024a). This makes online digital ads one of the most important channels via which politicians reach out to voters, and in the 2024 US election, 28 percent of political ads were online (see Statista Research Department 2024b).

Social media and the online experience today are heavily shaped by complex algorithms that collect data and enable platforms to guide the information that users receive. In most cases, we also know that the incentives of online platforms are to maximize engagement from users, collect data about user types and preferences, and create custom audiences for potential advertisers as a way of monetizing these data via digital ads.

The information ecosystem created by AI-powered online platforms can impact politics via several channels. First, social media algorithms can leverage the data that they have about users to decide which information individuals see and who communicates with whom, with potentially major effects on people's political attitudes. One potential impact of social media is therefore on voter beliefs, for example, increasing or reducing political polarization. Voter polarization, in turn, affects party platforms. Second, online platforms amplify the ability and incentives of parties to reach out to specific groups of voters with custom-made messages. This channel also affects both voter and party polarization. Third, AI tools can create new ways in which nonparty actors (e.g., civil society organizations or extremist groups) can reach users, and they also provide new means for users to check the veracity of certain claims and participate in new forms of interactions for democratic debate and information exchange. Fourth, AI algorithms can also change internal party dynamics. Finally, AI can have broader social effects, via the education system or social networks, increasing or reducing people's interest in politics or their willingness and ability to engage in activities such as voting and political debate. In this paper, we focus on the first two channels because they appear to have been more important so far, though the importance of the third channel may have grown over time (see Burton 2023; Mostagir and Siderius 2024).

Specifically, we build on our previous work in Acemoglu, Ozdaglar, and Siderius (2024), which considered a model of information exchange on a social media platform that algorithmically determines the pattern of information sharing between users, and on Acemoglu, Huttenlocher, et al. (2024), which considers a model of digital ad targeting by an online platform. These two models, therefore, bracket the two types of interactions that constitute our focus here. The first, which we refer to as the social media channel, is about how the AI-based news and content feeds affect voter polarization. The second, which we refer to as the digital ads channel, is about the effects of targeted digital ads. In both cases, we embed these online users in a model of political competition, comprising two parties that choose their platforms to attract voters and potentially buy digital ads targeting voters. In both cases, AI and digital business models play critical roles in platform incentives. In the former (social media channel that builds on Acemoglu, Ozdaglar, and Siderius 2024), a social media platform chooses the content sharing network between users by leveraging AI tools and with the objective of maximizing engagement so as to boost its digital ad revenues. In the latter (the digital ads channel, which builds on Acemoglu, Huttenlocher, et al. 2024), the social media platform uses AI tools to target digital ads to voters on behalf of political parties.

More specifically, the key decision in our model of social media is made by the platform about the structure of interactions between users. Users have a political belief (ideology), which they can update according to the information they receive. This information is contained in social media posts (articles), which come with a specific message (left-wing or right-wing) and a degree of reliability (observed perfectly by all players). Users decide whether to share, ignore, or dislike a message, and their main source of utility is from these social media interactions. Users also vote in a two-party election according to the alignment of their beliefs with the policy positions on offer. Since each individual is infinitesimal, voting behavior does not generate an incentive to change users' social media behavior.

As in Acemoglu, Ozdaglar, and Siderius (2024), the payoff structure is such that users like to share articles, but not if others dislike and tag them as misinformation. This creates a tendency for individuals to share articles that have a message congruent with their beliefs, since they (rationally) judge those to be less likely to contain misinformation. The key decision in our model is made by the platform and concerns how the algorithm of the platform shapes the newsfeed and connections of users (observing the prior beliefs and ideology of users, thanks to its AI-powered data crunching of their past behavior). In one extreme, the platform could choose a complete network, whereby posts by every user are equally likely to be seen by all other users, or an extreme filter bubble, whereby connections between users have complete "homophily," meaning that social media posts are only shared among people with the same prior beliefs or ideology. The main result in Acemoglu, Ozdaglar, and Siderius (2024), which we leverage here, is that when articles have low reliability and the population is already polarized, then filter bubbles are more profitable for the platform. A complete network could in principle generate engagement from a bigger base of users and generate more profits for the platform, but low-reliability articles presented to people with opposite ideology are likely to be identified and labeled as misinformation, reducing their circulation and thus the platform's revenue from engagement and digital ads. This channel implies that, when the relevant content does not have very high reliability to start with, social media algorithms increase voter polarization, and especially the polarization among the most extremist viewers. Given this type of polarization, parties choose more polarized policy positions, responding to their more extremist base. This is despite the fact that moderate voters retain identical or nearly identical political beliefs after their social media experience. Our result is consistent with evidence from Fiorina and Abrams (2008) suggesting that US polarization was long characterized by a relatively stable, moderate electorate and party positions shifting toward the extremes.

Our digital ads model extends Acemoglu, Huttenlocher, et al. (2024) and considers two political parties reaching voters with digital ads, crafted and targeted by AI, on an online entertainment platform. Users can be naive or sophisticated, with the key difference that naive users are easier to convince with incorrect information, while sophisticated users have the correct model of the world. The presence of naive voters increases the profitability of using digital ads for political purposes. When parties can use such ads, they have a greater ability to sway voters, and this weakens their incentives to moderate their policies. Hence, albeit from a very different channel, this model also implies that AI and digital ad-based business models cause greater voter and party polarization.

At a high level, therefore, our analysis of both channels indicates that AI-powered platforms act as a source of polarization among voters, and political parties respond to this by choosing more polarized policy positions (even more so than the voters). The ways the two channels work are quite different, however. The social media channel works via the platform's ability to manufacture filter bubbles and makes it more likely that left-leaning (right-leaning) users are exposed to more left-leaning (right-leaning) content. On the other hand, in the digital ads channel, it is the parties that tailor their messages for groups of voters who are more susceptible to believing the ads they receive and thus drive polarization. It is this ability to influence susceptible voters that makes digital ads more potent than other types of advertisement in informational outreach and more attractive to political parties. The overall result is again weaker incentives for parties to moderate their platforms.

In both cases, the results from the theoretical frameworks on which we are building also indicate that further competition among platforms does not ameliorate the polarization problem. We examine how certain regulations influence voter and party polarization in democracies. Specifically, we analyze the effects of a diversification standard, where platform users are exposed to more counterattitudinal content (in the spirit of proposals such as Sunstein 2018), and assess its potential to limit the creation of filter bubbles. In the context of digital ads, we study the implications of algorithmic regulations designed to enhance transparency and reduce the degree of ad targeting. Our analysis suggests that polarization, both among voters and in equilibrium party positions, responds to changes in digital awareness or literacy and the persuasiveness of ads.[1]

12.1.1 Related Literature

Our work is connected to three streams of literature: the first on social media, echo chambers, and filter bubbles, the second related to advertising in digital and nondigital settings, and the third about the politics of polarization. Although we build on the emerging empirical evidence in these areas, our contribution is theoretical and develops novel possible channels from the use of AI tools in social media and other platforms to voter and political party polarization.

In the context of the first literature, in a randomized-controlled experiment, Levy (2021) shows that Facebook's algorithm selectively chose pro-attitudinal political content to display to users based on their ideology, creating an endogenous echo chamber, or filter bubble. The negative effects of echo chambers are explored in an emerging empirical literature (Barberá 2020; Flaxman, Goel, and Rao 2016; Ross Arguedas et al. 2022) and have featured in a few theoretical studies as well (see Baumann et al. 2020; Golub and Jackson 2010; Mostagir and Siderius 2023; Törnberg 2018). Braghieri et al. (2024) and Molina (2024) study various channels by which social media interactions can lead to the emergence of echo chambers. Our contribution is distinguished from this literature because we explore mechanisms that have not yet been analyzed, in particular, the social media channel building on Acemoglu, Ozdaglar, and Siderius (2024). In this context, our analysis uncovers a novel pathway via which an AI-powered platform tends to amplify political biases and drive greater division in beliefs.

The second strand of literature studies the role of informational advertising (Butters 1977; Meurer and Stahl 1994) and manipulative advertising (Gupta 2023; Piccolo, Tedeschi, and Ursino 2018), where our earlier work in Acemoglu, Huttenlocher, et al. (2024) sits in between. Our focus is on targeted (and manipulative) digital advertising in the political domain, where we find that party competition entices online business models to monetize via digital advertising, which also induces greater polarization in political

1. Additionally, digital ad taxes that shift platforms toward a subscription-based model, discussed in detail in Acemoglu, Huttenlocher, et al. (2024), can also limit political polarization, but we do not analyze them in this paper.

beliefs. We refer to this as the digital ads channel, which is distinct from the social media channel, and is primarily driven by incentives of platforms to leverage AI for crafting individualized ads targeting users who are most susceptible to such ads. In turn, given this opportunity, parties pay to advertise to soften competition between each other, but in doing so, drive greater polarization in beliefs. When there is a single dominant political party, we find that the platform's business model gravitates toward subscription instead, and these polarizing forces disappear.

The last strand of literature contains both empirical articles (e.g., Barber et al. 2015; Callander and Carbajal 2022; Fiorina and Abrams 2008; McCarty 2007) and a few theoretical works on polarization. For example, Dixit and Weibull (2007), Acemoglu, Chernozhukov, and Yildiz (2016), and Mostagir and Siderius (2022b) explore how Bayesian learning can lead to polarization under certain circumstances, while Glaeser (2005), Glaeser, Ponzetto, and Shapiro (2005), Acemoglu, Egorov, and Sonin (2013), and Druckman and Levy (2022) investigate various reasons for parties shifting away from moderate policies. Berman (2021) discusses the political science literature on the rise of radical right-wing populism, while Guriev and Papaioannou (2022) survey the broader political economy literature on populism. Tucker et al. (2018) summarize the literature on the effects of social media and polarization.

12.1.2 Paper Outline

The remainder of this paper proceeds as follows. Section 12.2 introduces our model of voting and party competition. Section 12.3 introduces the platform's incentives and their profit-maximization problem, both through the social media and digital ads channels. Section 12.4 studies and extends the model in Acemoglu, Ozdaglar, and Siderius (2024) and derives the implications for political polarization of voters and parties, whereas Section 12.5 examines the impact of targeted digital ads on political beliefs, building on the model of Acemoglu, Huttenlocher, et al. (2024). We discuss the effects of various regulations in Section 12.6, and Section 12.7 concludes. The appendix contains the proofs of the main results stated in the text.

12.2 Our Model of Voting

We start with our model of politics, which will be common in our explorations of the social media and digital ads channels. There are two political parties and a continuum of voters that are on online platforms (with total measure normalized 1), as well as some voters that are completely offline.

Each online voter $i \in [0,1]$ participates both on an online platform and in an election. Voter i holds prior beliefs b_i about a binary, fixed state of the world $\theta \in \{L, R\}$ (e.g., whether the left-wing or right-wing candidate is a better fit for office). The cumulative density function (cdf) of the distribution of beliefs is denoted by $H : [0,1] \to [0,1]$ and describes the political leaning of the electorate, which we assume is symmetric about the median belief of $1/2$ and non-degenerate (i.e., has density function h with $h(\alpha) = h(1 - \alpha)$ for all $\alpha \in [0,1]$).

We now introduce an order that captures the extent of polarization. An electorate described by $\tilde{H}$ is more *polarized* than an electorate described by H (denoted by $\tilde{H} \succ H$) if $\tilde{H}^{-1}(\alpha) > H^{-1}(\alpha)$ for all $\alpha \in (1/2,1)$ and $\tilde{H}^{-1}(\alpha) < H^{-1}(\alpha)$ for all $\alpha \in (0,1/2)$, with $\tilde{H}^{-1}(1/2) = H^{-1}(1/2)$. In other words, our order means that $\tilde{H}$ has the same median voter as H but is more spread out to the left and the right.

There are two political parties, $P \in \{L, R\}$, which strategically choose and commit to positions x_L and x_R on the interval $[0,1]$. Party payoffs are assumed to take the following form:

$$U_P = \mathbf{1}_P \cdot \mathcal{R} - (x - \hat{x}_p)^2,$$

where $\mathbf{1}_p$ is the indicator function denoting whether party P comes to power, $\mathcal{R}$ is a rent/utility from coming to power, x is the policy that is implemented (by either this party or its rival) and $\hat{x}_P$ is party P's ideal point, so that the term $-(x - \hat{x}_P)^2$ corresponds to the disutility of the political party due to deviation of the actual policy from its ideal point. We assume that $\hat{x}_L < 1/2 < \hat{x}_R = 1 - \hat{x}_L$, so that the left-wing party is indeed left-wing and the right-wing party is indeed right-wing. Our model of politics therefore combines ideological differences between parties together with a desire to come to power, separate from policy considerations.

Agents observe the positions of the two parties (x_L, x_R), and, as in Quinn, Martin, and Whitford (1999), voter i casts her vote for party j stochastically with probability

$$\rho_j(b_i, x_L, x_R) = \frac{\exp[-(b_i - x_j)^2]}{\exp[-(b_i - x_L)^2] + \exp[-(b_i - x_R)^2]}, \tag{1}$$

with $\rho_L(b_i) + \rho_R(b_i) = 1$ for all b_i. This "soft max" is equivalent to agent i voting for her favored party j^*, given by $j^* \in \arg\min_{j \in \{L,R\}} |x_j - b_i|$ (i.e., picking the candidate closest to her own belief in absolute value), but trembling with exponential decaying weight in the squared-distance between b_i and x_j. This form can be micro-founded by assuming the presence of nonpolicy valence or idiosyncratic preference terms that affect the choice of each voter between the two parties, as in the probabilistic voting models (e.g., Coughlin 1992; Lindbeck and Weibull 1993). An important implication of this form is that voters with more extreme policy positions are more likely to vote for their preferred party than the more moderate voters.

The soft max in Equation 1 implies that candidate j captures a total share of votes from online voters given by

$$\chi_j = \int_0^1 \rho_j(b_i, x_L, x_R) h(b_i) di.$$

We model the voting behavior of offline voters, who are not influenced by any online activity in our model, in a reduced form. In particular, we assume that the total votes from this group for party j is stochastic and is given by $\zeta_j \sim$ Uniform[0,1], where the uniform assumption is adopted for simplicity. This implies that the total votes of party j will be $\chi_j + \zeta_j$ and those of party $-j$ will be $\chi_{-j} + \zeta_{-j} = 1 - \chi_j + 1 - \zeta_j$. Party j then wins the election and comes to power if

$$\chi_j + \zeta_j > (1 - \chi_j) + (1 - \zeta_j).$$

We consider the game where parties (L, R) choose positions (x_L^*, x_R^*) simultaneously, then online agents vote for candidates according to ρ and then the random variable ζ is realized.

Given the symmetry of H around the median, in what follows we focus on the antisymmetric Nash equilibrium of this game, where $|x_L^* - 1/2| = |x_R^* - 1/2|$, or in words, where the two parties locate and equidistant fashion relative to the median. Because uniqueness is not guaranteed, we also focus on the extremal antisymmetric Nash equilibria, whereby among all antisymmetric Nash equilibria, we pick the one that has the largest $|x_L^* - 1/2|$. This focus is motivated by our desire to carry out simple comparative statics.

Under the baseline Hotelling (1929) model (Downs 1957), we obtain the standard Downsian convergence result, where both political parties choose to cater to the median voter's preferences by setting $x_L^* = x_R^* = 1/2$ in the unique equilibrium. One of our key results will be that because of the effects of AI-powered online business strategies, we will generally have policy differentiation—$x_L^* < x_R^*$. This arises because voters near the poles are less likely to vote for a candidate that has a platform misaligned with their ideology, driving the parties' incentives to differentiate themselves (as opposed to the standard framework, where such forces are muted). Our next result characterizes this differentiation as a function of the belief distribution H.

LEMMA 1

(i) There exists at least one antisymmetric Nash equilibrium (x_L^*, x_R^*) *with* $x_R^* = 1 - x_L^*$ *and every equilibrium satisfies* $x_L^* < (1/2) < x_R^*$;

(ii) There exists a unique extremal antisymmetric Nash equilibrium $(\underline{x}_L^*, \overline{x}_R^*)$ *with* $\underline{x}_L^* \leq x_L^*$ *and* $\overline{x}_R^* \geq x_R^*$ *for any antisymmetric equilibrium pair* (x_L^*, x_R^*);

(iii) If $\tilde{H} \succ H$, *the extremal antisymmetric Nash equilibrium under* H, $(\underline{x}_L^*, \overline{x}_R^*)$, *and under* $\tilde{H}$, $(\underline{\tilde{x}}_L^*, \overline{\tilde{x}}_R^*)$, *satisfy* $\underline{\tilde{x}}_L^* < \underline{x}_L^*$ and $\overline{\tilde{x}}_R^* > \overline{x}_R^*$.[2]

Lemma 1(i) establishes the existence of an antisymmetric Nash equilibrium in our voting game where the two parties distinguish themselves from each other. In all such equilibria, we have $x_L^* < x_R^*$, and these policy posi-

2. To avoid cumbersome terminology, we often refer to "the equilibrium" as the extremal antisymmetric Nash equilibrium and denote it by (x_L^*, x_R^*), avoiding the more notation-intensive $(\underline{x}_L^*, \overline{x}_R^*)$, although they refer to identical entities.

tions lie on opposite sides of the median voter's most preferred policy. This is a consequence of the combination of uncertain election outcomes that depend smoothly on policy positions (due to probabilistic voting and the presence of stochastic offline voters) and the differences in the ideological positions (ideal points) of the two parties. Intuitively, policy convergence whereby $x_L^* = x_R^* = x$ for some x could never be an equilibrium. Such a point would deviate from the ideal point of at least one of the two parties, say, party R, and if this party moved toward its ideal point, this would have a second-order cost in terms of vote shares as derived in (1), but would always have a first-order gain in terms of moving closer to one's own ideal point.

While the existence of an antisymmetric Nash equilibrium is immediate (from a straightforward application of Brouwer's fixed point theorem given the continuity of vote shares in (1)), uniqueness is not guaranteed, because the trade-off—between being close to one's ideal point and gaining more votes from (1)—is often nonconvex. However, there can only be a finite number of symmetric Nash equilibria, and hence the existence of an extremal one is also guaranteed, as stated in part (ii).

The comparative static result in part (iii) of the lemma is important for the rest of our analysis. It states that a more polarized online electorate leads to more polarized policy positions among the two parties—in the sense that both parties move further away from the median voter's ideal point. There are two complementary intuitions for this result. To explain these, first note that we do not know in general whether x_L^* is to the left or to the right of $\hat{x}_L$ (and likewise for x_R^* relative to $\hat{x}_R$). Suppose first that it is to its right, meaning that party L (and symmetrically its rival) are moderating their positions to increase their probability of coming to power. In this scenario, a polarized electorate enables both parties to move closer to their ideal points, leading to a further polarization of party positions. Alternatively, both parties could already be more polarized than their ideal points in order to strongly cater to their more extreme voters. In this case, a further polarization of the electorate strengthens this effect and again intensifies the polarization of party positions. Both of these channels are rooted in the fact that, as (1) clarifies, extremist voters are more valuable to a party because the soft max in this expression has a steeper curvature for these voters. Also, both of these channels work even if only the most extremist voters in the party's base become more polarized, and this is in fact a common situation we will see in both the social media and digital ads channels.

12.3 Platform Incentives

We next describe the online platform's profit and choice of business model, which will also apply to both of our mechanisms explored in the next two sections. For ease of exposition, we take the perspective of a social media platform, though much of our analysis applies more generally to online platforms that monetize through subscription and/or digital advertising. We assume that the platform is revenue-maximizing (meaning that we ignore costs) and its revenues come from digital ads and potentially subscription income. Namely, the objective of the platform is to maximize

$$\Pi = I^S + \int_0^1 \delta z_i \, di, \tag{2}$$

where I^S is subscription income (if any) and the second term is total digital ad revenue. Specifically, z_i denotes the number of ads (in expectation) that can be presented to user i and δ is revenue per ad.

Under the social media model in the next section, we assume that there is no subscription income, δ is exogenously given, and z_i is proportional to the number of shares of posts that individual i engages in. Therefore, $\int_0^1 z_i \, di$ will be proportional to the total engagement of content on social media, incentivizing the platform to maximize engagement or shares. Under the digital ads model, the platform will choose between a subscription-based model where $I^S > 0$ and $\int_0^1 z_i \, di = 0$ or $I^S = 0$ and an ads-based business model with $\int_0^1 z_i \, di > 0$, or a mixture with both $I^S > 0$ and $\int_0^1 z_i \, di > 0$. In this case, δ will be optimally chosen by the platform as a function of the willingness of parties to pay for digital ads, and z_i will be related to the expected number of ads individual i will consume as we describe there.

12.4 Social Media and Content Sharing

We begin by describing our model of social media and content sharing, which is based on a simplified version of Acemoglu, Ozdaglar, and Siderius (2024). We then present theorem 3, our main result from Acemoglu, Ozdaglar, and Siderius (2024), which characterizes the platform's profit-maximizing sharing network and shows that, when the available social media content has low reliability, this sharing network takes the form of a filter bubble, where individuals see only articles shared by like-minded users. We use this characterization to pin down how the electorate's beliefs shift through the social media channel and to derive the corresponding impact on political party positions.

12.4.1 Our Model of Content Sharing

Users hold prior beliefs $b_i \in [0,1]$ about $\theta = R$ and communicates stochastically with other users on social media, according to a sharing network $\mathbf{P}$ determined algorithmically by the platform. We focus on "articles" users share over this network with each other.

Each article on social media has a three-dimensional type (r, v, m) indicating its reliability ($r \in [0,1]$), veracity ($v \in \{\mathcal{T}, \mathcal{M}\}$) and message ($m \in \{L, R\}$). The reliability specifies the likelihood that the article is truthful instead of containing misinformation. If the article is truthful, it is more likely to argue for the true θ, whereas an article with misinformation simply provides noise about θ. Formally, we have that $\mathbb{P}[m = \theta | \nu = \mathcal{T}] = p > (1/2)$ and $\mathbb{P}[m = \theta | \nu = \mathcal{M}] = (1/2)$. Importantly, both the reliability and the message are publicly observable, but the veracity is not—instead, this must be inferred from the observable characteristics of the article, using Bayes's rule, which will also depend on agent i's prior b_i about θ.

Each agent can decide between sharing, ignoring, or disliking a given article. The payoff to ignoring is 0, whereas the payoff to disliking is equal to $\tilde{u}\mathbf{1}_{\nu=\mathcal{M}} - \tilde{c}$, which implies that the agent gets some utility $\tilde{u}$ from calling out misinformation, but must exert some effort $\tilde{c}$ in order to do so (and incurs the cost regardless of whether the article actually contains misinformation).

There are two sources of utility and costs from sharing content. The first component is network-independent; agents receive utility that only depends on the nature of the content. Agents get positive utility, $u\mathbf{1}_{\nu=\mathcal{T}}$, from sharing truthful content and pay a cost, $c\mathbf{1}_{\nu=\mathcal{M}}$, for sharing misinformation. Second, when they share, their content gets passed onto their neighbors in the sharing network, as determined by $\mathbf{P}$. For every reshare received, the agent gets an additional marginal utility of κ, whereas for every dislike received, the agent pays a reputational cost d. The parameter κ can capture the degree of "sensationalism" of the article, representing the idea that some content is more sensational and thus generates more social benefit for the sender when it spreads virally.

12.4.2 Platform Incentives

The platform's objective is to maximize digital advertisement revenue, as specified in Equation 2. Since δ is fixed in this case, this is equivalent to maximizing $\int_0^1 z_i di$, which means maximizing the circulation of social media content by choosing the sharing network $\mathbf{P}$. We assume that this choice is without any constraints, meaning that the chosen network could be any element of the set of all possible stochastic sharing networks over nodes defined by the users on this platform. This is a simplification adopted for transparency and tractability, and the general conclusions are not affected if we assume that the sharing network is chosen to be a subset of the preexisting network structure, such as the exogenous online social network.

12.4.3 Filter Bubbles

Following the terminology in Acemoglu, Ozdaglar, and Siderius (2024), a sharing network has maximal connectivity if it is the complete network. It has maximal homophily if it can be represented by two islands with within-island link probability $p_s = 1$ and between-island link probability $p_d = 0$. Here, we first replicate theorem 3 from Acemoglu, Ozdaglar, and Siderius (2024):

PROPOSITION 4.1 *The platform's profit-maximizing sharing network is determined by a reliability threshold* $r_P \in (0,1)$ *such that:*

(i) *If* $r < r_p$*, the platform's profit-maximizing sharing network has maximal homophily and thus corresponds to a filter bubble.*

(ii) *If* $r > r_p$*, the platform's profit-maximizing sharing network has maximal connectivity.*

In a nutshell, when the relevant articles have low reliability in the sense of $r < r_p$ (where $r_P \in (0,1)$), the platform's profit-maximizing sharing network is a filter bubble, whereby the article is recommended only to some set of agents, $\mathcal{A}'$, which is made up of agents with the same ideological position and is consequently fully disconnected from the set of other agents, $\mathcal{A}''$. When $r > r_p$, the platform chooses the complete network. The intuition, as already hinted in Section 1, is that with low-reliability articles, the platform is worried about agents with different priors or political views calling out misinformation and thus slowing down or preventing the viral spread of articles, which is costly for the platform because it reduces engagement. One other noteworthy feature of this theorem is that it makes it natural for us to focus on extreme filter bubbles and complete networks, as the two types of sharing network structures that the profit-maximizing platform will choose.

In what follows, we focus on the case where $r < r_p$ and assume that the benchmark for comparison without AI is the complete network, since without AI and extensive data collection about users, the platform could not ensure that an article is only seen by those who have similar views to those it advocates. Moreover, to deliver our insights in the most transparent manner, we consider two articles (r_1, v_1, m_1) and (r_2, v_2, m_2), and suppose that (r_1, r_2, r) and $m_1 = L$ but $m_2 = R$.[3]

We next show that the reliability parameter r both determines the size and nature of the filter bubble and acts as a proxy for the quantity of misinformation in circulation on social media (with higher reliability indicating less pervasive misinformation).

PROPOSITION 4.2 *Suppose* $r < r_P$*. As r decreases further, the size (and the ideological heterogeneity) of the filter bubble also decreases. As* $r \to 0$*, only the online voters with the most extreme views aligned with the article are included in the filter bubble.*

The proof and the main idea of this proposition rely on proposition 4.1. As we have seen, when content is not too reliable ($r < r_P$), the profit-maximizing

3. The case where $r_1 \neq r_2$ will lead to fundamentally similar insights, but the distribution of beliefs after the articles are recommended, $\tilde{H}$, will depend on the difference between r_1 and r_2. Since we are interested in the role AI plays in its recommendation algorithm, we simplify along this dimension and focus on articles that have similar likelihood to contain misinformation. Likewise, the case of $m_1 = m_2 = R$ or $m_1 = m_2 = L$ is less interesting because one political party is "handicapped" by a lack of information it can push on the platform. If parties produced articles themselves, this would naturally ensure that $m_1 = L$ and $m_2 = R$.

sharing network **P*** induces an extreme filter bubble, sharing a given article only within an ideologically aligned community. Note, however, that even within this regime, the value of r determines the size of the filter bubble. When $r \approx r_P$, then the filter bubble is in fact quite similar to the complete network and includes a large fraction of all users. But as r declines further, the filter bubble gets smaller and more extreme, and in the limit, it includes a tiny and very extremist fraction of the population. What this implies, in particular, is that for sufficiently low r, moderate voters are not part of the filter bubble. This result, which is new relative to Acemoglu, Ozdaglar, and Siderius (2024), and is proved in the appendix.

12.4.4 Polarization of the (Online) Electorate

Once agents receive articles (regardless of the sharing network **P**), they update their priors b_i according to Bayes's rule to form posterior beliefs $\hat{b}_i$ about θ depending on the message of the article they observe. Importantly, we assume agents do not update their beliefs about θ for articles that may be hidden from them.[4] Political parties then choose their positions $(\tilde{x}_L^*, \tilde{x}_R^*)$, given the distribution of $\hat{b}_i$'s in the population, denoted by $\tilde{H}$. We say that $\tilde{H}$ is more polarized than an alternative H' according to the polarization definition above, and denote the distribution of beliefs under a filter bubble by $\tilde{H}_{FB}$ and under the complete network by $\tilde{H}_C$.

We also define $(\tilde{x}_L^{FB}, \tilde{x}_R^{FB})$ as the party positions under a filter bubble, and $(\tilde{x}_L^C, \tilde{x}_R^C)$ as party positions under a complete network. We say that parties are more polarized under filter bubbles if $\tilde{x}_L^{FB} < \tilde{x}_L^C$ and $\tilde{x}_R^{FB} > \tilde{x}_R^C$. Existence and uniqueness of the extremal antisymmetric equilibrium are guaranteed by lemma 1 in Section 4.2.

Our next result establishes the impact of filter bubbles on voter polarization. We refer to the individuals who are at the median among the left-leaning and the right-leaning voters, respectively (those that the midpoints between 0 and 1/2, and between 1/2 and 1, or mathematically, $\tilde{H}^{-1}(1/4)$ and $\tilde{H}^{-1}(3/4)$) as the left median and the right median:

Proposition 4.3 *There exist $0 < r_1 < r_2 < r_p < 1$ such that an article with reliability $r \in (r_1, r_2)$ leads to voter polarization in the sense that $\tilde{H}_{FB} \succ \tilde{H}_C$, but the left and the right medians remain identical under both belief distributions, i.e., $\tilde{H}_{FB}^{-1}(1/4) = \tilde{H}_C^{-1}(1/4)$ and $\tilde{H}_{FB}^{-1}(3/4) = \tilde{H}_C^{-1}(3/4)$.*

This is a critical result for our analysis. It not only establishes the presence of filter bubbles but also indicates that with sufficiently low reliability ($r < r_2$), social media content has no impact on moderate voters, including those between the left (respectively the right) median and the overall median at 1/2. The intuition is given by proposition 4.2. When $r < r_2$, the

4. Appendix C in Acemoglu, Ozdaglar, and Siderius (2024) provides a microfoundation for this feature.

profit-maximizing filter bubble on the left does not include the 25th quantile of the belief distribution, and thus only the beliefs of voters that are more extreme than this could be impacted by social media content. Put simply, low-reliability content on social media affects only extremist voters, not moderate ones. This finding is congruent with claims made in Fiorina and Abrams (2008), who have argued that the moderate electorate did not become more polarized, and US political polarization was driven by parties. Our theory suggests that this pattern may be the result of the polarization by extreme voters, to which party positions responded. This story is also in line with the work of Guess, Nyhan, and Reifler (2020) and Lazer et al. (2018), who argue that most of the misinformation in the American media diet came from a small percentage of social media users who were the most extreme on both sides of the political spectrum. To this result, we also add the possibility that AI-powered filter bubbles are making this polarization of the extremes even more intensive. The intuition in our case is exactly the same: While $\tilde{H}_{FB}$ is more polarized than $\tilde{H}_C$, the additional polarization is accounted for the most extremist social media participants.

It is also interesting to see why similar dynamics do not transpire under complete networks. In this case, all agents will see both articles, which have the same reliability but argue for opposite perspectives. In consequence, their overall effects will cancel each other, and the posterior belief distribution $\tilde{H}$ will continue to coincide with the prior distribution H, exhibiting no voter polarization. In more general settings, left-leaning and right-leaning articles may have different credibilities, and it is natural to assume that the right-leaning articles will have greater credibility when $\theta = R$, and vice versa. If so, then with a complete network, people will update their priors and posterior distribution will shift in the direction of the truth.

12.4.5 Polarization of Parties

Using lemma 1, we can establish the following consequence of proposition 4.3:

COROLLARY 4.1 *An article with reliability $r \in (r_1, r_2)$ induces parties to become more extreme in equilibrium, i.e., $\tilde{x}_L^{FB} < x_L^*$ and $\tilde{x}_R^{FB} > x_R^*$.*

When the reliability of social media content is not too low, then the most extreme right-wing agents will update their priors b_i to more extreme posteriors $\hat{b}_i > b_i$ after seeing message $m_2 = R$. Likewise, the most extreme left-wing agents will update their priors b_i to more extreme beliefs $\hat{b}_i < b_i$ after seeing message $m_1 = L$. This is because, in such a strong filter bubble, agents from these groups will not see the opposing messages. Then, from lemma 1(ii), this type of voter polarization will induce party polarization, with each party choosing more extreme policy positions.

To further highlight the role of content reliability, in the next proposition we show that the results of proposition 4.3 do not hold when content reliability is very high or very low:

PROPOSITION 4.4 *Fix* $\varepsilon > 0$. *There exist* $0 < \underline{r}^* < \overline{r}^* < 1$ *such that if* $r < \underline{r}^*$ *or* $r > \overline{r}^*$, *then*

$$|\tilde{x}_L^{FB} - x_L^*| < \varepsilon \text{ and } |\tilde{x}_R^{FB} - x_R^*| < \varepsilon.$$

This proposition therefore highlights that AI-powered social media is most likely to generate voter and party polarization when the reliability of news content is middling (or when there is sufficient uncertainty about the veracity of online content). Nevertheless, our reading of the evidence is that the middling reliability regime is the best approximation to the current political climate, which has sometimes been described as a "post-truth" era, where there is little agreement in society what is an objective truth (see Lewandowsky, Ecker, and Cook 2017; Rochlin 2017; see also Nyhan 2020; Pennycook and Rand 2019; Suarez-Lledo and Alvarez-Galvez 2021).

Several interesting comparative statics follow straightforwardly from this result. First, if we hold constant reliability r and increase the sensationalism of the article, κ, or decrease the reputational concerns, d, from sharing the article, then the platform's sharing network is less likely to induce a filter bubble. This will lead to less polarized political positions in equilibrium, which may at first appear paradoxical. However, in reality, highly sensational articles are also often unreliable (see Grinberg et al. 2019). Thus, if we consider a simultaneous increase in κ and a decrease in r is smaller, then filter bubbles can become more likely, and we can see more extreme political party positions, as stated in corollary 4.1.

We can also show, with similar arguments to those in Acemoglu, Ozdaglar, and Siderius (2024), that more divisive content (with higher p and lower q) is more likely to induce polarization among voters and thus between parties. This is for two related reasons. First, with higher p and lower q, the article leads to stronger belief updates, which then generate more polarized posterior beliefs. Second, when content is more divisive, it becomes more profitable for the platform to opt for a filter bubble, as shown in proposition 3 of Acemoglu, Ozdaglar, and Siderius (2024), and via this choice of platform architecture, more divisive content again promotes polarization.

Finally, we can also study the implications of the prior distribution of the electorate becoming more polarized. According to proposition 3 in Acemoglu, Ozdaglar, and Siderius (2024), when prior polarization becomes stronger, filter bubbles become more likely, which further drives belief polarization by proposition 4.3, and in turn, party polarization by corollary 4.1. In this sense, polarization is like Pandora's box: Once the electorate becomes polarized, social media fuels the flames of polarization through the AI's choice of algorithm, which further reinforces the polarization. This perpetuating cycle working via social media can lead to a positive feedback loop that exacerbates any initial polarization.

12.5 Digital Political Advertising

Next, we extend a simplified version of the model of Acemoglu, Huttenlocher, et al. (2024) of online business models and digital ads to study our second channel for political polarization.

12.5.1 Sophisticated and Naive Users

We let λ fraction of the users be sophisticated and $1 - \lambda$ fraction of the users be naive. There is a state of the world $\theta \in \{L, R\}$ as before, and we suppose that users hold prior beliefs $b_i \sim H$. Sophisticated users have a correctly specified subjective model of digital ads, which is that the signals s_i contain no information about the underlying state θ. On the other hand, naive agents believe that political ads contain information about θ and that false positives are relatively rare. In particular, we assume that naïfs hold the subjective model that $\mathbb{P}[s_i \neq \theta] = \phi \in [0,1/2]$. Both ϕ and λ encode the degree of targeting and manipulation possible from digital ads on the platform, as discussed in detail in Acemoglu, Huttenlocher, et al. (2024). Lower values of ϕ indicate a larger misspecification on the part of naive agents who believe that false positives are relatively rarer than they actually are. This allows political parties to send a positive signal, independent of how fit they are for office, to persuade naïfs to vote for them. Similarly, lower values of λ represent a larger fraction of naïfs in the population, who are more susceptible to digital ad targeting.[5] This structure implies that as ϕ and λ increase, we approach the standard model with fully rational agents (which is in fact the limit of our setting with $\lambda = 1$ or $\phi = 1/2$).

12.5.2 Digital Ads and Platform Choices

When there are multiple parties, we assume there are two different ads the platform can show (one for the left-wing candidate and one for the right-wing candidate) with ad loads $\alpha^{(L)}$ and $\alpha^{(R)}$ and total ad load $\alpha \equiv \alpha^{(L)} + \alpha^{(R)}$ (with the probability of the left-wing candidate's ad being shown with probability $\alpha^{(L)}/(\alpha^{(L)} + \alpha^{(R)})$). Existence and generic uniqueness of an equilibrium under this generalization with multiple parties follow immediately from proposition 8 in Acemoglu, Huttenlocher, et al. (2024). The parameter α here represents the overall frequency at which a political ad is displayed relative to organic content, such as entertaining videos. Users view the ad

5. In this context, "targeting" refers to the ability of AI-crafted messages to be more persuasive for naive agents, rather than targeting and reaching naive agents or those with a particular ideology more frequently. Such additional dimensions of targeting can also be incorporated, but we do not pursue them in our current work, since even without this feature, we show that digital ads polarize the electorate and induce further polarization between political parties.

a stochastic number of times $k \sim$ Poisson (αT). Each ad provides the same signal $s_i \in \{L, R\}$, depending on which party it comes. We assume that the left-wing party's ad always argues for the left-wing candidate being better and the right-wing party's ad always argues for the right-wing candidate. This implies that ad content is not truly informative about the underlying state θ. Sophisticated voters recognize this and do not update their beliefs b_i about θ in response to viewing ads.[6] Naive users, on the other hand, do not fully recognize this and, consequently, update their beliefs using Bayes's rule under the misspecified subjective model that $\mathbb{P}[s_i \neq \theta] = \phi \leq 1/2$.

A user receives no inherent value from the ads, whereas she collects an expected entertainment utility of $(1 - \alpha)T$ from viewing organic content.[7] This implies that more frequent ads have a cost in terms of lower entertainment utility for users. The platform makes a take-it-or-leave-it offer to the political parties in return for the digital ads that will be shown to users. These offers determine δ and the z_i's above.

12.5.3 Two-Party Competition

Our main result in this section characterizes the profit-maximizing platform business model as a function of the digital nature of advertising and the ad technology when there are two political parties:

PROPOSITION 5.1 *There exists* $\phi^*(\lambda) \in [0,1]$ *such that*

(i) If $\phi > \phi^*(\lambda)$, *the platform offers a subscription-based plan with* $P^* = T - v$ *and no advertising* $\alpha^* = 0$;

(ii) If $\phi < \phi^*(\lambda)$, *the platform offers an ad-based plan with* $P^* \subset [0, T - v)$ *and symmetric advertising loads* $\alpha^{(L)*} = \alpha^{(R)*} = \alpha^*/2 > 0$.

Moreover, $\phi^*(\lambda)$ *is decreasing in* λ.

The intuition for proposition 5.1 can be seen by varying the fraction of naive agents (lower λ) and/or the amount of false positive information in digital ads (lower ϕ). Under proposition 5.1(i), the fraction of naive agents is small and digital ads do not send many false positives or equivalently have little persuasiveness for naive agents. In this regime, the platform is better off monetizing via subscription fees because ads do little to sway the beliefs in the population, making parties unwilling to pay much to advertise

6. This assumption is similar to the result of Lemma 1 in Acemoglu et al. (2024), which shows that no surplus is generated from sophisticated voters who have linear demand over the advertised product. In our model with political digital ads, we impose a similar finding, which is that rational voters do not update their beliefs (because ads contain no information about θ) and thus, similarly, no surplus is generated from advertising to only rational agents.

7. The fact that users are atomless in voting and do not directly benefit from being better informed about the candidates is one key difference between our model of political digital ads and Acemoglu, Huttenlocher, et al. (2024), where agents recognize that the information in the ads will allow them to make better purchasing decisions. Another key difference is that candidates are vertically differentiated in this model, whereas products are horizontally differentiated in Acemoglu, Huttenlocher, et al. (2024).

on the platform. Consequently, the cost of showing ads is outweighed by the loss of revenue due to lower entertainment utility for users. In contrast, in proposition 5.1(ii), the population is more susceptible to digital ads and there are more naïfs in the population. In this case, advertising occurs in equilibrium, as both parties are willing to pay for digital ads to try to differentiate themselves from their rival and this compensates the platform for the loss in subscription revenue resulting from lower entertainment utility for users. The next proposition characterizes the implications of digital ads for the belief distribution of voters:

PROPOSITION 5.2 *Let density h be convex and continuous. Then:*
(i) If $\phi > \phi^*(\lambda)$, then the electorate has the same belief distribution H and political parties choose the same positions (x_L^*, x_R^*) in the extremal antisymmetric Nash equilibrium.
(ii) If $\phi < \phi^*(\lambda)$, then the electorate has a belief distribution $\tilde{H} \succ H$ and political parties choose $(\tilde{x}_L^*, \tilde{x}_R^*)$ in the extremal antisymmetric Nash equilibrium with $\tilde{x}_L^* < x_L^*$ and $\tilde{x}_R^* > x_R^*$.

Proposition 5.2 shows that political advertising in the regime where ads are targeted at naïfs tends to generate greater political polarization among the electorate, which in turn affects the polarization of political parties. Polarization of the electorate in regime (ii) is driven by the fact that agents receive more signals about the political parties, which naturally induces greater movements in their beliefs via Bayesian updating. While some agents become more moderate as a result of political advertising, the average movement of beliefs is toward the extremes. This can be seen from the fact that if all agents were sophisticated, advertising would induce a mean-preserving spread of beliefs (which follows from the Martingale property of Bayesian beliefs). However, with naive agents, belief movements are more pronounced and have a positive drift toward more extreme positions given the misspecification about the informativeness of political ads. Then, from lemma 1, such transitions to more extreme ideologies by the electorate also lead the parties to anchor to more polarizing positions as a result.

In proposition 5.2, as opposed to in proposition 4.3, we do not know where among the existing belief distribution polarization kicks in. The next corollary shows that this takes a form similar to proposition 4.3, with the extremes becoming more polarized, provided that the naive voters were already more extreme than sophisticates to start with. To state this result, we introduce the additional notation of H_N and H_S, which designate the belief distributions of naive voters and sophisticated voters, respectively, with $H = \lambda H_S + (1 - \lambda)H_N$:

COROLLARY 5.1 *Let H_N have support $[0, b_N^*] \cup [1 - b_N^*, 1]$ and H_S have support $[b_N^*, 1 - b_N^*]$. If $\lambda > 1/2$ and $\phi < \phi^*(\lambda)$, then voters at the medians on the left and the right ($\tilde{H}^{-1}(1/4)$ and $\tilde{H}^{-1}(3/4)$) continue to have the same b_i and $\tilde{b}_i$ after* *the introduction of the digital ads, but the overall distribution becomes more polarized, i.e.,* $\tilde{H} \succ H$, *which results in polarization in political party positions,* $\tilde{x}_L^* < x_L^*$ *and* $\tilde{x}_R^* > x_R^*$.

Corollary 5.1 establishes an analogous result to proposition 4.3, whereby relatively extreme voters become even more extreme in response to digital ads, while there is no similar polarization among moderate voters. The movements in the two extremes still lead to greater polarization on the part of the parties, however, with the same logic as in lemma 1(i). While we do not formally study it in this paper, corollary 5.1 opens up questions about the potential welfare implications of digital ads in driving parties to cater more to their most extreme supporters, at the cost of neglecting more moderate agents whose beliefs are less impacted via the digital ads channel.

12.5.4 Online Business Models with a Dominant Party

In this subsection, we consider a dominant party (e.g., an incumbent) that can advertise on the platform (which, without loss of generality, we suppose is the right-wing party). To model political dominance, we relax symmetry of the underlying belief distribution H, as well as symmetry of the ideal points $\hat{x}_L$ and $\hat{x}_R$ so that the dominant party wins probability $\chi_R^* > 1/2$ (without advertising).[8] We also assume, for simplicity, that under belief distribution H, the extremal equilibrium position x_R^* satisfies $x_R^* \geq \hat{x}_R$, so the equilibrium position the dominant party adopts is more extreme than its ideal point.

Our next result shows that, in this case, the platform's profit-maximizing business model is fully subscription based, rather than monetized via digital ads, independent of λ and ϕ:

PROPOSITION 5.3 *There exists* $\bar{\chi} > 0$ *such that if* $\chi_R^* > \bar{\chi}$, *the platform offers a subscription-based plan with* $P^* = T - v$ *and no advertising* $\alpha^* = 0$. *Moreover, the electorate has the same belief distribution* H *and political parties choose the same positions* (x_L^*, x_R^*) *in the extremal Nash equilibrium.*

The intuition for proposition 5.3 comes from considering the platform's incentives in setting its business model. If the dominant party decided to advertise, it would increase its vote share, as digital ads make the electorate more favorable toward it. However, the platform must weigh the revenue it earns from digital ads against the potential loss of subscription fees. When there is a dominant party, the incremental gain in vote share the party receives is small in comparison to the subscription revenue the platform forfeits by showing ads (given the party already has captured a substantial fraction χ_R^* of the vote). Importantly, this conclusion holds regardless of whether we are in part (i) or (ii) of proposition 5.1. Put differently, the

8. We prove in Appendix 8 that an extremal Nash equilibrium, this time defined only with reference to the dominant party, exists even when H is not symmetric (though the equilibrium will typically not be antisymmetric).

equilibrium business model may be subscription based even when there are many naive voters susceptible to digital ads (low λ and low ϕ), and the ad compensation from the dominant party may be insufficient to outweigh lost subscription revenue for the platform.

In contrast, as emphasized in proposition 5.1(ii), with sufficiently naive voters, competition between the two parties induces an equilibrium with digital ads. In this case, each party has an incentive to use digital ads to improve its position relative to its rival. The juxtaposition of these two results implies that, starting from a position in which there is a dominant party, as political competition intensifies, at some point, we may switch away from a subscription-based business model toward intensive use of digital political ads.

12.6 Effects of Regulations

In this section, we examine how certain online regulations might influence the polarizing effects of AI-powered platform economics. We analyze two types of interventions, one targeting the social media mechanism and another focusing on the digital ads mechanism, to study their potential impact on polarization dynamics.

12.6.1 Diversification Standards for Social Media

One tool that can be useful for countering the polarizing effects of AI-powered social media is a diversification standard, as advocated by Sunstein (2018). Let us consider the following type of diversification standard, denoted by γ: If the platform chooses a sharing network **P** that belongs to the class of island networks with parameters (k, p_s, p_d) (where k is the number of islands, p_s is the within-island link probability, and p_d is the between-island link probability), then the chosen network has to satisfy $p_s / p_d \equiv p^* \leq \gamma$. Notice that for $\gamma < \infty$ such a constraint will bind when $r < r_p$ because, as we have seen, the platform's profit-maximizing sharing network takes the form of an island network with $p_s = 1$ and $p_d = 0$. We think of γ as a *diversification* standard, requiring that agents be exposed to a certain fraction of cross-cutting perspectives:

Proposition 6.1 *There exists $\bar{r} < r_2$ such that for an article of reliability $r \in (0, \bar{r})$ and diversification standard $\gamma < \infty$, the platform chooses* **P** *from the class of island models (satisfying $p^* \leq \gamma$), and $\tilde{x}_L^* > x_L^{(FB)}$ and $\tilde{x}_R^* < x_R^{(FB)}$.*

Note that proposition 6.1 follows almost immediately from the proof of proposition 5 in in Acemoglu, Ozdaglar, and Siderius (2024). The key insight is that for a sufficiently light diversification standard γ, the platform is still incentivized to choose a sharing network that follows the (p_s, p_d) island structure from before. The only difference is that now some voters from the left will be exposed to counterattitudinal right-wing articles, and vice versa, and this can make the electorate less polarized and moderate party positions.[9]

12.6.2 Digital Ad Transparency

Another regulation, especially relevant in the context of the digital ads channel, is increasing the transparency of digital ads, which can be thought to reduce the fraction of naive agents in the population (increase λ) or reduce the effectiveness of ad targeting (increase ϕ), or both. We let λ' and ϕ' be the fraction of sophisticated agents and the power of the ad targeting post-intervention, whereas λ and ϕ are these corresponding quantities before the intervention:

Proposition 6.2 *Suppose $\phi < \phi^*(\lambda)$. There exist $\bar{\lambda} > 0$ and $\bar{\phi} > 0$ such that if $\lambda' > \bar{\lambda}$ or $\phi' > \bar{\phi}$, then digital ad transparency moderates electorate beliefs moderate to $\bar{H} \prec \tilde{H}$. Consequently, political parties choose more moderate positions $(\bar{x}_L^*, \bar{x}_R^*)$ with $\bar{x}_L^* > \tilde{x}_L^*$ and $\bar{x}_R^* < \tilde{x}_R^*$ in the extremal antisymmetric Nash equilibrium.*

Proposition 6.2 highlights the potential benefits of reducing the influence of targeted digital ads on naive voters. Note that proposition 6.2 does not follow directly from proposition 5.1, which requires both λ and ϕ to lie in a particular orthant of the parameter space, whereas proposition 6.2 considers a situation in which either λ *or* ϕ is increased.

We also note that a complementary tool to digital ad transparency is improving digital literacy among users. This might act in a similar fashion by making targeted digital ads less effective in influencing naive voters. Relatedly, Hudders, Van Reijmersdal, and Poels (2019) and Hobbs, Kanižaj, and Pereira (2019) discuss digital literacy and how it can make users more aware of misleading advertisements. Another complementary policy tool would be regulations that reduce the ability of the advertisement technology to microtarget very specific user groups and/or regulations on how generative AI can be used in such advertisements (see Golab-Andrzejak 2023; Simchon, Edwards, and Lewandowsky 2024).

12.6.3 Additional Interventions

Several insights from Acemoglu, Ozdaglar, and Siderius (2024) and Acemoglu, Huttenlocher, et al. (2024) can also be adapted to this environment, but we do not do so to avoid repetition. In particular, as in Acemoglu, Huttenlocher, et al. (2024), we examine how digital ad taxes might influence subscription-based business models and, through this channel, alter

9. Bail et al. (2018) show that over-exposure to counter-attitudinal news can have "backfire", leading to greater polarization. This suggests that too tight diversification standards may not achieve their desired intent.

the incentives for polarizing voter beliefs and consequently party positions. Our analysis suggests that digital ad taxes could lead to lower λ^* and ϕ^* in proposition 5.1 and proposition 5.2. The proof follows directly from proposition 15 in Acemoglu, Huttenlocher, et al. (2024): A tax on digital ad revenues would require that parties compensate the platform further for the corresponding loss in subscription revenues. For this to be profitable, a greater fraction of the population would need to be susceptible to ad targeting (lower λ) or digital ads would need to be more persuasive (lower ϕ), or some combination of the two. Additionally, we consider how watermarking schemes that tag reliable content on social media, along with other regulations, might also affect political polarization. However, as emphasized in Acemoglu, Ozdaglar, and Siderius (2024), these interventions can also generate offsetting effects, and if not carefully designed, they may have negative unintended consequences.

12.7 Concluding Remarks

It is now widely recognized that AI will transmute not just our economic and social lives, but also our politics. Yet, there is relatively little analysis of how, and through what channels, this political impact will work out in different kinds of societies. In this paper, we develop models to understand the effects of AI-powered social media and entertainment platforms on polarization and the political economy.

We focused on two types of influences, which we explored separately. In the first, which we refer to as the social media channel, AI's impacts work through the algorithms that a social media platform utilizes for determining the news and content feed of users, with the aim of maximizing engagement and the resulting digital ad revenue. The collection of data from users and powerful AI tools enable the platform to create "filter bubbles," whereby users only engage with the content passed on by like-minded other users. We established, following our previous work in Acemoglu, Ozdaglar, and Siderius (2024), that with low-reliability content, manufacturing filter bubbles is a profit-maximizing strategy for the platform, because it encourages the viral spread of news items, which would have otherwise been stopped and tagged as misinformation by users with different beliefs. We showed that such filter bubbles lead to the polarization of voters that already hold extreme views. Notably, even though moderate voters on the left and the right may not become much more polarized, political parties respond to the polarization at the tails by choosing more extreme policy positions.

In the second, which we call the digital ads channel, we consider an entertainment platform that intermixes content valued by users and digital ads from political parties. Following Acemoglu, Huttenlocher, et al. (2024), we suppose that there are both naive and sophisticated users, who have different susceptibilities to individualized ads, prepared and targeted by means of AI tools. We also allowed the platform to choose a business model based on subscriptions or one monetized via digital ads. We showed that with two parties from the two ends of the spectrum locked in neck-and-neck competition, monetization via digital ads is more profitable, and these digital ads sway naive voters to be more attached to their party. As a result, the electorate once again becomes more polarized, and parties similarly respond to such voter polarization by choosing more extreme policy positions. We show, in contrast, that the same outcome does not occur when platforms use a subscription-based model, and we also establish that it is the nature of political competition that makes digital ads more profitable; in fact, with one dominant party, the profit-maximizing business model would be the subscription-based one without this type of polarization. Hence, it is the interplay of AI-powered digital ads targeting naive users and intense political competition between the two parties that undergirds voter polarization, which then paves the way to political party polarization.

Overall, our analysis of both channels indicates that AI-powered platforms act as a source of polarization among voters, and political parties respond to this by choosing more polarized policy positions. We focused on the two channels separately, because they work in distinct ways and are impacted by different regulations differentially. In the social media channel, the AI's role is to enable sufficient data collection and processing in order to determine each user's ideological leanings and then create custom-made filter bubbles that make left-leaning (right-leaning) users more exposed to more left-leaning (right-leaning) content being transmitted by other left-leaning (right-leaning) users. For this reason, we also indicated how diversification standards for social media (e.g., as suggested by Sunstein 2018) could be an effective deterrent to further polarization. In the digital ads channel, AI is used for designing and targeting persuasive digital ads for naive users (with high susceptibility to targeted ads) from the two ends of the political spectrum. This suggests that different tools, in particular, digital ad transparency measures could be effective by reducing the susceptibility of naive users to such ads (see Golab-Andrzejak 2023; Simchon, Edwards, and Lewandowsky 2024). Additionally, digital ad taxes that push platforms toward a subscription-based model, as considered in Acemoglu, Huttenlocher, et al. (2024), could be effective in this case.

We view our paper as a first step in a vast landscape that involves multifaceted interactions between AI and politics. To start with, much more empirical work is necessary to delineate how online articles and messages impact people's political beliefs and how these translate into voting and other political actions in the offline world. Additionally, we have only touched upon a few of the ways AI impacts politics. It is useful to briefly discuss some of the other pathways, which are in principle equally important and also equally under-researched.

First, AI tools can create new ways in which both non-party actors (such as civil society organizations or extremist groups) and political parties can reach users in democracies. A few reports already discuss how platform algorithms created "rabbit holes" toward extremist groups in the 2010s, and more powerful AI models can significantly amplify these capabilities (see Brown et al. 2022; O'Callaghan et al. 2015). There are also understandable concerns about deepfakes enabling more manipulative outreach by both established and fringe actors (e.g., Langguth et al. 2021; Veerasamy and Pieterse 2022).

Second, AI can likewise provide new capabilities to nondemocratic regimes for indoctrination and spreading false information. There is relatively little work on what the limits of such indoctrination may be; for example, will the population ultimately understand the new capabilities in this domain and become immune to such indoctrination? There is both some theoretical work (e.g., Mostagir, Ozdaglar, and Siderius 2022) and empirical work (e.g., Hristakieva et al. 2022) that scratch the surface of such questions, while also raising important directions for future work in this area.

Third, existing research (e.g., Beraja et al. 2023; Beraja, Yang, and Yuchtman 2023; Zeng 2020) shows that AI capabilities have already been used effectively for surveillance and quelling dissent, which can transform politics both in nondemocratic and democratic systems. Nevertheless, there are relatively few theoretical and empirical studies of how intensified surveillance affects politics.

Fourth, a wealth of AI-generated content can reduce the population's interest and engagement in politics, with fairly uncertain but wide-ranging social and political implications. A version of this effect was anticipated by the philosopher Hannah Arendt when she wrote "If everybody lies to you, the consequence is not that you believe the lies, but rather that nobody believes anything any longer" (Berkowitz 2024). In practice, this and many other responses are possible in a world with more targeted, potentially more manipulative messages online (see Carroll et al. 2023; Chen and Papanastasiou 2021; Mostagir and Siderius 2022a).

Fifth, AI tools can conceivably enable users to check the veracity and reliability of claims and messages in social media, or can be deployed for creating new platforms for more reliable political communication and even new ways for consensus and compromise-building (see some discussions of this issue in chapter 10 of Acemoglu and Johnson 2023). These AI-driven systems could assess the credibility of sources, detect inconsistencies in narratives, and provide users with context or alternative perspectives to improve informed decision-making (e.g., see Gabriel et al. 2024). Additionally, AI could facilitate real-time content moderation by flagging or debunking misleading claims before they gain traction (see Lu et al. 2022). Beyond fact-checking, AI-powered platforms could foster more constructive political discourse by structuring debates, summarizing key arguments, and even suggesting areas of compromise based on common ground between opposing viewpoints (see Huerta et al. 2023).

Finally, the myriad other effects of AI working through automation, job loss, wealth and income inequality, and productivity enhancement can also have downstream effects on politics. Automation increases productivity but also displaces jobs, particularly in middle-skill occupations, worsening income and wealth inequality (Acemoglu and Restrepo 2020; Chen, Li, and Tang 2022; Gallego and Kurer 2022). These shifts can fuel populist movements, reshape labor policies, and drive debates on AI regulation and social safety nets. Moreover, AI-driven economic concentration may alter political alignments and policymaking, as wealth and power become increasingly centralized in tech-centric regions. AI's economic disruptions have significant political consequences, influencing governance, policy debates, and public sentiment.

We view all of these areas as fruitful directions for future research.

Appendix

A. Equilibria with a Dominant Party

Suppose there is a dominant party in power, which implies that the distribution of prior ideological beliefs, H, may not necessarily be symmetric (i.e., it is skewed toward the dominant party). This yields a slightly different version of the result in lemma 1. We will leverage this result in Section 12.5.4.

LEMMA A.1

(i) There exists a Nash equilibrium (x_L^*, x_R^*) *in potentially asymmetric strategies with* $x_L^* < x_R^*$;

(ii) There exists an extremal Nash equilibrium $(\bar{x}_L^*, \bar{x}_R^*)$ *with* $\bar{x}_R^* \geq x_R^*$ *for all Nash equilibria* (x_L^*, x_R^*);

(iii) If $\tilde{H} \succ_{FOSD} H$, *then for every Nash equilibrium* (x_L^*, x_R^*) *under belief distribution H, there exists a Nash equilibrium* $(\tilde{x}_L^*, \tilde{x}_R^*)$ *such that* $\tilde{x}_L^* > x_L^*$ and $\tilde{x}_R^* > x_R^*$.

PROOF OF LEMMA A.1. For part (i), consider the function $\varphi : [0,1]^2 \rightarrow [0,1]^2$ that maps an arbitrary position (x_L, x_R) into the best response positions (x_L^{BR}, x_R^{BR}), where the right-wing party takes the left-wing's party position as given, and vice versa. Similar to the proof of lemma 1, we have a continuous mapping from a compact, convex set onto itself. By Brouwer's theorem we are guaranteed a fixed point of φ such that $\varphi(x_L^*, x_R^*) = (x_L^*, x_R^*)$, which is the definition of a Nash equilibrium.

Then it just remains to show we cannot have $x_L^* = x_R^*$. We argue by contradiction, that $x_L^* = x_R^*$, which means at least one party is not at its ideal point, let's say party R without loss of generality. Then, when $x_L^* = x_R^*$, one can show similar to in lemma 1 that

$$\frac{\partial}{\partial x_R} \mathcal{R} \cdot \int_0^1 \frac{\exp(-(\beta - x_R)^2)}{\exp(-(\beta - x_R)^2) + \exp(-(\beta - x_L^*)^2)} h(\beta)\, d\beta \,\Big|_{x_R = x_R^* = x_L^*} = 0,$$

whereas $(\partial / \partial x_R)(x_R - \hat{x}_R)^2 = 2(x_R - \hat{x}_R) \neq 0$. Thus, there is a profitable deviation of party R closer to its ideal policy point, contradicting that this is an equilibrium. This establishes part (i).

To see part (ii), it is sufficient to argue that there exist finitely many Nash equilibria. Suppose that (x_L^*, x_R^*) is a Nash equilibrium and take a neighborhood $B_\epsilon(x_L^*, x_R^*)$ of radius $\epsilon > 0$. Now consider $\varphi' = \varphi - I$ where $I(\cdot)$ is the identity function. Then $\varphi'(x_L^*, x_R^*) = 0$ and given that 1 is not an eigenvalue of $d\varphi$ (which holds generically), we have that $\det(d\varphi') \neq 0$, and hence φ' is a local diffeomorphism by the inverse function theorem, implying that φ' is bijective over $B_\epsilon(x_L, x_R)$. This prevents another point $(x_L', x_R') \in B_\epsilon(x_L, x_R)$ such that $\varphi'(x_L', x_R') = 0$ (i.e., in other words, it bars the existence of another fixed point in the open-neighborhood of (x_L, x_R). Finally we leverage that $[0,1]^2$ is compact: Take an open cover around each fixed point of φ and the complement of the set of fixed points. There exists a finite subcover, so there must exist finitely many fixed points of φ.

To see part (iii), we define the function $\varphi : [x_L^*, 1]\, [x_R^*, 1] \rightarrow [x_L^*, 1][x_R^*, 1]$ as before but defined on a subspace of $[0,1]^2$, where we map arbitrary cutoffs in $(x_L, x_R) \in [x_L^*, 1] \times [x_R^*, 1]$ to best-response cutoffs (x_L^{BR}, x_R^{BR}) under distribution $\tilde{H}$. To see this is a well-defined mapping, note that for any $x_L \in [x_L^*, 1]$ it is a best response for party R to choose a position at least at x_R^*, and similarly for any $x_R \in [x_R^*, 1]$ it is a best response for party L to choose a position at least at x_L^*, given the first-order stochastic dominance shift in H to $\tilde{H}$. We can see this by noting that

$$\frac{\partial}{\partial x_R} \mathcal{R} \cdot \int_0^1 \frac{\exp[-(\beta - x_R)^2]}{\exp[-(\beta - x_R)^2] + \exp[-(\beta - x_L^*)^2]} \times h(\beta)\, d\beta - 2(x_R^* - \hat{x}_R) \Big|_{x_R = x_R^*} = 0,$$

by optimality of x_R^* for party R, which implies that

$$\frac{\partial}{\partial x_R} \mathcal{R} \cdot \int_0^1 \frac{\exp(-[\beta - x_R)^2]}{\exp[-(\beta - x_R)^2] + \exp[-(\beta - x_L^*)^2]} \times \tilde{h}(\beta)\, d\beta - 2(x_R^* - \hat{x}_R) \Big|_{x_R = x_R^*} > 0,$$

and moreover $\partial x_R^* / \partial x_L^* > 0$ everywhere. Thus, φ has a fixed point in this subspace of $[0,1]^2$, exactly as in claim (iii). ■

B. Proofs

Proof of Lemma 1. To prove (i), we establish the existence of an anti-symmetric Nash equilibrium. The utility for party j is equal to $U_p = R \cdot \mathbb{P}[\theta \geq 1 - \chi_j] - (x - \hat{x}_i)^2$, which is equivalent to

$$U_j = \mathcal{R} \cdot \int_0^1 \frac{\exp[-(\beta - x_i)^2]}{\exp[-(\beta - x_i)^2] + \exp[-(\beta - x_j)^2]} h(\beta)\, d\beta - (x_i - \hat{x}_i)^2.$$

First, We argue that $x_L^* \leq (1/2) \leq x_R^*$. Suppose not, and without loss generality, consider $x_R^* < (1/2)$. Then

$$\frac{\partial U_R(x_R^*)}{\partial x_R^*} = \mathcal{R} \cdot \int_0^1 \frac{2(\beta - x_R^*) e^{-(\beta - x_R^*)^2 - (\beta - x_L^*)^2}}{(e^{-(\beta - x_L^*)^2} + e^{-(\beta - x_R^*)^2})^2} h(\beta) d\beta - 2(x_R^* - \hat{x}_R) > 0,$$

given that $x_L', x_R' < (1/2)$, and H is symmetric. To see this, we just consider:

$$\int_0^1 \frac{2(\beta - x_R^*) e^{-(\beta - x_R^*)^2 - (\beta - x_L^*)^2}}{(e^{-(\beta - x_L^*)^2} + e^{-(\beta - x_R^*)^2})^2} h(\beta)\, d\beta$$

$$= \int_0^{x_R^*} \frac{2(\beta - x_R^*) e^{-(\beta - x_R^*)^2 - (\beta - x_L^*)^2}}{(e^{-(\beta - x_L^*)^2} + e^{-(\beta - x_R^*)^2})^2} h(\beta)\, d\beta + \int_{x_R^*}^{1/2} \frac{2(\beta - x_R^*) e^{-(\beta - x_R^*)^2 - (\beta - x_L^*)^2}}{(e^{-(\beta - x_L^*)^2} + e^{-(\beta - x_R^*)^2})^2} h(\beta)\, d\beta$$

$$+ \int_{1/2}^{1/2 + x_R^*} \frac{2(\beta - x_R^*) e^{-(\beta - x_R^*)^2 - (\beta - x_L^*)^2}}{(e^{-(\beta - x_L^*)^2} + e^{-(\beta - x_R^*)^2})^2} h(\beta) d\beta + \int_{1/2 + x_R^*}^{1} \frac{2(\beta - x_R^*) e^{-(\beta - x_R^*)^2 - (\beta - x_L^*)^2}}{(e^{-(\beta - x_L^*)^2} + e^{-(\beta - x_R^*)^2})^2} h(\beta) d\beta$$

And note by symmetry of H (and by virtue of $x_L^*, x_R^* < 1/2$), the first integral is smaller in absolute value than the third integral, while the second and fourth integrals are strictly positive. At the same time $2(x_R^* - \hat{x}_R) < 0$ given $x_R^* < 1/2 < \hat{x}_R$. Thus, it is a profitable deviation for party R to increase its x_R from any policy point $x_R^* < 1/2$, a contradiction of x_R^* being an equilibrium. An analogous argument shows that $x_L^* \leq 1/2$, so we must have $x_L^* \leq 1/2 \leq x_R^*$.

Next, we consider the map $\varphi : [0,1] \to [0,1]$ that maps an arbitrary position x_L into the complementary best-response position $1 - x_R^{BR}$, where x_R^{BR} solves the following (with x_L taken as given):

$$\max_{x_R \in [0,1]} U_R = \mathcal{R} \cdot \int_0^1 \frac{\exp(-(\beta - x_R)^2)}{\exp(-(\beta - x_L)^2) + \exp(-(\beta - x_R)^2)} h(\beta)\, d\beta - (x_R - \hat{x}_R)^2.$$

Utility U_R is quasi-concave when H is symmetric, so it must be the case that this admits a unique $x_R^*(x_L)$ which is a global maximum for U_R over all of $[0,1]$ (see Mas-Colell et al. 1995). Moreover, by the inverse function theorem, the solution $x_R^*(x_L)$ is continuous in x_L. By Brouwer's theorem, there exists a fixed point of φ such that $x_R^* = x_R^{BR}(1 - x_R^*)$, which by symmetry implies that $x_L^* = x_L^{BR}(x_R^*)$, and thus (x_L^*, x_R^*) is an antisymmetric Nash equilibrium by construction.

For part (ii), it is sufficient to argue that there exist finitely many antisymmetric Nash equilibria, and then we can let $(\underline{x}_L^*, \overline{x}_R^*)$ denote the most extremal antisymmetric Nash equilibrium. We use the Lefschetz fixed-point theorem to establish this (see Dold 2012). We prove that each fixed point of φ is a Lefschetz fixed point (i.e., it is isolated); consider a fixed point $(x_L^*, 1 - x_L^*)$. Note that there exists an open neighborhood $B_\epsilon(x_L^*)$ where $x_R^*(x_L)$ is bijective over $B_\epsilon(x_L^*)$ for small enough ϵ given that $(\partial x_R^* / \partial x_L)\,|_{x_L = x_L^*, x_R = 1 - x_L^*} \neq 1$, which holds for generic $\mathcal{R}$ by the inverse function theorem.

Thus, there exists a unique fixed point $x_L^* \in B_\epsilon(x_L^*)$ for small enough $\epsilon > 0$. Finally, it just remains to consider the following open cover of $[0,1]$: Take $B_\epsilon(x_L^*)$ around each of the fixed points x_L^*, and the complement of the set of fixed points (which is open because the set of fixed points is always closed). Since [0,1] is compact, there must be finitely many subcovers, which in particular, implies there exist finitely many Lefschetz fixed points.

By contradiction, suppose there exist infinitely many fixed points, so for any $\varepsilon > 0$, there exists $|\tilde{x}_L^* - \tilde{\bar{x}}_L^*| < \varepsilon$ such that

$$\frac{\partial U_R(x_R^*)}{\partial x_R^*} = \mathcal{R} \cdot \int_0^1 \frac{2(\beta - x_R^*)e^{-(\beta - x_R^*)^2 - (\beta - \underline{x}_L^*)^2}}{(e^{-(\beta - \underline{x}_L^*)^2} + e^{-(\beta - x_R^*)^2})^2} h(\beta)\, d\beta + 2(x_R^* - \hat{x}_R)$$

Consequently, fixed points are isolated As such, we consider open neighborhoods around the fixed points of $(x_L^*, 1 - x_L^*)$ and take an open cover around the fixed points of φ and the complement of the set of fixed points. Existence of a finite subcover (given that [0,1] is compact) guarantees there exist finitely many fixed points of φ.

Finally, it remains to show that $x_L' = x_R' = 1/2$ is not an equilibrium. Note that in this case we have that for party R, their payoff is given by

$$U_i = \mathcal{R} \cdot \int_0^1 \frac{\exp(-(\beta - x_R)^2)}{\exp(-\beta - x_R)^2 + \exp(-\beta - 1/2)^2} h(\beta)\, d\beta + (x_R - \hat{x}_R)^2$$

Taking a first-order condition with respect to x_R evaluated at proposed equilibrium $x_R' = 1/2$, we see that

$$\frac{\partial U_i}{\partial x_R}\left(x_R = \frac{1}{2}\right) = \mathcal{R} \cdot \int_0^1 \frac{\begin{Bmatrix} 4(\beta - 1/2)\exp[-2(\beta - 1/2)^2] \\ -4(\beta - 1/2)\exp[-2(\beta - 1/2)^2] \end{Bmatrix}}{4\exp[-2(\beta - 1/2)^2]} h(\beta)\, d\beta + 2(x_R - \hat{x}_R)$$
$$= 2(x_R - \hat{x}_R)$$

Thus, party R has an incentive to move some small ε to the right of $x_R' = 1/2$ (closer to its policy ideal point), while losing only a second-order fraction of voters by doing so. This is a contradiction of $x_L' = x_R' = 1/2$ being an equilibrium, as we wanted to show.

For part (ii), suppose for distribution H we have an extremal antisymmetric Nash equilibrium $(\underline{x}_L^*, \bar{x}_R^*)$ and let us consider distribution $\tilde{H}$ and extremal symmetric Nash equilibrium $(\underline{x}_L^*, \bar{\bar{x}}_R^*)$. Under $\tilde{H}$, we know that the best response of x_R given $\underline{x}_L^*$ is some $x_R^* > \bar{x}_R^*$ (and conversely, the new best-response position for party L satisfies $x_L^* < \underline{x}_L^*$ given $\bar{x}_R^*$). To see this, first notice that we have the following first-order condition

$$\frac{\partial U_R(x_R^*)}{\partial x_R^*} = \mathcal{R} \cdot \int_0^1 \frac{2(\beta - x_R^*)e^{-(\beta - x_R^*)^2 - (\beta - \underline{x}_L^*)^2}}{(e^{-(\beta - \underline{x}_L^*)^2} + e^{-(\beta - x_R^*)^2})^2} h(\beta)\, d\beta - 2(x_R^* - \hat{x}_R) = 0,$$

whereas under $\tilde{H}$, we leverage lemma A.3 in Acemoglu, Ozdaglar, and Siderius (2024), and compute the gain in voter share if an agent were originally at belief b_i under H (but now has belief $b_i + \epsilon_i$ under $\tilde{H}$) and consider a deviation slightly to the right:

$$\frac{\partial U_R}{\partial x_R^*} = \mathcal{R}\cdot\int_0^{1/2}\frac{2(\beta-\epsilon(\beta)-x_R^*)e^{-(\beta-\epsilon(\beta)-x_R^*)^2-(\beta-\epsilon(\beta)-\underline{x}_L^*)^2}}{(e^{-(\beta-\epsilon(\beta)\underline{x}_L^*)^2}+e^{-(\beta-\epsilon(\beta)-x_R^*)^2})^2}h(\beta)\,d\beta$$

$$+\mathcal{R}\cdot\int_{1/2}^{1}\frac{2(\beta+\epsilon(\beta)-x_R^*)e^{-(\beta+\epsilon(\beta)-x_R^*)^2-(\beta+\epsilon(\beta)-\underline{x}_L^*)^2}}{(e^{-(\beta+\epsilon(\beta)-\underline{x}_L^*)^2}+e^{-(\beta+\epsilon(\beta)-x_R^*)^2})^2}h(\beta)\,d\beta-\mathcal{R}$$

$$\cdot\int_0^1\frac{2(\beta-x_R^*)e^{-(\beta-x_R^*)^2-(\beta-\underline{x}_L^*)^2}}{(e^{-(\beta-\underline{x}_L^*)^2}+e^{-(\beta-x_R^*)^2})^2}h(\beta)\,d\beta.$$

By the fact that $\epsilon(\beta)=\epsilon(1-\beta)$ and via symmetry of H, we will argue that this expression is positive. To see this, observe that letting $f(\beta) = 2(\beta-x_R^*)(e^{-(\beta-x_R^*)^2-(\beta-\underline{x}_L^*)^2}/[e^{-(\beta-\underline{x}_L^*)^2}+e^{(-\beta-x_R^*)^2})^2]$, we obtain a relationship between the integrals $\int_0^{1/2} f(\beta-\epsilon(\beta),x_R^*,x_L^*)h(\beta)\,d\beta$, $\int_{1/2}^1 f(\beta+\epsilon(\beta),x_R^*,x_L^*)h(\beta)\,d(\beta)$ and $\int_0^1 f(\beta,x_R^*,x_L^*)h(\beta)\,d(\beta)$. Via second-order Taylor series approximation, we have that for a symmetric distribution H,

$$\int_0^{1/2} f[\beta-\epsilon(\beta)]h(\beta)\,d(\beta)+\int_{1/2}^1 f[\beta+\epsilon(b)]h(\beta)\,d\beta$$

$$\approx\int_0^1\left(f(\beta)+\frac{1}{2}\epsilon(\beta)^2 f''(\beta)\right)h(\beta)d(\beta)$$

and correspondingly we can see that our original expression can be approximated by $1/2\int_{\frac{1}{2}}^1\epsilon(\beta)^2 f''(\beta)h(\beta)\,d\beta$, which determines the sign of $\partial U_R/\partial x_R^*$. It just suffices then to look at $\text{sgn}[\int_{\frac{1}{2}}^1\epsilon(\beta)^2 f''(\beta)h(\beta)\,d\beta]$, which requires that $\text{sgn}[f''(1-\beta)+f''(\beta)]>0$ for all β given that H is symmetric, which can be straightforwardly verified when evaluated at $\overline{x}_R^*>1/2$, given that $\underline{x}_L^* = 1-\overline{x}_R^*<1/2$, as follows:

$$f'(\beta) = -\frac{2e^{(\beta-x_R^*)^2+(\beta-\underline{x}_L^*)^2}}{(e^{(\beta-x_R^*)^2}+e^{(\beta-\underline{x}_L^*)^2})^3}\cdot(e^{(\beta-x_R^*)^2}(-1-2\beta x_R^*+2(x_R^*)^2+2\beta\underline{x}_L^*-2x_R^*\underline{x}_L^*)$$

$$+e^{(\beta-\underline{x}_L^*)^2}\left[-1-2(x_R^*)^2+2\beta(x_R^*-\underline{x}_L^*)+2x_R^*\underline{x}_L^*)\right]$$

$$f''(\beta) = -\frac{8(x_R^*-\underline{x}_L^*)e^{(\beta-x_R^*)^2+(\beta-\underline{x}_L^*)^2}}{(e^{(\beta-x_R^*)^2}+^{(\beta-\underline{x}_L^*)^2})^4}\cdot(e^{2(\beta-x_R^*)^2}(\beta(\underline{x}_L^*-x_R^*)+(x_R^*)^2-x_R^*\underline{x}_L^*-1)$$

$$+e^{2(\beta-\underline{x}_L^*)^2}\left[\beta(\underline{x}_L^*-x_R^*)+(x_R^*)^2-x_R^*\underline{x}_L^*+1)+4(\beta-x_R^*)(x_R^*-\underline{x}_L^*)e^{(\beta-x_R^*)^2+(\beta-x_l^*)^2}\right].$$

Plugging in β and $1-\beta$ to $f''(\cdot)$ and summing yields the desired claim of positivity. Analogously, we see that the best response of x_L given $\overline{x}_R^*$ satisfies $x_L^*<\underline{x}_L^*$. The monotonicity of the equilibrium cutoffs $(\tilde{x}_R,\tilde{x}_L)$ under transformations of $\tilde{H}$ then follows from Milgrom and Shannon (1994).

Finally, it just remains to show that $(\underline{x}_L^*,\overline{x}_R^*)$ is not an equilibrium under $\tilde{H}$. But this has already been done in the first step above, by showing that party R has a profitable deviation to increase x_R above $\overline{x}_R^*$ (when party L plays $\underline{x}_L^*$) and party L has a profitable deviation to decrease x_L below $\underline{x}_L^*$ (when party R plays $\overline{x}_R^*$), given a shift in the underlying belief distribution to $\tilde{H}$. ■

Proof of Proposition 4.1. This follows immediately from the proof of theorem 3 in Acemoglu, Ozdaglar, and Siderius (2024). ■

PROOF OF PROPOSITION 4.2. First, we claim that if $m = R$, the filter bubble consists of agents with prior beliefs $b_i \in [\underline{b},1]$ for some $\underline{b} < 1$ given that $r < r_P$. By the proof of theorem 3 in Acemoglu, Ozdaglar, and Siderius (2024), the platform will choose the smallest $\underline{b} \in \{0,\varepsilon,\ldots,m\varepsilon,\ldots,1\}$ such that the fully connected network of beliefs $[\underline{b},1]$ induce all these agents to either share or ignore (known as the "filter bubble"). If there were a disconnected region, say $b_1 < b_2 < b_3$ with b_1 and b_3 in the filter bubble, but b_2 not, then the sharing network of the platform is not profit-maximizing, because by adding the agent with b_2 to the network, the payoff to agents with b_1 and b_3 increases or remains constant if agent b_2 shares, whereas b_2 is necessarily willing to share in some equilibrium if agent b_1 is willing to, given π_2 (agent i with belief b_2's posterior belief about article veracity) is higher than π_1. The result then follows from Topkis (1998) given our social media game is supermodular.

Second, we show that $\underline{b}$ increases as r decreases. Once again this is a direct consequence of Topkis (1998) and noting that the payoff to sharing uniformly decreases for all agents in the population as r decreases. Formally, the payoff to sharing is given by $U_i = u\pi_i - c(1-\pi_i) + \kappa S_i - dD_i$, and π_i is decreasing in r, and this has a supermodular form. We thus get monotone comparative statics on the network of agents with priors on $[\bar{b},1]$, with some agents potentially now disliking given the decrease in r. Consequently, the profit-maximizing sharing network per proposition 4.1 (and theorem 3 in Acemoglu, Ozdaglar, and Siderius (2024)) consists of agents with prior beliefs $[\underline{b}',1]$ with $\underline{b}' > \underline{b}$.

Third, we show that for any agent i on the platform with prior $b_i < 1$, there exists $\underline{r}$ such that if $r < \underline{r}$, ignoring is a better response than sharing. The payoff to sharing is upper bounded by $u\pi_i - c(1 - \pi_i) + \kappa N$ and the payoff to ignoring is 0. Whenever $\pi_i < [(c - \kappa N)/(u - c)]$, the payoff to ignoring is higher, and since $\pi_i \to 0$ as $r \to 0$ and $(\kappa < c)/N$ (see Section 2.6 of Acemoglu, Ozdaglar, and Siderius 2024), there exists such a value of r sufficiently small such that the agent of type b_i will not share. Moreover, we show there exists $\underline{r}'$ such that if $r < \underline{r}'$, disliking is a better response to ignoring, which makes disliking the best response. To see this, notice that the payoff to disliking is $\tilde{u}(1-\pi_i) - \tilde{c}$, and $1-\pi_i \to 1$ as $r \to 0$ and $\tilde{u} > \tilde{c}$. This implies that agent i will not be included in the filter bubble in the profit-maximizing sharing network. ■

PROOF OF PROPOSITION 4.3. First, notice that if an agent receives two articles of opposing messages with the same reliability, her posterior belief $\tilde{b}_i$ will remain unchanged. This is due to the symmetry of the two messages and the Martingale property of Bayesian beliefs; if their posterior changed after seeing both $m = L$ and $m = R$ of the same reliability r, then their prior belief must be miscalibrated. Thus, $\tilde{H}_C = H$, and the beliefs of the agents before and after the news sharing remain identical, so it just suffices to prove that $\tilde{H}_{FB} \succ H$.

It is clear from proposition 4.1 and proposition 4.2 that, for any $\underline{b}$, we can pick a value for r such that the agents with priors $[\underline{b},1]$ are the ones in the platform's profit-maximizing filter bubble (again, assuming message $m = R$). Let us pick r_2 such that $\underline{b} > H^{-1}(3/4)$, so then agents who receive article $m = L$ will be those with prior beliefs at most $b_i \in [0,1-\underline{b}]$ and the agents who receive article $m = R$ will be those with prior beliefs at most $b_i \in [\underline{b},1]$. Consequently, agents with beliefs $b_i \in [H^{-1}(1/4), H^{-1}(3/4)]$ do not view any article, and thus do not update their beliefs, so $\tilde{H}$ remains consistent with H over all beliefs $b_i \in [H^{-1}(1/4), H^{-1}(3/4)]$.

It finally remains to prove that agents with $b_i \in [\underline{b},1]$ who view an article $m = R$ update their beliefs to some $b_i + \epsilon_i$ (by lemma A.3 from Acemoglu, Ozdaglar, and Siderius (2024)). We find that

$$\tilde{b}_i = \frac{pb_i\pi_i}{pb_i + (1-p)(1-b_i)} + (1-\pi_i)b_i,$$

where

$$\pi_i = \frac{[pb_i + (1-p)(1-b_i)]r}{[b_i/2 + (1-b_i)/2](1-r) + [pb_i + (1-p)(1-b_i)]r}.$$

We get the simplification that

$$\tilde{b}_i - b_i = \pi_i\left(\frac{pb_i}{pb_i + (1-p)(1-b_i)} - b_i\right)$$

where clearly $pb_i/[pb_i + (1-p)(1-b_i)] > b_i$ given $p > 1/2$ and $b_i > 1/2$, so $\tilde{b}_i - b_i > 0$. It follows from an analogous argument that agents with $b_i \in [0,1-\underline{b}]$ who view an article $m = L$ update their beliefs to some $b_i - \epsilon_i$. The claim follows by choosing $r_1 < r_2$ but sufficiently large that the filter bubble is non-empty. ■

Proof of Corollary 4.1. This follows immediately from the results of proposition 4.3 and lemma 1(ii). ■

Proof of Proposition 4.4. Choose $r^* = r_P$; then the platform's profit-maximizing sharing network is fully connected. By the same arguments as in proposition 4.3, posterior beliefs do not change for any agents in the population because they view both articles, so in particular the inequality holds for $\varepsilon = 0$.

Next, note that $\pi_i \to 0$ as $r \to 0$, so it is sufficient to work with π_i. From the proof of proposition 4.3, for the right-wing agents who receive the $m = R$ article when reliability is low, we have the relationship that

$$\tilde{b}_i - b_i = \pi_i\left(\frac{pb_i}{pb_i + (1-p)(1-b_i)} - b_i\right) \leq \pi_i$$

By continuity of the voting game in Section 2, there exists a small enough ζ such that if $\pi_i \leq \zeta$, then the extremal antisymmetric Nash equilibrium changes by at most $\varepsilon > 0$ in both $\tilde{x}_L^{FB}$ and $\tilde{x}_R^{FB}$. ■

Proof of Proposition 5.1. Notice that naive and sophisticated agents always choose the same online plan because they have an atomless contribution to the outcome of the election and hence do not value the additional information that they will get via digital ads (even when they think such ads are informative, as is the case for naive agents). Hence, they get no inherent value from advertising, and they would simply both choose the plan that maximizes $(1-\alpha_\ell)T - P_\ell$. Offering two plans is, therefore, redundant and without loss of generality we can suppose the platform offers a single plan (this is in stark contrast to Acemoglu, Huttenlocher, et al. 2024).

First, for advertising intensities $(\alpha^{(L)}, \alpha^{(R)})$, the platform makes a maximal advertising revenue from naïfs of $(1-\lambda)m^*(\alpha^{(L)}, \alpha^{(R)})$ and can charge a subscription fee $P^*(\Sigma_{j\in[L,R]}\alpha^{(j)})$, which is decreasing in the total ad load; in particular, the optimal price the platform charges conditional on ad intensity $(\alpha^{(L)}, \alpha^{(R)})$ is just $P^* = (1-\alpha^{(L)}-\alpha^{(R)})T - v$. The platform then solves

$$\max_{(\alpha^{(L)},\alpha^{(R)})} (1-\lambda)m^*(\alpha^{(L)},\alpha^{(R)}) + P^*\left(\sum_{j\in\{L,R\}}\alpha^{(j)}\right) \tag{3}$$

Let us denote $[\alpha^{(L)*}(\lambda,\phi), \alpha^{(R)*}(\lambda,\phi)]$ as the solution to equation (3). Notably, $m^*[\alpha^{(L)*}(\lambda,\phi), \alpha^{(R)*}(\lambda,\phi)]$ is decreasing in ϕ by the arguments in the proof of lemma 2 in Acemoglu, Huttenlocher, et al. (2024). This implies that equation (3) is decreasing in ϕ, as we have for $\phi' > \phi$,

$$\begin{aligned}
&(1-\lambda)m^*_\phi(\alpha^{(L)*}(\lambda,\phi),\alpha^{(R)*}(\lambda,\phi)) + P^*\left(\sum_{j\in\{L,R\}}\alpha^{(j)}(\lambda,\phi)\right)\\
&\geq (1-\lambda)m^*_\phi(\alpha^{(L)*}(\lambda,\phi'),\alpha^{(R)*}(\lambda,\phi')) + P^*\left(\sum_{j\in\{L,R\}}\alpha^{(j)}(\lambda,\phi')\right)\\
&> (1-\lambda)m^*_{\phi'}(\alpha^{(L)*}(\lambda,\phi'),\alpha^{(R)*}(\lambda,\phi')) + P^*\left(\sum_{j\in\{L,R\}}\alpha^{(j)}(\lambda,\phi')\right),
\end{aligned}$$

where m^*_ϕ is the ad revenue under parameter ϕ. Fixing λ, we can first check whether setting $\phi = 0$ yields $(\alpha^{(L)*}, \alpha^{(R)*}) = (0,0)$, in which case we set $\phi^*(\lambda) = 0$. Otherwise one can find the supremal value $\phi^* > 0$ such that

$$m^*[\alpha^{(L)*}(\lambda,\phi^*),\alpha^{(R)*}(\lambda,\phi^*)] + P^*\left(\sum_{j\in\{L,R\}}\alpha^{(j)*}(\lambda,\phi^*)\right) > T - v \tag{4}$$

which has a unique solution $\phi^*(\lambda)$ because the LHS is decreasing in ϕ, the RHS is constant, the function

$$m^*[\alpha^{(L)*}(\lambda,0),\alpha^{(R)*}(\lambda,0)] + P^*\left(\sum_{j\in\{L,R\}}\alpha^{(j)*}(\lambda,0)\right) > T - v$$

by assumption, and when $\phi = 1/2$, we have

$$m^*\left\{\left[\alpha^{(L)*}\left(\lambda,\frac{1}{2}\right),\alpha^{(R)*}\left(\lambda,\frac{1}{2}\right)\right]\right\} + P^*\left\{\left[\sum_{j\in\{L,R\}}\alpha^{(j)*}\left(\lambda,\frac{1}{2}\right)\right]\right\} < T - v$$

given that the maximal transfer from the firm satisfies

$$m^*\left\{\left[\alpha^{(L)*}\left(\lambda,\frac{1}{2}\right),\alpha^{(R)*}\left(\lambda,\frac{1}{2}\right)\right]\right\} = 0$$

and

$$P^*\left[\sum_{j\in\{L,R\}} \alpha^{(j)*}\left(\lambda,\frac{1}{2}\right)\right] < T - v$$

unless $\alpha^{(L^*)} = \alpha^{(R^*)} = 0$. We thus have the desired result, that for $\phi > \phi^*(\lambda)$, the platform offers a fully subscription-based model whereas when $\phi < \phi^*(\lambda)$, the platform offers at least some advertising $\alpha^* = \alpha^{(L)*} + \alpha^{(R)*} > 0$, by construction of ϕ^*.

Second, it remains to show that $\phi^*(\lambda)$ is decreasing in λ. As in the proof of proposition 7 of Acemoglu, Huttenlocher, et al. (2024), we know that $m^*\{[\alpha^{(L)*}(\lambda, \phi^*), \alpha^{(R)*}(\lambda, \phi^*)]\}$ is decreasing in λ, so the expression $(1 - \lambda)$ $m^*\{[\alpha^{(L)*}(\lambda, \phi^*), \alpha^{(R)*}(\lambda, \phi^*)]\}$ is decreasing in λ, and the LHS of equation (4) is decreasing in λ (by the same reasoning as the chain of inequalities for ϕ). Thus for higher values of λ, the subscription model becomes more viable for the platform, which in turn implies that $\phi^*(\lambda)$ decreases in λ.

Finally, we argue that the advertising loads are symmetric in equilibrium. To see this, consider the map $\psi : [0,1] \to [0,1]$ that maps left-wing advertiser's load, $\alpha^{(L)}$, to advertising load of the right-wing party, $\alpha^{(R)}$, that would maximize the gains for the right-wing party from advertising. Generically, this map is well-defined (there is a single global maximum, see Ott and Yorke 2005), continuous and maps a convex set onto itself, and thus by Brouwer's theorem has a fixed point $\Psi(\alpha^*/2) = \alpha^*/2$ for some total advertising load $\alpha^* > 0$. By symmetry, when the right-wing party is advertising at $\alpha^*/2$, it is also a best response for the left-wing party to advertise at $\alpha^*/2$. Thus, the proposed contract from the platform to the firm in equilibrium involves $(\alpha^{(L)*},\alpha^{(R)*}) = (\alpha^*/2, \alpha^*/2)$. ■

Proof of Proposition 5.2. Part (i) follows immediately from noting that the electorate has $\tilde{H} = H$ under a fully subscription-based model, and so the extremal antisymmetric Nash equilibrium does not change from $(x_L^{\dagger}, x_R^{\dagger})$.

For part (ii), we use lemma A.3 in Acemoglu, Ozdaglar, and Siderius (2024) to show that for every $b_i > 1/2$, there exists $\epsilon_i > 0$ such that $\tilde{h}(b_i) \geq h(b_i - \epsilon_i)$, and similarly for every $b_i > 1/2$, there exists $\epsilon_i > 0$ such that $\tilde{h}(b_i) \geq h(b_i + \epsilon_i)$. For the former, this corresponds to some $1/2 < b_i' < b_i$ where $b_i' + \epsilon_i' = b_i$ under $\tilde{H}$, and note that there may exist other b_i'''s such that $b_i'' + \epsilon_i'' = b_i$ (hence, the inequality, $\tilde{h}(b) \geq h(b_i - \epsilon_i)$). For the latter, analogously, we have that this corresponds to $b_i < b_i' < 1/2$, where $b_i = b_i' - \epsilon_i'$ under $\tilde{H}$, and note that there may exist other b_i'''s such that $b_i = b_i'' - \epsilon_i''$ (hence, the inequality $\tilde{h}(b) \geq h(b + \epsilon_i)$). Under the advertising-based model, with probability $1 - e^{-\alpha^* T}$ agents receive a signal $s_i \in \{L, R\}$ with equal probability and update their beliefs as follows:

$$\tilde{b}_i = \begin{cases} \dfrac{(1-\phi)b_i}{(1-\phi)b_i + \phi(1-b_i)}, & \text{if m = R} \\[2ex] \dfrac{\phi b_i}{\phi b_i + (1-\phi)(1-b_i)}, & \text{if m = L,} \end{cases}$$

whereas with probability $e^{-\alpha^* T}$ agents receive no signal and leave their beliefs unchanged, $\tilde{b}_i = b_i$. Note then that for $\tilde{b}_i > 1/2$, we have that

$$\tilde{h}(\tilde{b}_i) = (1 - e^{-\alpha^* T})\left[\frac{1}{2}h\left(\frac{\phi\tilde{b}_i}{(1-\tilde{b}_i) + \phi(2\tilde{b}_i - 1)}\right) + \frac{1}{2}h\left(\frac{(1-\phi)\tilde{b}_i}{\phi + \tilde{b}_i - 2\tilde{b}_i\phi}\right)\right]$$

$$+ e^{-\alpha^* T}h(\tilde{b}_i) \geq h(\tilde{b}_i - \tilde{\epsilon}_i)$$

for $\tilde{\epsilon}_i < \tilde{b}_i - 1/2$, by virtue of $\phi \in [0,1/2]$ and convexity of h. To see this, notice that

$$\frac{(1 - e^{-\alpha^* T})}{2}\frac{\phi\tilde{b}_i}{(1-\tilde{b}_i) + \phi(2\tilde{b}_i - 1)} + \frac{(1 - e^{-\alpha^* T})}{2}\frac{(1-\phi)\tilde{b}_i}{\phi + \tilde{b}_i - 2\tilde{b}_i\phi} + e^{-\alpha^* T}\tilde{b}_i < \tilde{b}_i,$$

by the same reasoning as that of lemma 2 in Acemoglu, Huttenlocher, et al. (2024), where the naive users drift more toward the extremes, so tend to come from less extreme positions to begin with. Similarly for agents with $\tilde{b}_i > 1/2$, we can leverage the related fact that

$$\tilde{h}(\tilde{b}_i) = (1 - e^{-\alpha^* T})\left[\frac{1}{2}h\left(\frac{\phi\tilde{b}_i}{(1-\tilde{b}_i) + \phi(2\tilde{b}_i - 1)}\right) + \frac{1}{2}h\left(\frac{(1-\phi)\tilde{b}_i}{\phi + \tilde{b}_i - 2\tilde{b}_i\phi}\right)\right]$$

$$+ e^{-\alpha^* T}h(\tilde{b}_i) \geq h(\tilde{b}_i + \tilde{\epsilon}_i)$$

for $\tilde{\epsilon}_i > (1/2) - \tilde{b}_i$, by virtue of $\phi \in [0, 1/2]$ and convexity of h. This establishes that $\tilde{H} \succ H$, and the resulting antisymmetric Nash equilibrium shift follows exactly from lemma 1(ii).■

Proof of Corollary 5.1. Given $\lambda > 1/2$, and H_N and H_S do not have overlapping support, we see that the sophisticates always make up the distribution $H^{-1}(\alpha) = \tilde{H}^{-1}(\alpha)$ for all $\alpha \in (1/4, 3/4)$, and do not change their beliefs in response to digital political ads. Conversely, by proposition 5.1(ii), we see that $\tilde{H}_N \succ H_N$ when $\phi < \phi^*(\lambda)$ and the platform adopts an advertising-based business model. Consequently, $\tilde{H} \succ H$, so applying lemma 1(ii) we see that the political parties become more polarized in response to increased polarization of the naïfs.■

Proof of Proposition 5.3. Recall the utility of the dominant party R is given by

$$U_R = \mathcal{R} \cdot \int_0^1 \frac{\exp[-(\beta - x_R^*)^2]}{\exp[-(\beta - x_R^*)^2] + \exp[-(\beta - x_L^*)^2]} h(\beta;\alpha)d\beta - (x_R^* - \hat{x}_R)^2,$$

where the belief distribution $h(\beta; \alpha)$ depends on the advertising α from the dominant party. From advertising, the party improves the first part of its payoff by at most $(\partial/\partial\alpha)\mathcal{R}(1 - \chi_R^*)(1 - \lambda)(1 - e^{-\alpha T}) = \mathcal{R}\alpha(1 - \lambda)(1 - \chi_R^*)e^{-\alpha T}$, which comes from assuming the remaining $1 - \chi_R$ share who would not vote for party R, would necessarily then vote for party R conditional on viewing a political ad in favor of R (which is a stronger outcome than the political ad would have). Thus, we get the upper bound

$$\frac{\partial}{\partial \alpha}\mathcal{R}\int_0^1 \frac{\exp[-(\beta - x_R^*)^2)]}{\exp[-(\beta - x_R^*)^2)] + \exp[-(\beta - x_L^*)^2)]} h(\beta;\alpha)d\beta$$

$$\leq \mathcal{R}\alpha(1-\lambda)(1-\chi_R^*)e^{-\alpha T} \leq \mathcal{R}\alpha(1-\lambda)(1-\chi_R^*).$$

Moreover, it is easy to see that $\partial x_R^* / \partial \alpha > 0$ from lemma 2(ii), which decreases the second part of the payoff to party j under the assumption that $\hat{x}_R < x_R^*$.

Thus, for any positive amount of advertising $\alpha^* > 0$, the party is willing to compensate the firm at most $\mathcal{R}\alpha^*(1-\lambda)(1-\chi_R^*)$, but the platform takes a loss in subscription revenue of $\alpha^* T$, for which it must be compensated for it to be willing to offer an advertising-based plan. Setting $\overline{\chi} > 1 - T/\mathcal{R}$ achieves the desired result for all values of $\lambda \in [0, 1]$ (and $\phi \in [0, 1/2]$) where the platform opts for a subscription-based business model. Consequently, $\tilde{H} = H$ and the set of Nash equilibria (which exist by lemma 2(i)) are the same both with and without the potential for political ads, given a dominant party. ■

Proof of Proposition 6.1. Before the diversification standard, an agent with prior belief $[0,\underline{b}]$ receives an article $m = L$ of reliability $r \in (r_1, r_2)$ with probability 1 and receives an article $m = R$ of the same reliability with probability 0. Similarly, an agent with prior belief $[1-\underline{b},1]$ receives an article $m = L$ of reliability $r \in (r_1, r_2)$ with probability 0 and receives an article $m = R$ of the same reliability with probability 1.

By the proof of proposition 7 in Acemoglu, Ozdaglar, and Siderius (2024), the platform chooses a $\mathbf{P}$ that is still an island network structure but satisfies the diversification standard $p_s/p_d \leq \gamma$. In particular, this implies that an agent with prior belief $[0,\underline{b}]$ receives an article $m = L$ of reliability $r \in (r_1, r_2)$ with probability $\zeta < 1$ and receives an article $m = L$ of the same reliability with probability $\xi > 0$. At the same time an agent with prior belief $[1-\underline{b},1]$ receives an article $m = L$ of reliability r with probability $\xi > 0$ and receives an article $m = R$ of the same reliability with probability $\zeta < 1$.

Notice that agent with prior belief $b_i < \underline{b}$ updates their posterior under the new diversification standard according to

$$\tilde{b}_i = \begin{cases} \underline{b}_i, \text{with probability} \zeta(1-\xi) \\ b_i, \text{with probability} (1-\zeta)(1-\xi) + \zeta\xi, \\ \tilde{\tilde{b}}_i, \text{with probability} (1-\zeta)\xi \end{cases}$$

where $\underline{b}_i$ is the belief from proposition 4.3 for a left-wing agent and $\tilde{b}_i < 1/2$ for $\overline{r}$ sufficiently small. Similarly, notice that for an agent with prior belief $b_i > \overline{b}$, she updates her posterior under the new diversification standard according to

$$\tilde{b}_i = \begin{cases} \tilde{\tilde{b}}_i, \text{with probability} \zeta(1-\xi) \\ b_i, \text{with probability} (1-\zeta)(1-\xi) + \zeta\xi, \\ \underline{b}_i, \text{with probability} (1-\zeta)\xi \end{cases}$$

where $\tilde{\tilde{b}}_i$ is the belief from proposition 4.3 for a right-wing agent and $\tilde{\underline{b}}_i > 1/2$ for $\bar{r}$ sufficiently small. It is clear that $\tilde{H} \prec H$ as a result of the diversification standard, so by lemma 1(ii), we know that both political party positions moderate in response to the standard. ∎

Proof of Proposition 6.2. Similar to the proof of proposition 14 in Acemoglu, Huttenlocher, et al. (2024), the maximal revenue the platform can collect from the firms (and specifically from the naïfs) is given by $m^*(\alpha^{(L)},\alpha^{(R)}) \leq L_\lambda(\alpha^{(L)} + \alpha^{(R)})$ for some constant $L_\lambda > 0$. The total advertising revenue is thus bounded above $(1-\lambda)L_\lambda(\alpha^{(L)} + \alpha^{(R)})$, but the loss in subscription revenue from the platform from advertising is $(\alpha^{(L)} + \alpha^{(R)})T$. For $\bar{\lambda} = 1 - T / L_\lambda$, if $\lambda' > \bar{\lambda}$, then the platform opts for a fully subscription-based business model instead, with the sophisticated users protecting the naive ones from an ad-based plan that fails to generate sufficient revenue to compensate for the loss in subscription. This leads posterior beliefs to equal $\bar{H} = H \prec \tilde{H}$, which by lemma 1(ii) moderates the positions of the political parties (undoing the effect identified in proposition 5.2(ii)).

Likewise, the maximal revenue the platform can collect from the firms (and specifically from the naïfs) is given by $m^*(\alpha^{(L)},\alpha^{(R)}) \leq L_\phi(1/2 - \phi)(\alpha^{(L)} + \alpha^{(R)})$ for some constant $L_\phi > 0$, as we did in the proof of proposition 14 in Acemoglu, Huttenlocher, et al. (2024). To see this, one can just let L_ϕ to be defined as the maximal change in advertising revenue following a decrease in the technology ϕ, i.e., $L_\phi = \max_{\phi\in[0,1/2]}|\partial m^*[\alpha^{(L)*}(\phi,\lambda),\alpha^{(R)*}(\phi,\lambda)] / \partial\phi| < \mathcal{R}$. For $\bar{\phi} = (1/2) - (T / L_\phi)$, if $\phi' > \bar{\phi}$, then the platform opts for a fully subscription-based business model instead, leading to the same effect as with $\lambda' > \bar{\lambda}$, following from lemma 1(ii). ∎

References

Acemoglu, Daron, Victor Chernozhukov, and Muhamet Yildiz. 2016. "Fragility of Asymptotic Agreement Under Bayesian Learning." *Theoretical Economics* 11: 187–225.

Acemoglu, Daron, Georgy Egorov, and Konstantin Sonin. 2013. "A Political Theory of Populism." *Quarterly Journal of Economics* 128: 771–805.

Acemoglu, Daron, Daniel Huttenlocher, Asuman Ozdaglar, and James Siderius. 2024. "Online Business Models, Digital Ads, and User Welfare." Technical report. National Bureau of Economic Research.

Acemoglu, Daron, and Simon Johnson. 2023. *Power and Progress: Our Thousand-Year Struggle over Technology and Prosperity*. Hachette UK.

Acemoglu, Daron, Asuman Ozdaglar, and James Siderius. 2024. "A Model of Online Misinformation." *Review of Economic Studies* 91: 3117–50.

Acemoglu, Daron, and Pascual Restrepo. 2020. "Robots and Jobs: Evidence from US Labor Markets." *Journal of Political Economy* 128: 2188–2244.

Associated Press. 2024. "About 20 Percent of Americans Regularly Get Their News from Influencers on Social Media, Report Says." https://apnews.com/article/influencers-election-trump-harris-news-eacd42bce73d6e11cbc760caf28c993a.

Bail, Christopher A., Lisa P. Argyle, Taylor W. Brown, John P. Bumpus, Haohan Chen, M. B. Fallin Hunzaker, Jaemin Lee, Marcus Mann, Friedolin Merhout, and Alexander Volfovsky. 2018. "Exposure to Opposing Views on Social Media Can Increase Political Polarization." *Proceedings of the National Academy of Sciences* 115: 9216–21.

Barber, Michael, Nolan McCarty, Jane Mansbridge, and Cathie Jo Martin. 2015. "Causes and Consequences of Polarization." *Political Negotiation: A Handbook* 37: 39–43.

Barberá, Pablo. 2020. "Social Media, Echo Chambers, and Political Polarization." *Social Media and Democracy: The State of the Field, Prospects for Reform*, 34–55.

Baumann, Fabian, Philipp Lorenz-Spreen, Igor M. Sokolov, and Michele Starnini. 2020. "Modeling Echo Chambers and Polarization Dynamics in Social Networks." *Physical Review Letters* 124: 048301.

Beraja, Martin, Andrew Kao, David Y. Yang, and Noam Yuchtman. 2023. "AI-tocracy." *Quarterly Journal of Economics* 138: 1349–1402.

Beraja, Martin, David Y. Yang, and Noam Yuchtman. 2023. "Data-Intensive Innovation and the State: Evidence from AI Firms in China." *Review of Economic Studies* 90: 1701–23.

Berkowitz, Roger. 2024. "On Fake Hannah Arendt Quotations." *AmorMundi.*

Berman, Sheri. 2021. "The Causes of Populism in the West." *Annual Review of Political Science* 24: 71–88.

Braghieri, Luca, Sarah Eichmeyer, Ro'ee Levy, Markus M. Mobius, Jacob Steinhardt, and Ruiqi Zhong. 2024. "Level Slant and Polarization of News Consumption on Social Media." Available at SSRN 4932600.

Brown, Megan A., James Bisbee, Angela Lai, Richard Bonneau, Jonathan Nagler, and Joshua A. Tucker. 2022. "Echo Chambers, Rabbit Holes, and Algorithmic Bias: How YouTube Recommends Content to Real Users." Available at SSRN 4114905.

Burton, Joe. 2023. "Algorithmic Extremism? The Securitization of Artificial Intelligence (AI) and Its Impact on Radicalism, Polarization and Political Violence." *Technology in Society* 75: 102262.

Butters, Gerard R. 1977. "Equilibrium Distributions of Sales and Advertising Prices." *Review of Economic Studies* 44: 465–91.

Callander, Steven, and Juan Carlos Carbajal. 2022. "Cause and Effect in Political Polarization: A Dynamic Analysis." *Journal of Political Economy* 130: 825–80.

Carroll, Micah, Alan Chan, Henry Ashton, and David Krueger. 2023. "Characterizing Manipulation from AI Systems." In *Proceedings of the 3rd ACM Conference on Equity and Access in Algorithms, Mechanisms, and Optimization*, 1–13.

Chen, Li, and Yiangos Papanastasiou. 2021. "Seeding the Herd: Pricing and Welfare Effects of Social Learning Manipulation." *Management Science* 67: 6734–50.

Chen, Ni, Zhi Li, and Bo Tang. 2022. "Can Digital Skill Protect Against Job Displacement Risk Caused by Artificial Intelligence? Empirical Evidence from 701 Detailed Occupations." *PLOS One* 17: e0277280.

Coughlin, Peter J. 1992. *Probabilistic Voting Theory*. Cambridge University Press.

Dixit, Avinash K., and Jörgen W. Weibull. 2007. "Political Polarization." *Proceedings of the National Academy of Sciences* 104: 7351–56.

Dold, Albrecht. 2012. *Lectures on Algebraic Topology*. Vol. 200. Springer Science & Business Media.

Downs, Anthony. 1957. "An Economic Theory of Political Action in a Democracy." *Journal of Political Economy* 65: 135–50.

Druckman, James N., and Jeremy Levy. 2022. "Affective Polarization in the American Public." In *Handbook on Politics and Public Opinion*, 257–70. Edward Elgar Publishing.

Feezell, Jessica T., John K. Wagner, and Meredith Conroy. 2021. "Exploring the Effects of Algorithm-Driven News Sources on Political Behavior and Polarization." *Computers in Human Behavior* 116: 106626.
Fiorina, Morris P., and Samuel J. Abrams. 2008. "Political Polarization in the American Public." *Annual Review of Political Science* 11: 563–88.
Flaxman, Seth, Sharad Goel, and Justin M. Rao. 2016. "Filter Bubbles, Echo Chambers, and Online News Consumption." *Public Opinion Quarterly* 80: 298–320.
Gabriel, Saadia, Liang Lyu, James Siderius, Marzyeh Ghassemi, Jacob Andreas, and Asu Ozdaglar. 2024. "MisinfoEval: Generative AI in the era of 'Alternative Facts.'" arXiv preprint arXiv:2410.09949.
Gallego, Aina, and Thomas Kurer. 2022. "Automation, Digitalization, and Artificial Intelligence in the Workplace: Implications for Political Behavior." *Annual Review of Political Science* 25: 463–84.
Glaeser, Edward L. 2005. "The Political Economy of Hatred." *Quarterly Journal of Economics* 120: 45–86.
Glaeser, Edward L., Giacomo A. M. Ponzetto, and Jesse M. Shapiro. 2005. "Strategic Extremism: Why Republicans and Democrats Divide on Religious Values." *Quarterly Journal of Economics* 120: 1283–1330.
Golab-Andrzejak, Edyta. 2023. "The Impact of Generative AI and ChatGPT on Creating Digital Advertising Campaigns." *Cybernetics and Systems*: 1–15.
Golub, Benjamin, and Matthew O. Jackson. 2010. "Naive Learning in Social Networks and the Wisdom of Crowds." *American Economic Journal: Microeconomics* 2: 112–49.
Grinberg, Nir, Kenneth Joseph, Lisa Friedland, Briony Swire-Thompson, and David Lazer. 2019. "Fake News on Twitter During the 2016 US Presidential Election." *Science* 363: 374–78.
Guess, Andrew M., Brendan Nyhan, and Jason Reifler. 2020. "Exposure to Untrustworthy Websites in the 2016 US Election." *Nature Human Behaviour* 4: 472–80.
Gupta, Aastha. 2023. "Deceptive Advertising, Regulation and Naive Consumers." *International Journal of Industrial Organization* 91: 103026.
Guriev, Sergei, and Elias Papaioannou. 2022. "The Political Economy of Populism." *Journal of Economic Literature* 60: 753–832.
Hobbs, Renee, Igor Kanižaj, and Luis Pereira. 2019. "Digital Literacy and Propaganda." *Media Studies* 10: 1–7.
Hotelling, Habold. 1929. "Stability in Competition." *Economic Journal* 39: 41–57.
Hristakieva, Kristina, Stefano Cresci, Giovanni Da San Martino, Mauro Conti, and Preslav Nakov. 2022. "The Spread of Propaganda by Coordinated Communities on Social Media." In *Proceedings of the 14th ACM Web Science Conference 2022*, 191–201.
Hruska, Jan, and Petra Maresova. 2020. "Use of Social Media Platforms Among Adults in the United States—Behavior on Social Media." *Societies* 10: 27.
Hudders, Liselot, Eva A. Van Reijmersdal, and Karolien Poels. 2019. "Digital Advertising and Consumer Empowerment." *Cyberpsychology: Journal of Psychosocial Research on Cyberspace* 13.
Huerta, E. A., Ben Blaiszik, L. Catherine Brinson, Kristofer E. Bouchard, Daniel Diaz, Caterina Doglioni, Javier M. Duarte, Murali Emani, Ian Foster, Geoffrey Fox, et al. 2023. "Fair for AI: An Interdisciplinary and International Community Building Perspective." *Scientific Data* 10: 487.
Kemp, Simon. 2020. *Digital 2020: Global Digital Overview*. https://datareportal.com/reports/digital-2020-global-digital-overview.
Langguth, Johannes, Konstantin Pogorelov, Stefan Brenner, Petra Filkuková, and

Daniel Thilo Schroeder. 2021. "Don't Trust Your Eyes: Image Manipulation in the Age of Deepfakes." *Frontiers in Communication* 6: 632317.

Lazer, David M. J., Matthew A. Baum, Yochai Benkler, Adam J. Berinsky, Kelly M. Greenhill, Filippo Menczer, Miriam J. Metzger, Brendan Nyhan, Gordon Pennycook, David Rothschild, et al. 2018. "The Science of Fake News." *Science* 359: 1094–96.

Levy, Ro'ee. 2021. "Social Media, News Consumption, and Polarization: Evidence from a Field Experiment." *American Economic Review* 111: 831–70.

Lewandowsky, Stephan, Ullrich K. H. Ecker, and John Cook. 2017. "Beyond Misinformation: Understanding and Coping with the 'Post-Truth' Era." *Journal of Applied Research in Memory and Cognition* 6: 353–69.

Lindbeck, Assar, and Jörgen W. Weibull. 1993. "A Model of Political Equilibrium in a Representative Democracy." *Journal of Public Economics* 51: 195–209.

Lu, Zhuoran, Patrick Li, Weilong Wang, and Ming Yin. 2022. "The Effects of AI-Based Credibility Indicators on the Detection and Spread of Misinformation Under Social Influence." *Proceedings of the ACM on Human-Computer Interaction* 6: 1–27.

Mas-Colell, Andreu, Michael Dennis Whinston, Jerry R. Green, et al. 1995. *Microeconomic Theory*. Vol. 1. Oxford University Press.

McCarty, Nolan. 2007. "The Policy Effects of Political Polarization." In *The Transformation of American Politics: Activist Government and the Rise of Conservatism*, 223–55. Princeton University Press

Meurer, Michael, and Dale O. Stahl. 1994. "Informative Advertising and Product Match." *International Journal of Industrial Organization* 12: 1–19.

Milgrom, Paul, and Chris Shannon. 1994. "Monotone Comparative Statics." *Econometrica: Journal of the Econometric Society* 62 (1): 157–80.

Molina, Carlos Molina. 2024. *Essays on Political Economy*. PhD diss., Massachusetts Institute of Technology.

Mostagir, Mohamed, Asuman Ozdaglar, and James Siderius. 2022. "When Is Society Susceptible to Manipulation?" *Management Science* 68: 7153–75.

Mostagir, Mohamed, and James Siderius. 2022a. "Learning in a Post-Truth World." *Management Science* 68: 2860–68.

Mostagir, Mohamed, and James Siderius. 2022b. "Naive and Bayesian Learning with Misinformation Policies." Technical report. Massachusetts Institute of Technology.

Mostagir, Mohamed, and James Siderius. 2023. "Social Inequality and the Spread of Misinformation." *Management Science* 69: 968–95.

Mostagir, Mohamed, and James Siderius. 2024. "When Should Platforms Break Echo Chambers?" Technical report. Massachusetts Institute of Technology.

Nayak, Sameera S., Timothy Fraser, Costas Panagopoulos, Daniel P. Aldrich, and Daniel Kim. 2021. "Is Divisive Politics Making Americans Sick? Associations of Perceived Partisan Polarization with Physical and Mental Health Outcomes Among Adults in the United States." *Social Science & Medicine* 284: 113976.

Nyhan, Brendan. 2020. "Facts and Myths About Misperceptions." *Journal of Economic Perspectives* 34: 220–36.

Ott, William, and James Yorke. 2005. "Prevalence." *Bulletin of the American Mathematical Society* 42: 263–90.

O'Callaghan, Derek, Derek Greene, Maura Conway, Joe Carthy, and Pádraig Cunningham. 2015. "Down the (White) Rabbit Hole: The Extreme Right and Online Recommender Systems." *Social Science Computer Review* 33: 459–78.

Pennycook, Gordon, and David G. Rand. 2019. "Fighting Misinformation on Social

Media Using Crowdsourced Judgments of News Source Quality." *Proceedings of the National Academy of Sciences* 116: 2521–26.

Pew Research Center. 2014. "Political Polarization in the American Public." June 12. https://www.pewresearch.org/politics/2014/06/12/political-polarization-in-the-american-public/.

Pew Research Center. 2020. "Americans Who Mainly Get Their News on Social Media Are Less Engaged, Less Knowledgeable." July 30. https://www.pewresearch.org/journalism/2020/07/30/americans-who-mainly-get-their-news-on-social-media-are-less-engaged-less-knowledgeable/.

Pew Research Center. 2024. "Social Media and News Fact Sheet." September 17. https://www.pewresearch.org/journalism/fact-sheet/social-media-and-news-fact-sheet/.

Piccolo, Salvatore, Piero Tedeschi, and Giovanni Ursino. 2018. "Deceptive Advertising with Rational Buyers." *Management Science* 64: 1291–1310.

Quinn, Kevin M., Andrew D. Martin, and Andrew B. Whitford. 1999. "Voter Choice in Multi-Party Democracies: A Test of Competing Theories and Models." *American Journal of Political Science*: 1231–47.

Rathje, Steve, Claire Robertson, William J. Brady, and Jay J. Van Bavel. 2024. "People Think That Social Media Platforms Do (But Should Not) Amplify Divisive Content." *Perspectives on Psychological Science* 19: 781–95.

Rochlin, Nick. 2017. "Fake News: Belief in Post-Truth." *Library Hi Tech* 35: 386–92.

Ross Arguedas, Amy, Craig Robertson, Richard Fletcher, and Rasmus Nielsen. 2022. "Echo Chambers, Filter Bubbles, and Polarisation: A Literature Review." *Reuters Institute for the Study of Journalism.*

Simchon, Almog, Matthew Edwards, and Stephan Lewandowsky. 2024. "The Persuasive Effects of Political Microtargeting in the Age of Generative Artificial Intelligence." *PNAS Nexus* 3: pgae035.

Statista Research Department. 2024a. "Media Usage in the US—Statistics and Facts." https://www.statista.com/topics/1536/media-use/.

Statista Research Department. 2024b. "Political Advertising in the US—Statistics and Facts." https://www.statista.com/topics/4942/political-advertising-in-the-us/.

Suarez-Lledo, Victor, and Javier Alvarez-Galvez. 2021. "Prevalence of Health Misinformation on Social Media: Systematic Review." *Journal of Medical Internet Research* 23: e17187.

Sunstein, Cass. 2018. *# Republic: Divided Democracy in the Age of Social Media.* Princeton University Press.

Topkis, Donald M. 1998. *Supermodularity and Complementarity*. Princeton University Press.

Törnberg, Petter. 2018. "Echo Chambers and Viral Misinformation: Modeling Fake News as Complex Contagion." *PLOS One* 13: e0203958.

Tucker, Joshua A., Andrew Guess, Pablo Barberá, Cristian Vaccari, Alexandra Siegel, Sergey Sanovich, Denis Stukal, and Brendan Nyhan. 2018. "Social Media, Political Polarization, and Political Disinformation: A Review of the Scientific Literature." *Political Polarization, and Political Disinformation: A Review of the Scientific Literature.* March 19.

Veerasamy, Namosha, and Heloise Pieterse. 2022. "Rising Above Misinformation and Deepfakes." In *International Conference on Cyber Warfare and Security* 17: 340–48.

Zeng, Jinghan. 2020. "Artificial Intelligence and China's Authoritarian Governance." *International Affairs* 96: 1441–59.

Comment Joshua Tucker

In the spirit of the conference, what follows is a prose version of Tucker's discussant slides as drafted by ChatGPT4o (and then heavily edited by Tucker) based on the following two prompts:

- *Prompt 1: I recently attended a conference where I was the discussant for a paper entitled "Online Business Models, Digital Ads, and User Welfare." I created a slide deck for my discussant remarks, and now I need to turn that slide deck into a written article of about 1,500 words. I am now uploading the slide deck. Can you try to convert the slide deck to a written article of about 1,500 words?*
- *Prompt 2: OK, that was really helpful. However, I'd like you to drop the numbers and bullet points and just make it all prose. The length of the article you gave me is only 910 words, so you should feel free to add more length.*

For those who are interested in these sorts of things, note that Tucker did not show ChatGPT the original paper at all, so the only information it had was what was contained in Tucker's slides presented at the conference.

Acemoglu, Huttenlocher, et al. (2024) delve into the complex dynamics among platforms, advertisers, and users, aiming to model how these relationships influence welfare outcomes in digital environments. I very much enjoyed reading the paper and thinking about its broader implications, particularly in relation to political advertising. I do, however, want to provide the caveat to readers that I am a political scientist who works on the intersection of social media, digital media, and politics, but I do not study online advertising per se; therefore, both the substance and methods of the paper are outside my areas of expertise. Hopefully, then, this commentary can be read in the spirit of the potential value-added from interdisciplinary assessments.

The paper presents a well-constructed framework that models interactions between users of platforms, firms that advertise on these platforms, and the platforms themselves. One of the paper's most compelling features is its effort to articulate how advertising functions as a source of information for users. The theoretical progression of the paper is particularly commendable, building from simpler models to more complex versions that incorporate additional real-world dynamics. Even for readers outside the field

Joshua Tucker is a Julius Silver, Roslyn S. Silver, and Enid Silver Winslow Professor, a professor of politics, an affiliated professor of Russian and Slavic studies, and an affiliated professor of data science at New York University.

For acknowledgments, sources of research support, and disclosure of the author's material financial relationships, if any, please see https://www.nber.org/books-and-chapters/political-economy-artificial-intelligence/comment-artificial-intelligence-and-political-economy-tucker.

of economics, the clarity of the approach makes the arguments accessible. Furthermore, the authors' attempt to use the model to explore potential policy interventions, as well as their emphasis on the critical importance of data access for both research and policymaking, adds value to their analysis.

Turning now to questions, comments, and suggestions, let me first start with one of the central concepts, ad intensity, which could benefit from greater clarification. The idea that ads provide valuable information to users is clear, but it remains ambiguous what specific type of information ads are delivering and how a greater volume of ads amplifies this informational signal. If advertising is primarily a means of signaling product quality, why does the effectiveness of the signal increase with volume? One idea I have is perhaps to invoke Zaller's (1992) classic model of public opinion formation, which theorizes that individuals vary in their level of resistance to new opinions. From this perspective, might more ads lead to a greater likelihood of overcoming resistance to belief in the product's quality? If this was the case, then we would have a reason for why ad intensity is important: the more ads there are, the more people who can be convinced by the ad (i.e., if low levels of ad intensity only convince people with no or little resistance, perhaps higher levels of ad intensity could convince people with higher levels of resistance as well, and therefore higher ad intensity leads to more desire for the product?). Even if this is not the idea the authors had in mind, I think it would be valuable to provide more of a sense of why, if ads are supposed to deliver information, more ads delivering the same information are more likely to do so than fewer ads.

This focus on the ways consumers might differ from one another leads nicely into a question I had about the role of sophisticated users in the theoretical framework. The paper suggests that these users are willing to pay subscription fees to avoid ads, but this raises a question: if sophisticated users are capable of extracting meaningful signals from ads, why would they choose to pay to avoid them? Conversely, if they are sophisticated enough to ignore ads, then it seems inconsistent for these users to pay to remove them? In my mind, this raised the question of whether the paper would benefit from a model of user preferences that considers the value of time and cognitive effort required to filter content. This approach might give us some sense of the cost borne by sophisticated users when they choose not to pay subscription fees and thus help further to explain why they do choose to pay those fees.

Another question I would like to highlight regards the distinction between users, firms, and influencers. The paper's framework largely treats these groups as distinct, which may align well with traditional platforms like streaming services but is less applicable to social media ecosystems. On platforms such as TikTok, users often act as both consumers and producers of content (for which advertising can then be sold), blurring the lines between these roles. This influencer-driven dynamic introduces unique considerations, especially when users generate value not just as consumers of ads but as creators who drive engagement with the platform (and ultimately advertising revenue or subscription fees).

I also found myself wondering about the dichotomy between offline and online markets. I read the paper as assuming that the products being advertised were products that one could find offline as well (e.g., Nike sneakers are also sold in stores). However, my guess is that many digital ads today promote products that exist exclusively in online marketplaces. This shift has implications for the model, raising the question of what it means for the model's predictions if there is no offline market. This links back to the question of the role of influencers, who in this case may be entirely responsible for producing the goods for sale in the online market, as well as for driving interest in those goods.

The differences between social media platforms and streaming services also warrant more attention in the paper. While both types of platforms employ digital ads and (potentially) subscription fees, they operate under fundamentally different paradigms. Social media platforms rely heavily on user-generated content and network effects, where the value of the platform increases with the size and activity of its user base. Streaming services, on the other hand, do not depend on user-generated content to the same extent, and network effects are less central to their value proposition. While of course streaming services depend on data from their users to drive their recommendation algorithms, the actual *content* people are consuming on a streaming platform like Netflix is not produced by Netflix subscribers. Developing tailored models for these categories, or exploring hybrid approaches, could enhance the applicability of the paper's findings across different platform types.

I also want to raise the question of ad quality. While the model emphasizes user sophistication as a determinant of ad effectiveness, it does not fully explore how the quality of the ads themselves might vary. Is it possible that some ads may inherently provide low-quality signals that fail to provide useful information even to naive users? If so, might platforms, in turn, have incentives to curate ad quality to enhance user trust and engagement? This dynamic adds another layer of complexity that could be incorporated into future iterations of the model.

As a political scientist, I was particularly interested in how the paper's framework could be extended to political advertising. More specifically, could we think of the distinction between naive and sophisticated consumers as mirroring the divide between uninformed and informed voters? Of course, political ads introduce additional complexities, such as partisanship, which would likely influence voter behavior in ways distinct from consumer behavior in markets for products. One thought in this regard is whether we can think of partisanship in the realm of political ads as playing a similar role to brand loyalty in the realm of the market for products? Another potentially important distinction around political advertising is that political campaigns also often operate with vastly unequal resources. While of course firms too have different advertising budgets, I don't think I saw differences in firm resources reflected in the model. Finally, how should we think about the role of misinformation in political advertising? Can it simply be folded into the model in the paper as a form of low-quality signaling? Or is there something fundamentally different about a political ad with misinformation because the goal of that ad is precisely to propagate low-quality information?

Turning to the policy implications of the paper, I wondered from where the authors thought the political support for their proposals would come. The idea of taxing digital advertisements and using the proceeds to subsidize platforms or firms may have theoretical merit, but selling this policy to the public poses challenges. While taxing firms may be politically palatable, providing subsidies to large technology companies is unlikely to be popular. I wondered whether such measures could be reframed to emphasize their benefits for users, particularly in terms of improving welfare outcomes.

Finally, in the spirit of the conference's theme, the implications of artificial intelligence for digital advertising merit closer attention. AI offers tools to target ads more effectively, potentially ratcheting up the exploitation of the paper's naive users. At the same time, it could also provide opportunities for users to filter out low-quality ads. I also found myself wondering whether the model in the paper had any insights for understanding how the consumer market for generative AI tools like ChatGPT might evolve in the future. I currently see this market as operating on a "freemium" model—could this paper offer any insights as to whether that model is likely to continue in the longer run?

In conclusion, the paper represents an important contribution to the study of digital platforms and their impact on user welfare. By raising important questions and suggesting avenues for further research, it provides a foundation for understanding the complex interplay between advertising, user behavior, and platform incentives. As the digital economy continues to evolve, this work will undoubtedly serve as a valuable resource for scholars and policymakers alike.

References

Acemoglu, Daron, Daniel Huttenlocher, Asuman Ozdaglar, and James Siderius. 2024. "Online Business Models, Digital Ads, and User Welfare." NBER Working Paper No. 33017. National Bureau of Economic Research.

Zaller, John. 1992. *The Nature and Origins of Mass Opinion*. Cambridge University Press.

Author Index

Subject Index

Page numbers in italics refer to tables and figures.